It's
Been
a
Good
Life

ISAAC ASIMOV

It's

Been

a

Good

Life

Edited by

JANET JEPPSON ASIMOV

Prometheus Books

59 John Glenn Drive
Amherst, New York 14228-2197

Published 2002 by Prometheus Books

Reprinted by permission of the Estate of Isaac Asimov and Doubleday:

Excerpts from the autobiographies of Isaac Asimov:

In Memory Yet Green, copyright © 1979 by Nightfall, Inc.
In Joy Still Felt, copyright © 1980 by Nightfall, Inc.
I. Asimov, copyright © 1992 by The Estate of Isaac Asimov

The short story:

"The Last Question" from *The Complete Stories, Vol. 1,*
copyright © 1990 by Nightfall, Inc.

Selected photographs (as indicated) © Jay Kay Klein

Inquiries should be addressed to
Prometheus Books
59 John Glenn Drive
Amherst, New York 14228–2197
VOICE: 716–691–0133, ext. 207
FAX: 716–564–2711
WWW.PROMETHEUSBOOKS.COM

06 05 04 03 02   5 4 3 2 1

Library of Congress Cataloging-in-Publication Data forthcoming

ISBN 1–57392–968–9

Printed in the United States of America on acid-free paper

CONTENTS

PROLOGUE

Human life is, or should be, an adventure in self-discovery, learning what talents one has and using them successfully. Isaac Asimov knew he'd had this adventure to the fullest and, at the end, said "It's been a good life."

No one but Isaac could tell the genuine story of that good life. Fortunately, he did—in short pieces, letters, and three large, detailed volumes of autobiography. Much of this autobiographical material is now out of print or has never been collected in book form.

At the request of Prometheus Books, I have tried to create a one-volume condensation of his autobiography that is not primarily chronological but concentrates on what Isaac wrote about his life as a writer and as a humanist. I have also used excerpts of letters—only those he wrote to me—and I've added his favorite story and an essay on his thoughts about science.

The epilogue is a revised version of one I wrote for the posthumously published third volume of his autobiography. His daughter, Robyn, and I decided that the new epilogue should reveal the true story of Isaac's final illness and death.

Throughout the book, my own comments and explanations are in brackets.

Janet J. Asimov

BRIEF CHRONOLOGY OF ISAAC ASIMOV'S LIFE

1920	— born in Petrovichi, USSR
1922	— entered the United States with parents and sister, Marcia
1929	— brother, Stanley, born
1935	— graduated from Boy's High School
1938	— sold first short story
1939	— B.S. Columbia University
1941	— M.A. Columbia University
1942	— married to Gertrude Blugerman
1942–45	— wartime work at Naval Air Experimental Station in Philadelphia
1945–46	— in army
1948	— Ph.D. Columbia University
1950	— first novel published
1950	— teaching at Boston University School of Medicine
1951	— son, David, born
1955	— daughter, Robyn, born
1958	— job at B.U. Medical School ends, retains title
1966	— first Hugo Award
1969	— father's death
1969	— hundredth book published
1970	— separation, moved to New York City
1973	— mother's death
1973	— divorce, second marriage, to Janet Jeppson

1977	—	*Isaac Asimov's Science Fiction Magazine* begins
1977	—	heart attack
1979	—	promoted to full professor at B.U. Medical School
1979, 1980	—	first two volumes of autobiography
1982	—	first best-seller
1983	—	triple bypass surgery
1984	—	"Humanist of the Year"
1987	—	Grand Master Award
1990	—	finished third volume of autobiography
1991	—	finished *Asimov Laughs Again*
1992	—	first draft of *Forward the Foundation*
1992	—	death

One.

RUSSIA

I am not impressed by ancestry, since if I could trace my origins to Judas Maccabeus or to King David, that would not add one inch to my stature, either physically, mentally, or ethically. It's even possible that my ancestry might not move in the direction of ancient Israel at all.

About 600 C.E., a Turkish tribe, the Khazars, lived in what is now southern Russia. They established an empire that reached its peak about 750 C.E., [and] about that time, the Khazars adopted Judaism as the state religion, [probably] to keep from falling under the influence of either the Byzantine Christians or the Arab Moslems, who were busily engaged in the first part of their centuries-long duel.

After 965, the Khazars were through as an organized power, but Judaism may have remained, and it may well be that many East European Jews are descended from Khazars and the people they ruled. I may be one of them. Who knows? And who cares?

My mother [Anna Rachel Berman] had blue eyes, and in her youth, light hair. Though my father [Judah] was brown-eyed and brown-haired, there must have been a recessive blue-eyed gene there too, for my brother, my sister, and I all have blue eyes. My hair was brown, but both my brother and sister had reddish hair. My brother's daughter has bright red hair and blue eyes; my own daughter has blond hair and blue eyes. What's more, I've got high Slavic cheekbones.

Where did all this come from? Surely not from any Mediterranean or Turkish people. It had to be of Slavic origin and Scandinavian beyond that—plus a bit of Mongol to account for my B-type blood.

The date of my birth, as I celebrate it, was January 2, 1920. It could not have been later than that. It might, however, have been earlier. Allowing for the uncertainties of the times, of the lack of records, of the Jewish and Julian calendars, it might have been as early as October 4, 1919. My parents were always uncertain and it really doesn't matter.

I was born in the little town of Petrovichi, in the USSR, fifty-five miles due south of Smolensk (where a great battle was fought during Napoleon's invasion of 1812, and another during Hitler's invasion of 1941). It is farther north than the territory of any of the states but Alaska.

According to my father's golden memories, I was "the healthiest possible" baby for two years and then I got double pneumonia. In later years, my mother told me that seventeen infants had fallen ill and that I was the only survivor [because after] the doctor had given me up she held me in her arms without ever letting go until I had recovered.

My father was fluent in Hebrew, Yiddish, and Russian. My mother was literate and could read and write both Russian and Yiddish. They spoke Russian to each other when they wanted to discuss something privately. Had they spoken to *me* in Russian, I would have picked it up like a sponge and had a second world language.

It would have been good to know the language of Pushkin, Tolstoy, and Doestoevski. [But] allow me my prejudice: surely there is no language more majestic than that of Shakespeare, Milton, and the King James Bible, and if I am to have one language I know as only a native can know it, I consider myself unbelievably fortunate that it is English.

Two.

THE UNITED STATES

In 1922, after my sister, Marcia, was born, my father decided to emigrate to the United States. My mother had a half brother living in New York who was willing to guarantee that we would not become a charge on the country; that, plus permission from the Soviet Government, was all we needed.

I am not sorry we left. I dare say that if my family had remained in the Soviet Union, I would have received an education similar to the one I actually did get, that I might well have become a chemist and even a science-fiction writer. On the other hand, there is a very good chance that I would then have been killed in the course of the German invasion of the Soviet Union in 1941 to 1945, and while I hope I would have done my bit first, I am glad I didn't have to. I am prejudiced in favor of life.

My father came to the United States in the hope of a better life for his children, and this he certainly achieved. He lived to see one son a successful writer, another son a successful journalist, and a daughter happily married. However, this was at great cost to himself.

In Russia, he was part of a reasonably prosperous merchant family, an educated man looked up to by those about him for his learning. In the United States, he found himself penniless . . . and virtually illiterate, for he could not read or even speak English. He turned his hand to any job he could get and after three years had saved enough money for a down payment on a small mom-and-pop candy store and our future was assured—and shaped.

In Russia, my mother had been the oldest of numerous siblings and had to take care of them in addition to working in her mother's store. In the United States, she had to raise three children and work endless hours in the candy store . . .

All in all, my family was never together and I never interacted with any of them except in the context of the candy store. It was in that respect that I was orphaned in a functional sense. In another sense, matters were quite the reverse. My parents were *always* home; I *always* knew where they were, so that I was too densely sheltered.

Then again [thanks to the long working hours], we could have no social life, so I interacted with no one *but* my immediate family. That, too, twisted and distorted my life and my personality in ways that must be all too apparent even now.

Despite all that education and experience can do, I retain a certain level of unsophistication that I cannot eradicate and that my friends find amusing . . . I suspect that I am never quite as unsophisticated as they think I am, but I don't mind.

No one can possibly have lived through the Great Depression without being scarred by it. . . . No "Depression baby" can ever be a yuppie. No amount of experience since the Depression can convince someone who has lived through it that the world is safe economically. One constantly waits for banks to close, for factories to shut down, for the pink slip of discharge.

Well, the Asimov family escaped. Not by much. We were *poor*, but we always had enough to put food on the table and to pay the rent. Never were we threatened by hunger and eviction. And why? The candy store. It brought in enough to support us. Only minimally, to be sure, but in the Great Depression, even minimally was heaven [with the price of incredibly long working hours for Isaac's parents and for him]. . . .

I am still and forever in the candy store. Of course, I'm not taking money and making change; I'm not forced to be polite to everyone who comes in (in actual fact, I was never very good at that). I am, instead, doing things I very much want to do—but the schedule is there; the schedule that was ground into me; the schedule you would think I would have rebelled against once I had the chance.

I can only say that there were certain advantages offered by the candy store that had nothing to do with mere survival, but, rather, with overflowing happiness, and that this was so associated with the long hours as to make them sweet to me and to fix them upon me for all my life. [And Isaac goes on to describe finding science-fiction magazines for sale in the candy store] . . .

The science-fiction magazines were the first pulp magazines I was allowed to read. That may have been part of the reason that, when the time came for me to be a writer, it was science-fiction that I chose as my medium.

Another reason was science fiction's more extended grasp on the young imagination. It was science fiction that introduced me to the universe, in particular to the solar system and the planets. Even if I had already come across them in my reading of science books, it was science fiction that fixed them in my mind, dramatically and forever . . .

However trashy pulp fiction might be, it had to be *read*. Youngsters avid for the corny, lightning-jagged, cliché-ridden, clumsy stories had to read words and sentences to satisfy their craving. It trained everyone who read it in literacy, and a small percentage of them may then have passed on to better things . . .

In general, the trend over the last half century or so has been away from the word to the picture. The comic magazines increased the level of looking, decreased the level of reading. The television set has carried this to an extreme. Even the slick magazines found themselves dying because of competition with the picture magazines of the 1940s and the girlie magazines that followed.

In short, the age of the pulp magazine was the last in which youngsters, to get their primitive material, were forced to be literate. Now . . . true literacy is becoming an arcane art, and the nation is steadily "dumbing down."

Three.
CITY CHILD

[About neighborhood games] I refused to play for keeps. What I wanted to do was merely win for the honor of winning and I did not want to confuse this with material gain. This was called "playing for fun." . . . My father approved of my refusal to play for keeps. In fact, he was dubious about my playing for fun, since he felt that my time could be spent much more instructively practicing my reading or studying or trying to think great thoughts.

To my father, any boy who played ball in the street was a "bum" and was clearly in training to become a "gangster." . . . "Remember, Isaac," he would say, "if you hang around with bums, don't think for a minute you will make a good person out of the bum. *No!* That bum will make a bum out of you."

The result was that since I didn't play punchball often enough to develop real skill, I was an undesirable choice for a team. I developed a series of solitary ball games . . .

[In the neighborhood] the cheers, the arguments, the screaming must have been unbearable to people trying to carry on ordinary occupations. The thunk-thunk-thunk, steady and unwearying over the house, of my ball against a wall must have driven many a person insane, too. The noise was an inseparable part of the world.

And, of course, it was pleasure. I have never been able to work up much sympathy for those who mourn the plight of city children crowded into their nasty streets. When I think back on the children of my childhood, all I can remember is that those nasty streets belonged to us and that the boisterous competition and the noisy excitement were the very breath of life to us.

Night was a wonderful time in Brooklyn in the thirties, especially in warm weather. Everyone would be sitting on their stoops, since air conditioning was unknown except in movie houses, and so was television without exception. There was nothing to keep one in the house. Furthermore, few people owned automobiles, so there was nothing to carry one away. That left the streets and the stoops, which were thus full, and the very fullness served as an inhibition to street crime. People were everywhere, talking, laughing, gossiping, and the roadways were relatively empty.

I would walk all over the neighborhood, daydreaming. In later years I channeled the daydreams into material for fiction, but in Decatur Street, I still hadn't reached that stage of practicality, and my daydreams were just invented and thrown away.

To those who are not bookworms, it must be a curious thought that someone would read and read, letting life with all its glory pass by unnoticed, wasting the carefree days of youth, missing the wonderful interplay of muscle and sinew. There must seem something sad and even tragic about it, and one might wonder what impels a youngster to do it.

But life is glorious when it is happy; days are carefree when they are happy; the interplay of thought and imagination is far superior to that of muscle and sinew. Let me tell you, if you don't know it from your own experience, that reading a good book, losing yourself in the interest of words and thoughts, is for some people (me, for instance) an incredible intensity of happiness.

If I want to recall peace, serenity, pleasure, I think of myself on those lazy summer afternoons, with my chair tipped back against the wall [outside the candy store], the book on my lap, and the pages softly turning. There may have been, at certain times in my life, higher pitches of ecstasy, vast moments of relief and triumph, but for quiet, peaceful happiness, there has never been anything to compare to it.

Four.
RELIGION

 One of the ways [in the USSR] a Jew could . . . work for a new world of social equality, of civil liberty, of democracy, would be to shake off the dead hand of Orthodox Judaism [which] dictates one's every action at every moment of the day and enforces differences between Jew and Gentile that virtually make certain the persecution of the weaker group.

It followed, then, that my father, when he came to the United States and was freed of the overwhelming presence of his father, could turn to a secular life. Not entirely, of course. Dietary laws are hard to break, when you've been taught that the flesh of swine is the broth of hell. You can't entirely ignore the local synagogue; you are still interested in biblical lore.

However, he didn't recite the myriad prayers prescribed for every action, and he never made any attempt to teach them to me. He didn't even bother to have me bar mitzvahed at the age of thirteen—the rite whereby a young boy becomes a Jew with all the responsibilities of obeying the Jewish law. I remained without religion simply because no one made any effort to teach me religion—any religion.

To be sure, at one period in 1928, my father, feeling the need for a little extra money, undertook to serve as secretary for the local synagogue. To do so, he had to show up at the synagogue services and, on occasion, took me with him. (I didn't like it.) He also, as a gesture, entered me in Hebrew school, where I began to learn a little Hebrew.

Since that meant learning the Hebrew alphabet and its pronunciation, and since Yiddish makes use of the Hebrew alphabet, I found I could read Yiddish.

My father didn't stay secretary long; he couldn't swing both it and the candy store. After some months, therefore, I was taken out of Hebrew school, to my great relief, for I didn't like it either. I didn't like the rote learning, and I didn't see the value of learning Hebrew.

I may have been mistaken in this. Learning *anything* is valuable, but I was only eight years old and hadn't quite got that into my head. One thing, though, remained from this early period and from my father's lectures which he would illustrate with biblical quotations. I gained an interest in the Bible. As I grew older, I read the Bible several times, [but] science fiction and science books had taught me their version of the universe and I was not ready to accept the Creation tale of Genesis or the various miracles described throughout the book. My experience with the Greek myths (and later, the grimmer Norse myths) made it obvious to me that I was reading Hebrew myths.

There was no trauma about it, no soul-searching, no internal crisis, no troubled discussions with my parents or anyone else. There merely came a time, probably before I was thirteen, when I found myself accepting atheism as matter-of-factly as I had previously accepted religion. Nor have I ever wavered in this point of view since. The universe I live in consists of matter and energy only, and that doesn't make me in the least bit uncomfortable.

I am sometimes suspected of being nonreligious as an act of rebellion against Orthodox parents. That may have been true of my father, but I have rebelled against nothing. I have been left free and I have loved the freedom. The same is true of my brother and sister and our children.

I have never, not for one moment, been tempted toward religion of any kind. The fact is that I feel no spiritual void. I have my philosophy of life, which does not include any aspect of the supernatural and which I find totally satisfying. I am, in short, a rationalist and believe only that which reason tells me is so.

[Letter] Have I told you that I prefer "rationalism" to "atheism"? The word "atheist," meaning "no God," is negative and defeatist. It says what you don't believe and puts you in an eternal position of defense. "Rationalism" on the other hand states what you DO believe; that is, that which can be understood in the light of reason. The question of God and other mystical objects-of-faith are outside reason and therefore play no part in rationalism and you don't have to waste your time in either attacking or defending that which you rule out of your philosophy altogether.

[Isaac had already written his *Guide to the Bible* when he appeared for a taping of the *David Frost Show*. Frost] said, with neither warning nor preamble, "Dr. Asimov, do you believe in God?"

That rather took my breath away. It was a dreadful way of putting a person on the spot. To answer honestly, "No," with millions of people watching, could arouse a great deal of controversy I didn't feel much need of. Yet I couldn't lie, either. I played for time, in order to find a way out.

He said, "Dr. Asimov, do you believe in God?"

And I said, "Whose?"

He said, a little impatiently, "Come, come, Dr. Asimov, you know very well whose. Do you believe in the Western God, the God of the Judeo-Christian tradition?"

Still playing for time, I said, "I haven't given it much thought."

Frost said, "I can't believe that, Dr. Asimov." He then nailed me to the wall by saying, "Surely a man of your diverse intellectual interests and wide-ranging curiosity must have tried to find God?"

(Eureka! I had it! The very nails had given me my opening!) I said, smiling pleasantly, "God is much more intelligent than I am—let him try to find me."

The audience laughed its head off and, to my relief, Frost changed the subject. He essayed one more probe into mysticism by saying, "Do you consider it possible, Dr. Asimov, that there may be forces and energies in the universe we have not yet discovered?"

"If so," I answered, "we have not yet discovered them." . . .

I had an attack of superstition after the taping. I had often stated that I didn't think that God, even if he existed, would be angry with an honest atheist who voted his convictions. Would he, however, tolerate a *wiseguy* atheist? Of course, no lightning bolt had struck me on the spot when I virtually dared him to find me, but the show was only a taping. What would happen when it was actually aired on September 5? . . .

September 5 . . . at 5 A.M. . . . I woke with the familiar agony [of a kidney stone]. There followed a nine-hour period of unbearable pain, the worst and most prolonged I have ever experienced. At one point, I could only gasp, "All right, God, you found me! Now let go!"

[He went to the hospital, and the doctor tried to give him an injection of morphine.] As he approached, the pain ebbed away. Whatever it was the kidney stone was doing, it stopped doing it.

I said, vigorously, "No, don't. Don't use the hypodermic. The pain has stopped. It's really stopped." I must have seemed like a faker afraid of the needle, but no one with an acute kidney-stone attack can sit up in bed and smile. The pain had to have left. (Try it yourself and see.) The doctor had no choice but to let me go home, and I managed to catch the *David Frost Show*.

[Isaac had to add] I was with a group of people about a week later, and one of them said, "I saw you on the *David Frost Show*."

A young man of nineteen was part of the group and he said, with genial insolence, "And what did you do, Dr. Asimov? Read commercials?"

With a haughty determination to squelch the young cockerel at once by a thrust too outrageous to parry, I said, "Not at all! I was demonstrating sexual techniques."

"Oh," he said, smiling sweetly, "you remembered?"

I was wiped out completely.

[Letter about a letter from a minister] I have shaken his faith in God. This bothered me for while I am perfectly content with my own rationalist view of the universe, I would not wish to take Linus's blanket from him just because I can live without one (or perhaps because my blanket is of another sort). So I wrote back to the effect that people who limited God to a tiny universe six thousand years old and required him to be forever interfering with his creation in order to make it work and to concern himself with a single planet and a single life-form were perhaps sacrilegiously limiting his powers; and trying to cut him down to man-size.

[Written in his last autobiography, when he was terminally ill] The afterlife is accepted by the vast majority, even in the absolute absence of any evidence for its existence. How did it all start? My . . . speculation is this—As far as we know, the human species is the only one that understands that death is inevitable, not only in general but in every individual's case. No matter how we protect ourselves against predation, accident, and infection, each of us will eventually die through the sheer erosion of our body—*and we know it.*

There must have come a time when this knowledge first began to permeate a human community, and it must have been a terrible shock. It amounted to the "discovery of death." All that could make the thought of death bearable was to suppose that it didn't really exist; that it was an illusion. After one *apparently* died, one continued to live in some other fashion and in some other place. This was undoubtedly encouraged by the fact that dead people often appeared in the dreams of their friends and relatives and the dream appearances could be interpreted as representing a shade or ghost of the still-living "dead" person.

So speculations about the afterworld grew more and more elaborate. The Greeks and the Hebrews thought that much of the afterworld (Hades or Sheol) was a mere place of dimness and all but nonexistence. However, there were special places of torment for evildoers (Tartarus) and places of delight for men who were approved of by the gods (Elysian Fields or Paradise). These extremes were seized on by people who wished to see themselves blessed and their enemies punished, if not in this world, then at least in the next.

Imagination was stretched to conceive of the final resting place of evil people or of anyone, however good, who didn't subscribe to quite the same mumbo jumbo that the imaginer did. This gave us our modern notion of Hell as a place of eternal punishment of the most vicious kind. This is the drooling dream of a sadist grafted onto a God who is proclaimed to be all-merciful and all-good.

Imagination has never managed to build up a serviceable Heaven, however. The Islamic Heaven has its houris, ever available and ever virginal, so that it becomes an eternal sex house. The Norse Heaven has its heroes feasting at Valhalla and fighting each other between feasts, so that it becomes an eternal restaurant and battlefield. And our own Heaven is usually pictured as a place where everyone has wings and plunks a harp in order to sing unending hymns of praise to God.

What human being with a modicum of intelligence could stand any of such Heavens, or the others that people have invented, for very long? Where is there a Heaven with the opportunity for reading, for writing, for exploring, for interesting conversation, for scientific investigation? I never heard of one.

If you read John Milton's *Paradise Lost* you will find that his Heaven is described as an eternal sing-along of praise to God. It is no wonder that one-third of the angels rebelled. When they were cast down into Hell, they *then* engaged in intellectual exercises (read the poem if you don't believe me) and I believe that, Hell or not, they were better off. When I read it, I sympathized strongly with Milton's Satan and considered him the hero of the epic, whether Milton intended that or not.

But what is *my belief*? Since I am an atheist and do not believe that either God or Satan, Heaven or Hell, exists, I can only suppose that when I die, there will only be an eternity of nothingness to follow. After all, the Universe existed for 15 billion years before I was born and I (whatever "I" may be) survived it all in nothingness.

People may well ask if this isn't a bleak and hopeless belief. How can I live with the specter of nothingness hanging over my head?

I don't find it a specter. There is nothing frightening about an eternal dreamless sleep. Surely it is better than eternal torment in Hell or eternal boredom in Heaven. And what if I'm mistaken? The question was asked of Bertrand Russell, the famous mathematician, philosopher, and outspoken atheist. "What if you died," he was asked, "and found yourself face to face with God? What then?"

And the doughty old champion said, "I would say, 'Lord, you should have given us more evidence.' "

[Recently] I dreamed I had died and gone to Heaven. I looked about and knew where I was—green fields, fleecy clouds, perfumed air, and the distant, ravishing sound of the heavenly choir. And there was the recording angel smiling broadly at me in greeting.

I said, in wonder, "Is this Heaven?"

The recording angel said, "It is."

I said (and on waking and remembering, I was proud of my integrity), "But there must be some mistake. I don't belong here. I'm an atheist."

"No mistake," said the recording angel.

"But as an atheist how can I qualify?"

The recording angel said sternly, "*We* decide who qualifies. Not you."

"I see," I said. I looked about, pondered for a moment, then turned to the recording angel and asked, "Is there a typewriter here that I can use?"

The significance of the dream was clear to me. I felt Heaven to be the act of writing, and I have been in Heaven for over half a century and I have always known this.

A second point of significance is the recording angel's remark that Heaven, not human beings, decides who qualifies. I take that to mean that if I were not an atheist, I would believe in a God who would choose to save people on the basis of the totality of their lives and not the pattern of their words. I think he would prefer an honest and righteous atheist to a TV preacher whose every word is God, God, God, and whose every deed is foul, foul, foul.

I would also want a God who would not allow a Hell. Infinite torture can only be a punishment for infinite evil, and I don't believe that infinite evil can be said to exist even in the case of Hitler. Besides, if most human governments are civilized enough to try to eliminate torture and outlaw cruel and unusual punishments, can we expect anything less of an all-merciful God?

I feel that if there were an afterlife, punishment for evil would be reasonable and of a fixed term. And I feel that the longest and worst punishment should be reserved for those who slandered God by inventing Hell.

But all that is just playing. I am firm in my beliefs. I am an atheist and, in my opinion, death is followed by an eternal and dreamless sleep.

Five.
PRODIGY

My father was a small storekeeper, with no knowledge of American culture, with no time to guide me, and no ability to do so even if he had the time. All he could do was to urge me to get good marks in school, and that was something I had every intention of doing anyhow.

In other words, circumstances conspired to allow me to find my own happy level, which turned out to be sufficiently prodigious for all purposes and yet kept the pressure at a sufficiently reasonable value to allow me to chug along rapidly with no feeling of strain whatever. It meant that I kept my "prodigiousness" for all my life, in one way or another.

In fact, when asked if I was an infant prodigy (and I *am* asked this with disconcerting frequency), I have taken to answering, "Yes, indeed, and I still am."

I learned to read before I went to school. Spurred on by my realization that my parents could not yet read English, I took to asking the older children on the block to teach me the alphabet and how each letter sounded. I then began to sound out all the words I could find on signs and elsewhere and in that way I learned to read with a minimum of outside help.

When he found out I could read, [my father bought] me a small dictionary, "so you can look up words and know how to spell them."

My first thought was that it was surely impossible to find some one word among all the incredible number, but after I studied the book for a while, the workings of "alphabetical order" became plain and I asked my father if that was how the words were arranged. My father had clearly held back the information to see if I could work it out for myself, and was terribly pleased.

[All this] gave my father the idea that there was something strange and remarkable about me. Many years later, he looked through one of my books and said, "How did you learn all this, Isaac?"

"From you, Pappa," I said.

"From me? I don't know any of this."

"You didn't have to, Pappa," I said. "You valued learning and you taught me to value it. Once I learned to value it, the rest came without trouble."

I did not realize that my memory was remarkable until I noticed that my classmates didn't have memories like it. After something had been explained to them, they would forget and would have to have it explained *again* and *again*. In my case it was only necessary that I be told once.

Actually, my memory for things that are of no particular interest to me is not much better than normal, and I can be guilty of appalling lapses when my self-absorption gets the better of me.

Early in my school career, I turned out to be an incorrigible disciplinary problem. No, I wasn't destructive, or disobedient, or difficult in any way. The point was that since I understood what the teacher was saying as fast as she could say it, I found time hanging heavy on my hands, so I would occasionally talk to my neighbor. That was my great crime. I talked in school.

I may have been gifted with a delightful memory and a quick understanding at a very early stage, but I was not gifted with great experience and a deep understanding of human nature. I did not realize that other children would not appreciate the fact that I knew more than they did and could learn more quickly than they did . . . I cheerfully made it clear, at all times, that I was very bright.

I was small for my age, weak for my age, and younger than anyone else in the class (eventually two and a half years younger due to my being shoved ahead periodically). . . . I was scapegoated, with diminishing intensity, right into my early twenties . . . [but] in the end, I did learn. There is still no way of hiding the fact that I am unusual, considering the vast number of books I have written and published, and the vast number of subjects I have covered in those books, but I have learned, in ordinary life, to "turn it off" and meet people on their own terms.

If only an infant prodigy could be prodigious in grasping human nature and not in memory and quickness of intellect alone. But then, not everything is inborn. The truly important parts of life develop slowly with experience, and that person is lucky who can learn them more quickly and with greater ease than I did.

Once I could read, and as my ability to read improved rapidly, I had nothing to read. My schoolbooks lasted me just a few days. I finished every one of them in the course of the first week of the term and thereafter was educated for that half year. The teacher had very little to tell me . . .

The candy store was filled with reading material but [at first] my father wouldn't let me touch it. He felt it to be trash . . . and I chafed. What to do? My father got me a library card. . . . Had my father had the time, and had he been of American culture . . . he might have directed me to what he considered good literature and, without meaning it, have narrowed my intellectual horizons.

However, he couldn't. I was on my own. My father assumed that any book that was in a public library was suitable reading and so he made no attempt to supervise the books I took out. And I, without guidance, sampled everything.

By the purest of circumstances, I found books dealing with the Greek myths. I mispronounced all the Greek names and much of it was a mystery to me, but I found myself fascinated. In fact, when I was a few years older, I read the *Iliad* over and over and over, taking it out of the library every chance I could, and starting all over again with the first verse as soon as I had completed the last.

You could recite any verse at random and I could tell you where it would be found. I also read the *Odyssey* but with lesser pleasure, for it wasn't as bloody . . .

One thing leads to another, even accidents. Once, when I was ill and couldn't go to the library, I persuaded my poor mother to go for me, promising that I would read any book she brought me. What she brought back was a fictionalized life of Thomas Edison. That disappointed me, but I had promised, so I read it and that *might* have been my introduction to the world of science and technology.

Then, too, as I grew older, fiction drew me to nonfiction. It was impossible to read Alexandre Dumas's *The Three Musketeers* without becoming curious about French history . . .

I read *The Jealous Gods* by Gertrude Atherton (thinking it was mythology, I imagine). I found myself reading about Athens and Sparta, and about Alcibiades, in particular. The picture I have of Alcibiades, as drawn by Atherton, has never left me.

Again, *The Glory of the Purple* by William Stearns Davis introduced me to the Byzantine Empire and to Leo III (the Isaurian), to say nothing of Greek fire. Another of his books introduced me to the Persian War and Aristides.

All this led me to history itself . . .

When I grew a little older, I discovered Charles Dickens (I have read *Pickwick Papers* twenty-six times and *Nicholas Nickleby* some ten times) . . . Dickens's pictures of poverty and misery always had the leaven of humor, which made it more tolerable [than the books by Eugene Sue].

I also read a justly forgotten book, *Ten Thousand a Year* by Samuel Warren, which had an excellent villain by the name of Oily Gammon. I think that was the first time I realized that a villain, not a "hero" might be the true protagonist of a book.

I read almost the entire gamut of nineteenth-century fiction. Because so much of it was by British authors, I became a spiritual Englishman and a conscious Anglophile.

About the only thing that was almost totally left out of my reading was twentieth-century fiction. (Not twentieth-century nonfiction, which I read voluminously.) Perhaps the libraries I went to were themselves poor in modern fiction . . .

That childish bent has remained. . . . Most twentieth-century *serious* fiction is beyond me. Mysteries and humor are another matter. Of all the twentieth-century writers the two I have read [and reread] most thoroughly, and with undiminished delight, are Agatha Christie and P. G. Wodehouse.

All this incredibly miscellaneous reading, the result of lack of guidance, left its indelible mark. My interest was aroused in twenty different directions and all those interests remained. I have written books on mythology, on the Bible, on Shakespeare, on history, on science, and so on. Even my lack of reading modern fiction has left its mark, for I am perfectly aware that there is a certain old-fashioned quality about my writing . . .

I received the fundamentals of my education in school, but that was not enough. My *real* education, the superstructure, the details, the true architecture, I got out of the public library. For an impoverished child whose family could not afford to buy books, the library was the open door to wonder and achievement, and I can never be sufficiently grateful that I had the wit to charge through that door and make the most of it.

Now, when I read constantly about the way in which library funds are being cut and cut, I can only think that the door is closing and that American society has found one more way to destroy itself.

Six.
BECOMING A WRITER

 [About 1927] I briefly made the acquaintance of a remarkable youngster [who] had the ability to tell stories that held me enthralled . . . for the first time, I realized stories could be invented, and that was a terribly important thing to learn. Until then, I had naturally assumed that stories existed only in books and had probably been there, unchanged, from the beginning of time, and that they were without human creators.

If I couldn't afford to buy science-fiction magazines, neither could my friends at the junior high school. I could, at least, read the stories [in the candy store—his father thought they were okay because they were about science]. . . . I discovered that I owned a valuable commodity—the ability to *tell* stories.

I took over the role of my story-telling friend . . . and now it was others who listened to me. Of course, the stories weren't my own, and I made no pretense that they were. I carefully explained that I had read them in science-fiction magazines.

During lunch hour, we would sit on the curb in front of the school, each with our sandwiches and, to anywhere from two to ten eager listeners, I would repeat the stories I had read, together with such personal embellishments as I could manage. It increased my pleasure in science fiction and I discovered, for the first time in my life, that I loved to have an audience. I found that I could speak before a group, even when some of them were strangers to me, without embarrassment.

It was about then [1931] that, for the first time, I began to write stories of my own. . . . The story I usually tell is that I felt bad about not having any *permanent* reading material, only books that had to be returned to the library or magazines that had to be returned to the racks. It occurred to me I might copy a book and keep the copy. I chose a book on Greek mythology for the purpose and, in five minutes, realized this was an impractical procedure. Then, finally, I got the further idea of writing my own books and allowing them to be my permanent library.

Undoubtedly this was a factor, but it can't be the entire motive. I must simply have had the terrible urge to make up a story.

Why not? Surely many people have the urge to make up a story. It has to be a common human desire—a restless mind, a mysterious world, a feeling of emulation when someone tells a story. Isn't storytelling what one does when one sits around a campfire? Aren't many social gatherings devoted to reminiscences and doesn't everyone like to tell a story of something that really happened? And aren't such stories inevitably embroidered and improved until the resemblance to reality becomes distant?

One can imagine early man sitting about campfires telling stories of great hunting feats that exaggerate the truth ridiculously but which are not questioned because every other person present intends to tell similar lies. A particularly good story would be repeated over and over and attributed to some ancestor or some legendary hunter.

And some people would, inevitably, be especially skilled at telling a story, and their talents would be in demand when there was some leisure time. They might even be rewarded with a haunch of meat if the story was really interesting. This would make them labor to invent bigger, better, and more exciting tales, naturally.

I don't see how there can be any doubt about it. The storytelling impulse is innate in most people, and if it happens to be combined with enough talent and enough drive, it cannot be suppressed. That was so in my case.

I just *had* to write. . . . Writing was exciting because I never planned ahead. I made up my stories as I went along and it was a great deal like reading a book I *hadn't* written. What would happen to the characters? How would they get out of the particular scrape they were in? The excitement was all I wrote for in those early years. In my wildest dreams it never occurred to me that anything I wrote would ever be published. I didn't write out of ambition.

As a matter of fact, I still write my fiction in that manner—making it up as I go along—with one all-important improvement. I have learned that there's no use in making things up as you go along if you have no clearly defined resolution to your story . . .

What I do now is think up a problem *and a resolution to that problem.* I then begin the story, making it up as I go along, having all the excitement of finding out what will happen to the characters and how they will get out of their scrapes, but working steadily toward the known resolution, so that I don't get lost en route. When asked for advice by beginners, I always stress that. Know your ending, I say, or the river of your story may finally sink into the desert sands and never reach the sea.

In the fall of 1931 . . . just before my twelfth birthday . . . I was going to write a series book, the first of many, I decided (apparently I always had the instinctive knowledge that I would be prolific), and I called it *The Greenville Chums at College.* I had seen a book called *The Darewell Chums at College,* and it seemed to me that by substituting Greenville for Darewell I had made all possible concessions to the need for originality.

I wrote two chapters that evening, making it up as I was going along (something that is still my system), and my mind was full of it the next morning. That day at lunch, I said to one of the youngsters who was particularly assiduous in attending my story-telling sessions: "Hey, let me tell you a story."

And tell him I did, in full detail, and just about word for word, up to the point where I had faded out. He was listening, rapt with attention, and when I stopped, he demanded I continue. I explained that it was all I had so far and he said, "Can I borrow the book when you've finished reading it?"

I was astonished. I had either neglected to make it clear to him, or he had failed to understand, that I was *writing* the book. He thought it was another already printed story I was retelling. The implied compliment staggered me, and from that day on, I secretly took myself seriously as a writer. I remember the name of the young man whose remark unwittingly did this for me. It was Emmanuel Bershadsky.

I never saw him again after I left junior high school, but thank you Emmanuel, wherever you are.

Still, *The Greenville Chums At College* did not continue forever. It petered out after eight chapters . . . a junior-high-school youngster living in a shabby neighborhood in Brooklyn knows very little about small-town life and even less about college. Even I, myself, was forced eventually to recognize the fact that I didn't know what I was talking about (especially when the plot made it necessary to describe what went on inside a chemistry laboratory) . . .

Just the same, from that time on, I never stayed away from my copybooks for long. Every once in a while I would drift back to try my hand at writing again. Nothing lasted very long for quite a number of years, but I never quit altogether.

[In 1935 his father bought him a used Underwood typewriter for ten dollars.] How old it was, I don't know, but it worked perfectly . . . I sat at the typewriter and typed by the hunt-and-peck method.

I was at it every day until my father, coming up one day for his afternoon nap, stopped to watch his son type. He frowned and said, "Why do you type with one finger, instead of with all your fingers like on a piano?"

I said, "I don't know how to do it with all my fingers, Pappa."

My father had an easy solution for that. "Learn!" he thundered. "If

I catch you typing with one finger again, I will take away the type-writer."

I sighed, for I knew he would. Fortunately there was Mazie, who lived across the street and for whom [I had a] pure and puppyish passion. . . . She knew how to type. She showed me how to place my hands on the typewriter keys and which fingers controlled which keys. She watched while, very slowly, I typed the word "the" with the left-hand-first finger, right-hand-first finger, and left-hand-middle finger. She then offered to give me periodic lessons.

An excuse to be alone with her every once in a while was just what I was looking for, but I had my pride. No one was ever allowed to teach me any more than I required to begin teaching myself. "That's all right," I said. "I'll practice."

And I did. . . . Once I was typing, of course, I had much more incentive to write. I remember distinctly that the first piece of fiction I ever wrote on the typewriter involved a group of men wandering on some quest through a universe in which there were elves, dwarves, and wizards, and in which magic worked. It was as though I had some pre-monition of J. R. R. Tolkien's *Lord of the Rings*. I can't remember what it was that inspired me in this direction. I had read *The Arabian Nights*, the E. Nesbit fantasies (particularly her stories about the psam-mead) and all sorts of books of magic and legendry, but none of them stick in my mind as sufficient.

I wrote better than forty pages, both sides, single-space, no margins, and I imagine I must have turned out nearly thirty thousand words before I ran down. But run down I did, and it cured me. I had my fill of fantasy and I didn't try again for years—and never in any lengthy way.

The next item of fiction I tried to write, possibly in 1936, was, at last, *and for the first time*, science fiction. Again, it was a long-winded attempt at writing an endless novel . . . [which] died just as my previous efforts did. What I now remember about my science-fiction epic is that there was a great deal of talk about the fifth dimension at the start and that later on there was some catastrophe that destroyed photosynthesis (though not on Earth, I think). I remember one sentence, and one sentence only. It was "Whole forests stood sere and brown in midsummer." Why I remember that, I don't know, but that is the earliest existing Asimovian science-fiction sentence.

It is rather embarrassing . . . to realize how little I learned about writing through careful study and intelligent consideration of what I read, and how much I made my way forward through mere intuition. Until I was a published writer, I remained completely ignorant of the fact that there were books on how to write and college-level courses on the subject. . . . [But they] would have spoiled my natural style; made me observe an artificial caution; would have hedged me about with rules that I could not have followed without wearing myself out.

All of that, however, is probably simple rationalization designed to resign me to things as they are.

Seven.
SCIENCE-FICTION FAN

[In 1937 the family moved to a larger apartment and for the first time Isaac had a room of his own—in a railroad flat.] The privacy was virtually nil [for] anyone wanting to go from the living room to their bedroom had to go through *my* bedroom. Still, at least there was no one actually in the room with me.

Then, too, I was even given a closet of my own and permission to keep my magazines there. After seven years of reading science-fiction magazines, I found myself more enamored of the stories than ever. They were, as a rule, every bit as exciting as the pulp adventures of the "Shadow" and "Doc Savage," which I also read, and, in addition, brought me into a fantastic world beyond anything earthbound literature could offer.

The horizons in science fiction were limitless, and the excitement of outer space, of time travel, of the far future seemed a continually unsurpassable delight. It was the pleasure of magic combined with the discipline of science. It was just enough of a slipping of bonds to give freedom, and not enough to seem folly and anarchy. It was the use of imagination to give the effect of a roller coaster loop-the-loop, with the use of the laws of nature to keep you on the track and bring you safely home.

[Finding kindred souls] I had become a science-fiction "fan" (the word is short for "fanatic"—I'm not joking) by the mid-1930s. By that I mean that I did not confine myself merely to the reading of science fiction. I tried to participate in the machinery. The simplest way was to write letters to the editor.

The science-fiction magazines all had letters columns, and readers were encouraged to write. The magazine that most attracted me was *Astounding Stories* . . . [to which] I wrote my first letter in 1935, and it was printed. I listed the stories I liked and disliked, said why, and asked for smooth edges, rather than the typical messy rough edges of the pulps that shredded and left paper lint everywhere. (The magazine did provide smooth edges, eventually. Nor were they holding back out of callousness. Smoothing the edges cost money.) . . .

There were other ways of being a fan, too. Individual fans might get to know each other (perhaps from the letters column, since names and addresses were given). If they were within reach of each other, they could get together, discuss the stories, swap magazines, and so on. This developed into "fan clubs." In 1934, one of the magazines invented the Science Fiction League of America and fans who joined could make friends over still wider areas.

Stuck in the candy store as I was, I knew nothing about the fan clubs and it never occurred to me to join the League. However, a young man who had gone to Boys High with me noted my name on the letters in *Astounding* and sent me a card in 1938 inviting me to attend meetings of the Queens Science Fiction Club . . .

On September 18, 1938, I met, for the first time, other science-fiction fans. However, between the first invitation and a second card giving me instructions on how to get to the meeting place, there had been a split in the Queens club, and a small splinter group formed a new fan organization. (Eventually, I came to understand that science-fiction fans were a quarrelsome and contentious bunch and that clubs were forever splitting up into hostile factions.)

My high school friend belonged to the small splinter group and, in all ignorance that I was not going to the Queens club, I joined them. The splinter group had broken off because they were activists who felt that science-fiction fans ought to take a stronger anti-Fascist stand, while the main group held that science fiction was above politics. Had

I known about the split I would have resolutely sided with the splinter group, so that by ending up there I came to the right place.

The new group gave themselves a rather long and grandiloquent name but they are popularly known as the Futurians and they were certainly the most astonishing fan club that was ever founded. They consisted of a group of brilliant teenagers who, as nearly as I could tell, all came from broken homes and had led miserable, or, at the very least, insecure childhoods.

Once again, I was an outsider, for I had a tightly knit family and a happy childhood, but in other respects I was charmed by all of them and felt that I had found a spiritual home.

To tell you how my life changed, I must explain my views on friendship—

One often hears in books, and movies, of childhood friendships that last throughout life; of onetime schoolmates who associate with each other through the years; of army buddies who are constantly getting drunk and reliving the joys of barracks life; of college chums helping each other through life for the sake of the old school tie.

It may happen, but I am always skeptical. It seemed to me that people who went to school together or were in the army together were living in a state of forced intimacy that they had not chosen for themselves. A kind of friendship-by-custom-and-propinquity might exist among those who happened to like each other independently or who were thrown into social togetherness outside of the artificial environments of school or army, but not otherwise.

In my own case, I had not one school friendship that survived school and not one army friendship that survived the army. Partly this was because there was no opportunity for social interaction outside either school or army and partly it was because of my own self-absorption.

However, once I met the Futurians, everything changed. Here, although there was little chance for social interaction most of the time, although I sometimes remained out of touch with this one or that one for a long period of time, I made close friendships which lasted in some cases for half a century, right down to the present.

Why?

At last I met people who burned with the same fire I did; who loved science fiction as I did; who wanted to write science fiction as I did; who had the same kind of erratic brilliance that I had. I did not have to recognize a soul mate consciously. I felt it at once without the necessity of intellectualizing it. In fact, in some cases, both within the Futurians and without, I felt soul-matehood and eternal friendship even with people whom I didn't really like.

Eight.
STARTING TO WRITE
SCIENCE FICTION

[After preparing an elaborate index-card system on science-fiction stories which] made me conscious of stories as literary items, as never before and, after six years of writing amorphous, disconnected, unending—and therefore dying—fictional items, it finally occurred to me to write a *story* . . . on May 29, 1937. I remembered the date a few years later and jotted it down, and still have the jotting, so I know . . . I was nearly seventeen and a half at the time. The story I began to compose . . . was entitled "Cosmic Corkscrew."

In it I viewed time as a helix (that is, something like a bedspring). Someone could cut across from one turn directly to the next, thus moving into the future by some exact interval, but being incapable of traveling one day less into the future. (I didn't know the term at the time, but what I had done was to "quantize" time travel.)

As far as I knew then, the notion of helical time was original with me. [It may have been inspired by] the neutrino. The existence of the neutrino had been postulated five years earlier and it had not been detected. Indeed, at the time it was thought it might never be detected.

Of course, the reason it wasn't detected was that it had neither electric charge nor mass, so that it offered no handle to the detecting techniques of the time—but that was prosaic.

What if the neutrino could not be detected because it went off into the past or the future? I had a vision of neutrinos flashing through time, backward and forward, and thought of them as a vehicle for time travel.

That turned out to be typical of my science fiction. I usually thought of some scientific gimmick and built a story about that. In this case, the time-as-helix notion came only afterward as a way of limiting my hero's freedom of action and creating the plot complication.

My protagonist made the cut across time and found Earth deserted. All animal life was gone, yet there was every sign that life had existed until very shortly before—and no indication at all of what had happened to bring about the disappearance. It was told in the first person from a lunatic asylum, because the narrator had, of course, been placed in one when he returned and tried to tell his tale.

In this story, I had the full panoply of pulp style, for I knew nothing else. I read enormous quantities of pulp magazines, to say nothing of the florid fiction of the nineteenth century and, without even thinking about it, I loaded my sentences with adjectives and adverbs and had my characters crying out, and starting back, and shrieking madly, and screaming curses. Everything was in jagged, primary colors.

But as far as possible I was interested in realistic science, or the illusion of it. Even in that first story, I went to some trouble to explain about neutrinos as authentically as I could, for instance, even if I did introduce the time-travel angle out of left field.

With time, the pulpish aspects of my writing became subdued and faded out, though perhaps not as rapidly as they would have were I better acquainted with contemporary writing by literary masters. My concern for realistic science stayed, however, and I quickly became and remained a writer of "hard" science fiction.

[Another characteristic of pulp fiction] Though women were routinely threatened by the villains, the nature of the threat was never explicitly stated. It was a period of strong sexual repression, and sexual acts and threats could only be referred to in "family magazines" in the most distant way. Of course, no one minded if there was a continuous display of violence and sadism—that was all right for the family—but no sex.

This reduced women to little mannikin figures who never contributed actively to the plot. . there solely to make the villains more villainous, the heroes more heroic. And in being rescued, they played a purely passive role, their part consisting mostly of screaming. I can't recall (though I'm sure there must have been rare cases) any woman trying to join the fight and help the hero; any woman picking up a stick or rock and trying to lambaste the villain. No, they were like does, idly cropping the grass while they waited for the stags to stop fighting so that they would know which harem they would belong to.

Under the circumstances, any red-blooded male reading pulp fiction (like me) grew very impatient with the introduction of females. Knowing in advance they would merely be stumbling blocks, I wanted them out. I remember writing letters to magazines complaining about women characters—their very existence.

This was one of the reasons (not the only one) that in my own early stories I omitted women. In most cases, I left them out altogether. It was a flaw, and another sign of my pulpish origins.

[His favorite science-fiction magazine, *Astounding*, was late in appearing.] I had enough money to make the subway trip to Street and Smith, Inc., and to buy a copy of *Astounding* there if I wished.

Choosing my mother as the softer touch in this case, I argued her into giving me permission to take off two hours that otherwise I would have to spend in the store—choosing two hours during my father's afternoon nap, so that I would not have to ask his permission as well. (Fortunately, it was finals week, and I had no classes to attend, merely exams to take.)

Then off I went. I might have been over eighteen by now, but a sheltered life is a sheltered life. It was one of the first times I had ever taken a subway into Manhattan on my own, except to go to school. I was going to wander about streets I did not know in order to make my way into strange buildings and ask questions of strange people. It made me uneasy.

I got there. It was not really a difficult task. The Street and Smith offices were at 79 Seventh Avenue, not far away from a subway station I passed through every day going to and from school. I placed my case before the elevator man, who gave me directions, and on the fifth floor I met a Mr. Clifford, who explained to me that the publication date had been changed from the second Wednesday to the third Friday. When I craved certainty, he showed me a printed schedule, and there was *Astounding* listed under Friday, May 20. Assuming it would actually come Thursday, May 19, it meant I had two more days to wait.

On Thursday, May 19, the June issue of *Astounding* came, and although it was raining that day, the sun shone brilliantly for me. It was the day of my chemistry finals, but I bothered with no last-minute studying. Until the moment I had to leave for school, I read the magazine. (It's all right. I did well in the exam.)

I had not entirely forgotten "Cosmic Corkscrew," which I had begun just a year before and which I had worked at in very desultory fashion for a few months. In the spring I had even taken the manuscript out of the drawer and thought about it, and, on occasion, had written a page or two, or had rewritten a passage.

Now, however, after the incident with *Astounding*, I was galvanized into activity. In the first place, the days during which I had imagined the magazine to be lost forever had revealed to me the extent to which science fiction had seized upon me. It made me realize something that until then had been only subliminal—that one of my ambitions in life was to be a science-fiction writer.

I did not want to be simply a writer, you understand. Nor was I interested in making money. Neither of these two items ever occurred to me. What I wanted was to write a *science-fiction* story and to have it appear in a *science-fiction* magazine. That would be to join the company of the demi gods whose names I knew and idolized: Jack Williamson, Nat Schachner, E. E. Smith, Edmund Hamilton, John W. Campbell, and all the rest.

In the second place, my visit to Street and Smith had somehow reduced the great gulf that separated myself and the demi gods. Street and Smith, and therefore *Astounding*, had become attainable. It existed in a real building in a real space, a building I could reach and enter and it contained people who would speak to me.

In the third place, my junior year at college [Columbia University] was completed and I would have more time on my hands.

With all these factors meeting . . . I finished "Cosmic Corkscrew" on June 19, 1938. It was actually the first piece of fiction I had ever completed with a view to possible publication. The next question was what to do with it. I hadn't the faintest idea as to how one went about submitting a story to a magazine. Nowadays, there are many youngsters who don't know, and all of them (it sometimes seems to me) write to me for advice. I wasn't even smart enough at that time to write to anyone for advice.

I knew I might mail it, but even if I could figure out what I was supposed to say in the letter, there was a problem. As I said in my diary, "If I mail it, it will cost a mint of money as the damn thing weighs four ounces."

Mail was three cents an ounce, so that the "mint of money" came to twelve cents.

We counted the pennies in those days. Just a few days earlier my father had refused to have a plumber fix a leaking gas pipe because the job would cost three dollars and he went shopping for a more reasonable plumber.

Again, through sharp bargaining, my father managed to get someone to agree to fix a fountain pen for thirty-four cents . . . [he explained] that he managed this low price by leaving out a new clip for an additional twenty-five cents. . . . I told him, rather forcefully, that a fountain pen was useless without a clip, and he called up to have that added to the tab.

None of this, at the time, seemed to represent the cruelty of poverty to us. We were used to it. We were aware at all times of the exact amount of money we had in our pockets, right down to the penny, and every outgo, however small, was carefully considered.

It did not escape me that a round-trip subway fare would cost me ten cents, or two cents less than to mail the story. Furthermore, the subway fare would enable me to check once again on the lateness of *Astounding*. On June 21, with the July issue still not at the store, I discussed the matter with my father.

I had till then kept the matter of my writing entirely to myself. I had viewed it merely as a hobby, a way of spending my time doing something interesting. It was for my own amusement only. . . . I had the instinctive feeling even then that I would not welcome criticism. Even when I came to my father with this purely tactical problem of how to submit a story, I did not offer to let him read it. Nor did he ask to read it; but if he had done so, I would have refused. (I haven't changed . . . I still don't discuss my stories when they are in the process of being written, and I still don't welcome criticism.)

Of course, as to such collateral matters as *submitting* a story, I was willing, even eager, to seek advice, and my father's suggestion was that I not only make the trip by subway, but also that I hand the manuscript to Mr. Campbell himself.

The thought was a frightening one. It became even more frightening when my father further suggested that necessary preliminaries included a shave and my best suit. That meant I would have to take additional time, but the day was already wearing on, and I didn't have very much time. I had to be back for the afternoon newspaper delivery, just in case the delivery boy didn't show up.

I compromised. I shaved, but did not bother changing suits, and off I went.

I was convinced that for daring to ask to see the editor of *Astounding Science Fiction* I would be thrown out of the building bodily, and that my manuscript would be torn up and thrown out after me in a shower of confetti. My father, however, who had lofty notions, was convinced that a writer (by which he meant anyone with a manuscript) would be treated with the respect due an intellectual. He had no fears in the matter, for had he himself not braved the Soviet bureaucracy? Maybe so, but it was I who had to brave Street and Smith.

I put off the crisis [by asking about the publication delay and was told] that the new publication date was the fourth Friday every month.

There was now no excuse to delay any further. I went into the main building and asked to see the editor. The girl behind the desk spoke briefly into the phone and said, "Mr. Campbell will see you."

I was astonished. I had asked to see him only because my father had told me to, but I was convinced that this was just my father's lack of sophistication. I assumed I would be asked to leave the manuscript with the receptionist, and this I was prepared to do.

What I did not know was that Campbell's invitation was what would have happened in many cases of this sort. John Campbell was a most unusual fellow who loved to talk and who would seize almost anyone as an audience. Furthermore, and this may have been a crucial point, he knew me from my recent letters—my name was familiar to him—and that meant he certainly wouldn't turn me away.

What if I hadn't written those letters? What if I didn't live on the subway line? What if I lived—I wouldn't say Nebraska—but in Westchester, Jersey City, Staten Island; anywhere that made Campbell reachable only by spending more than ten cents in fares?

In that case, I would not have traveled to Street and Smith, but would have mailed the story. Or if I had gone there, without having written letters to the magazine, he might conceivably not have seen me at all. And without personal contact, everything might have been different.

But it wasn't different; it was the way it was. The receptionist directed me through a large, loftlike room filled with huge rolls of paper and enormous piles of magazines and permeated with the heavenly smell of pulp.

And there, in a small room on the other side, was Mr. Campbell . . . not quite twenty-eight years old at the time.

Under his own name, and under his pen name of Don A. Stuart, he was one of the most famous and highly regarded authors of science fiction, but he was about to bury his writing reputation forever under the far greater renown he was to gain as editor.

Campbell was a large man, an opinionated man, who smoked and talked constantly, and who enjoyed above anything else, the production of outrageous ideas, which he bounced off his listener and dared him to refute. And it was difficult to refute Campbell even when his ideas were absolutely and madly illogical. And illogical they certainly seemed to be to *me*, for he was always an idiosyncratic conservative in his view of life, whereas I was an idiosyncratic liberal—and we never agreed on anything. Yet although he stood somewhere to the right of Attila the Hun in politics, he was, in person, as kind, generous, and decent a human being as I have ever met.

He was the quintessential editor, who fertilized and nourished a whole generation of writers . . . it didn't matter that he rejected you. There was an enthusiasm about him and an all-encompassing friendliness that was contagious. I always left him eager to write further.

Many years later I asked Campbell (with whom I had, by then, grown to be on the closest of terms) why he had bothered with me at all, since the first story was surely utterly impossible.

"Yes, it was impossible," he said frankly, for he never flattered. "On the other hand, I saw something in *you*. You were eager and listened and I knew you wouldn't quit no matter how many rejections I handed you. As long as you were willing to work hard at improving, I was willing to work with you."

That was Campbell. I wasn't the only writer, whether newcomer or old-timer, he was to work with in this fashion. Patiently, and out of his own enormous vitality and talent, he built up a stable of the best science-fiction writers the world had, till then, ever seen.

[Back to that fateful day at Street and Smith—in 1938, Isaac's senior year at Columbia] Campbell promised to read my story that night and to send a letter, whether acceptance or rejection, the next day. He promised also that in case of rejection he would tell me what was wrong with the story so that I could improve.

He lived up to both promises. Two days later, on June 23, the manuscript came back. It was a rejection.

As my diary put it: "At 0:30 I received back 'Cosmic Corkscrew' with a polite letter of rejection. He didn't like the slow beginning, the suicide at the end."

Campbell also didn't like the first-person narration and the stiff dialog. He pointed out that the length (nine thousand words) was inconvenient—too long for a short story, too short for a novelette. Magazines had to be put together like jigsaw puzzles, you see, and certain lengths for individual stories are more convenient than others.

I was off and running. The joy of having spent an hour or more with Campbell, the thrill of talking face to face with an idol, had already filled me with the ambition to write another science-fiction story, one that was better than the first, so that I could have occasion to meet him again.

In fact, by the time I returned to the store on the day of that visit, I had worked out another story in my mind, one I intended to call "Stowaway," and I waited only to hear from Campbell before starting it. His letter of rejection, when it arrived, was so cordial and helpful that it did not in the least dampen my spirits, either.

Rather the reverse, for I began "Stowaway" as soon as the rejection came, being careful to use the third person, begin quickly, and make it the proper length—six thousand words . . .

On June 23, 1938, the July 1938 *Astounding* finally arrived, and I found it an anticlimax. I [had] this to say in my diary: "Somehow this business of contributing seems to have spoiled some of my joy in *Astounding*. When I read *Astounding* now, I'm consumed with jealousy. I think that even if one of my stories is ever accepted that I won't return to my old enjoyment. . . . However, maybe I'm unduly pessimistic."

I wasn't. The loss was permanent. The bliss that the science-fiction magazine brought me, which had increased to an almost unbearable height after I had started keeping, saving, and cataloguing the magazines in 1937, slowly faded, and never returned to that peak again.

Yet I can't very well complain. I might, with far greater justice, say that I had emerged from a chrysalis into a far better form and world, for if I left one Eden, I entered another, that of writing. And this Eden, in one shape or another, I have never left, nor has it ever palled on me.

A strange change came over my diary, too. Until the day I visited Campbell I filled every page (with very few exceptions) from top to bottom and left to right—leaving no margins—with microscopic writing. After that day, I rarely finished a page and I totally omitted the detailed baseball analyses, which I suddenly outgrew and to which I never returned. I wrote more briefly and succinctly, because I wanted to spend more time on writing "Stowaway" and the stories that followed.

Almost at once, I gathered that ideally all the writing I did should be for publication; that anything I *had* to write for personal reasons, whether diary or mail, would have to be brief. I have followed that principle ever since.

[Two stories rejected, he tried writing his third] My old second-hand Underwood No. 5, which had given me good service for three years, was breaking down and . . . would have to be repaired. Ordinarily, my father would have seen to it that it was repaired, but he reasoned that the repair would be expensive, that the machine would break down again for an additional expensive repair and that it might, therefore, represent long-term economy to invest in a new machine. The mere fact that I had written and submitted two stories had made me, in my father's eyes, a literary man, and the rejections had not tarnished that image. As a literary man, he felt I deserved the best . . .

We spent four hours comparison shopping before we bought a late-model Smith-Corona portable typewriter, the first new typewriter I ever owned.

It cost sixty dollars, though from that sum we can deduct seventeen dollars as a trade-in for the Underwood. In other words, after three years of use, we got back seven dollars more on the old typewriter than we had spent for it, which, of course, made us feel good.

My letters in *Astounding* had not yet ended their usefulness. On September 1, 1938, I received a letter from Brainerd, Minnesota.

It was from Clifford D. Simak, who was at that time a minor science-fiction writer. [According to my diary] I had "hated" [Simak's story] "Rule 18," which had appeared in the July 1938 issue. In my letter to *Astounding* I gave it a very low rating.

Now Simak was writing to me to ask details so that he might consider my criticisms and perhaps profit from them. (Would that I could react so gently and rationally to adverse criticism—but I grew to know Cliff well in later years, though we rarely met, and I learned that gentle rationality was the hallmark of his character.)

I reread the story in order to be able to answer properly and found, to my surprise, that there was nothing wrong with it at all. What he had done was to write the story in separate scenes with no explicit transition passages between. I wasn't used to that technique, so the story seemed choppy and incoherent. The second time around I saw what he was doing and realized that not only was the story not in the least incoherent, but also that it moved with a slick speed that would have been impossible if all the dull bread-and-butter transitions had been inserted.

I wrote to Simak to explain and to apologize, and adopted the same device in my own stories. What's more, I attempted, as far as possible, to made use of something similar to Simak's cool and unadorned style.

I have sometimes heard science-fiction writers speak of the influence upon their style of such high-prestige literary figures of Kafka, Proust, and Joyce. This may well be so for them, but for myself, I make no such claim. I learned how to write science fiction by the attentive reading of science fiction, and among the major influences on my style was Cliff Simak.

By October 21, 1938, I had completed six stories, five of which I had submitted to Campbell and which he had rejected. The stories had piled up four other rejections among themselves, so that the box score was six stories, nine rejections, no sales.

I might have been dejected by this were it not for my monthly trips to Campbell . . . [and on] October 21, exactly four months after my first visit to Campbell, [I sold] my third story, "Marooned off Vesta," . . . [and another] called "The Weapon Too Dreadful to Use" to *Amazing Stories*.

The first story I sold to John Campbell was called "Trends," and it appeared in the July 1939 *Astounding* . . .

John Campbell was a great believer in nice simple names for his writers, and I am sure that he would ordinarily have asked me to use a pseudonym on the order of John Smith, and I would have absolutely refused to do so, and perhaps aborted my writing career.

However, those two early stories in *Amazing* appeared under my real name—Isaac Asimov. . . . Perhaps because the deed was done and my name, such as it was, had graced the contents page of a science-fiction magazine, Campbell uttered not a murmur and my name appeared in *Astounding*'s august pages in its proper form.

[More about "Trends," originally called "Ad Astra"] I was working for Bernhard J. Stern [a sociology professor at Columbia] . . . and since he was writing a book on social resistance to technological change, he had me reading a great many books that might conceivably be of use to him. My orders were to take note of any passages that dealt with the subject and to copy them down.

It was a liberal education for me and I was particularly struck by a whole series of [old] articles by astronomer Simon Newcomb, which I read at Stern's direction. Newcomb advanced arguments that demonstrated the impossibility of heavier-than-air flying machines, and maintained that one could not be built that would carry a man. While these articles were appearing, the Wright brothers flew their plane. Newcomb countered with an article that said, essentially, "Very well, one man, but not two."

Every significant social advance aroused opposition on the part of many, it seemed. Well, then, shouldn't space flight, which involved technological advances, arouse opposition too?

Yet I had never read a science-fiction story in which such opposition was described. Either the public role did not enter into the story at all, or if it was there, it was described as wildly approving—rather on the line of the public reaction to Lindbergh's solo flight across the Atlantic in 1927, eleven years before (which I just barely remembered).

I determined therefore to write a story about the first attempts to reach the moon, and to have opposition to space flight play an important role. It was because of that that I used "Ad Astra" as the title. This was from the Latin proverb, "Per aspera ad astra" ("through difficulties to the stars").

[In 1968, at a meeting of the Modern Languages Association] I made the comment in the course of the session that I didn't think I had ever made any successful prediction in my science-fiction stories. From the floor, Phil [Klass, writer William Tenn] said that, on the contrary, in my story "Trends," I had, in 1939 [when it was published], predicted popular opposition to space exploration, an opposition that no one else had foreseen and that had actually developed.

After that, I frequently gave that as an example of one of my successful predictions and, in fact, have a talk I entitle "The Science-Fiction Writer as Prophet," which virtually always gets a standing ovation from college-student audiences.

As I look back on those days of the late 1930s, it is clear to me now that science fiction was approaching a fork in the line of its progress. Science-fiction pulp, which I had been reading with such love and avidity, was declining, and a new generation of writers was arising, writers who had some feeling for science.

Amazing was still slanted toward mad professors with beautiful daughters, toward malevolent monsters and hectic action, and it would even continue to have some commercial success with it.

Campbell, however, was pushing for quieter, more thoughtful stories, in which the science was realistic, and in which scientists, inventors, and engineers talked and acted like recognizable human beings. That was the direction of progress, and it was the one in which I tended of my own accord to move. Since that was also the direction in which Campbell drew me, my progress was rapid.

Thanks to Campbell, science fiction was entering what has ever since been called its "Golden Age," and thanks to the accident of my being there at the right time—and in the right place—with the right impulses—I was able to become part of it.

Nine.
WRITING PROGRESS

On April 12 [1940], I visited Campbell again after he had had the third version of "Homo Sol" for over two weeks. I talked about other things for a while, cravenly staying away from the real point of interest, until he finally said, "Oh yes, your story? You haven't got it yet?"

My heart sank. Was this to be another "Pilgrimage"—three strikes and out? I remained abashed and mute and he said, "It's up in the accounting room now."

The "it" he was asking me if I had yet got was the check and not the story. He had bought it—my second sale to Campbell in nearly two years of trying. It came just in time, too, for it just covered what I still owed on my tuition in that first year of graduate work [Columbia University where his B.S., M.A., and Ph.D. were in chemistry].

The clearest thing I remember about that check is an incident that took place that evening in the candy store. I had placed the check on the cash register, so that my father could deposit it when he next went to the bank (after I had endorsed it over to him, of course), and I was engaged in dealing out cigarettes, collecting payment, making change, and so on, as I had done every night for eleven years now.

One customer took offense at my neglecting to say "Thank you" as I made the change—a crime I frequently committed because, very often, I was working without conscious attention but was concentrating deeply on the plot permutations that were sounding hollowly within the cavern of my skull.

The customer decided to scold me for my obvious inattention and for my apparent lack of industry.

"My son," he said, "made fifty dollars through hard work last week. What do you do to earn a living besides standing here?"

"I write," I said. "And I got this for a story today," and I held up the check for him to see.

It was a very satisfactory moment.

[At graduate school] At one time, I remember, I received a fairly low mark on one of my lab reports—one that dealt with the elevation of boiling points in solutions. I was not overly surprised at this, since my expectations in lab courses were never exuberantly high, but I thought I might as well see Professor Joseph Mayer, under whom I was taking the course, and attempt negotiation.

I took my paper with me and he went over it patiently. I was quite prepared to be told that I had done the experiment sloppily or that I had collected my data thoughtlessly. That wasn't it, however. Professor Mayer looked up at me and said:

"The trouble with you, Asimov, is that you can't write."

For a horrified moment, I stared at him. Then, no longer interested in negotiation, I gathered up the report and, before leaving, said to him, as stiffly and as haughtily as I could, "I'll thank you, Professor Mayer, not to repeat that slander to my publishers."

[In August 1940, after receiving the September *Astounding* in which "Homo Sol" appeared] I read the story, of course, for my own stories always interest me. In doing so, I am always aware of any changes forced on me by editors that go against my natural predilection, and in this story those changes were particularly noticeable and particularly bothersome.

For instance, in the story I made certain distinctions between the emotional reactions of Africans and Asians as compared with those of

Americans and Europeans. Campbell had suggested the passage rather forcefully and I had included it reluctantly, since I wanted to sell the story.

Then even after I had made a number of changes to please him, Campbell had, on his own hook, inserted several paragraphs that did not ring true in my ears. They were in his style, not in mine, and even if no one else could tell that, I could. What's more, they emphasized, with approval, Earthman's proficiency at warmaking.

It was August 1940 . . . Great Britain was standing alone against the victorious Nazis. Everyone was expecting a Nazi invasion attempt daily. I was in no mood to find racist and militaristic remarks in my stories, however mild and innocent they might seem.

After that, I did my best to wriggle out of such situations. When Campbell suggested bits of business here and there, either in preliminary discussions or during a request for revision, I would agree, but then if I disapproved, I would just forget to include it, or I would twist it into something I found inoffensive. I'm not sure I always succeeded, but I did almost all the time certainly.

In a way, then, my unhappiness over "Homo Sol" paved the way for my two most popular groups of science-fiction stories . . .

I began work on another story, "History." I wrote it during the first two weeks of September, which was precisely the period during which the great Blitz on London began. For night after night as I wrote, London was bombed, blasted, and burned, and there seemed no way in which it could endure. Great Britain would have to give in, it seemed. Certainly I could see no hope for her.

Yet, apparently, I still clung to a certainty that Hitler would be defeated. In "History," I made a brief reference to the fact that he died on Madagascar (presumably in exile, as was the case with Napoleon and Kaiser Wilhelm II).

[1940. The Robot series of stories] After reading "Robbie" in cold print in the magazine, I decided I liked it more than any other story I had written yet. It also occurred to me that robot stories would not involve me in any superiority-inferiority hassle with Campbell. Why not, then, write another?

Furthermore, clever devil that I was, I remembered Campbell's penchant for introducing religious motifs into stories where nothing of the sort had originally existed . . . I decided to push his buttons, therefore, by putting in a bit of religion to begin with.

My notion was to have a robot refuse to believe he had been created mechanically in a factory, but to insist that men were only his servants and that robots were the peak of creation, having been created by some godlike entity. What's more, he would prove his case by reason, and "Reason" was the title of the story.

On October 23 I presented the idea to Campbell, and he was immediately enthusiastic (as I had judged he would be). We talked it over and I went home to begin the story. . . . In this case, pushing Campbell's buttons was easier than pushing the typewriter keys. I made four starts in the course of the following week, and tore each up after a couple of pages. Ordinarily, when I had this kind of trouble with a story, I took it as a sign that the idea was not one I could handle and I would drop it. . . . This time, though, I dared not quit—not after having sold Campbell on the idea so effectively. On October 31, therefore, I crawled back to him with my troubles.

He listened carefully and then gave me one of those pieces of advice that were worth untold gold. What he said was, "Asimov, when you have trouble with the beginning of a story, that is because you are starting in the wrong place, and almost certainly too soon. Pick out a later point in the story and begin again."

For me, that was good advice. I started later in the story and had no trouble thereafter. Ever since then, I have always started my stories as late in the game as I thought I could manage, and if I had trouble getting off the ground, I would make myself start still later. And what about the portion of the story that comes before the beginning? That can be made clear in the course of dialog or, if necessary, in a flashback.

[December 1940] I wrote "Christmas on Ganymede," which dealt with a comic Christmas celebration involving Ganymedan natives who didn't understand what it was all about. I was trying to be funny, of course.

I had this terrible urge to be *funny*, you see, and had already indulged in humor in more than one story. Writing humor, however, is harder than digging ditches . . .

Handing in "Christmas on Ganymede" [to Campbell, on December 23, 1940] was of small account. It was rejected, and it deserved to be. What was far more important was that I wanted to write another robot story. This time I wanted to write a story about a robot that, through some mistake on the assembly line, turned out to be capable of reading minds.

Again, Campbell became interested and we talked it over at length—what complications would arise out of robotic telepathy, what a robot would be forced to lie about, how the matter could be resolved, and so on. At one point, Campbell said:

"Look, Asimov, in working this out, you have to realize that there are three rules that robots have to follow. In the first place, they can't do any harm to human beings; in the second place, they have to obey orders without doing harm; in the third, they have to protect themselves, without doing harm or proving disobedient. Well . . ."

That was it. Those were the Three Laws of Robotics. Eventually I phrased them like this:

THE THREE LAWS OF ROBOTICS

1. A robot may not injure a human being or, through inaction, allow a human being to come to harm.
2. A robot must obey the orders given it by human beings except where such orders would conflict with the First Law.
3. A robot must protect its own existence as long as such protection does not conflict with the First or Second Laws.

These Three Laws of Robotics have been used by me as the basis for over two dozen short stories and three novels (one a juvenile) about robots. I am probably more famous for them than for anything else I have written, and they are quoted even outside the science-fiction world. The very word "robotics" was coined by me.

The Three Laws revolutionized science fiction. Once they were well established in a series of stories, they made so much sense and proved so popular with the readers that other writers began to use them. They couldn't quote them directly, of course, but they could simply assume their existence, knowing well that the readers would be acquainted with the Laws and would understand the assumption.

I never minded that. On the contrary, I was flattered. Besides, no one could write a *stupid* robot story if he used the Three Laws. The story might be bad on other counts, but it wouldn't be stupid.

And yet I heard the Three Laws first from John Campbell, and I am always embarrassed to hear myself given the credit. Whenever I tried to tell Campbell himself, however, that he was the originator, he would always shake his head and grin and say, "No, Asimov, I picked them out of your stories and your discussions. You didn't state them explicitly, but they were there."

It's true I had made a remark that sounded like the First Law even in "Robbie," but I think Campbell was just trying to do what he always did—let the writer have the credit.

Or perhaps we were both right and, as Randall Garrett said many years later, both of us invented the Laws as a result of our peculiar symbiotic relationship.

[Women in the robot stories] In "Liar" [1941] I introduced my first successful female character. She was a "robopsychologist," and the story centered about her. She was more intelligent and more capable than any of the men in the story and I was very fond of her and wanted to write more stories about her.

The notion of using a woman scientist [arose] out of [knowing] Professor Mary Caldwell, my gentle and understanding graduate adviser. The character in "Liar" was nothing at all like Professor Caldwell in appearance and behavior, but I called her "Susan Caldwell" just the same.

After the story was accepted, I had qualmish second thoughts. It didn't strike me that Professor Caldwell would like the use of her name and I didn't want her annoyed with me.

On my next visit to Campbell, I found him out with the flu but I talked to his secretary, Katherine Tarrant, and explained the situation to her.

She said, with a sigh, "I suppose you want me to go through the manuscript and change the name wherever it appears."

"Yes," I said eagerly. "Would you?"

"What name do you want instead?"

Desperately I thought of a change that would involve the fewest letters. "Calvin," I said.

It was done and Susan Calvin has been the heroine of some ten stories of mine so far.

This brings up one of the reasons why I don't take critics seriously. Some critics, in discussing my robot stories, make much of the name "Calvin," assuming that I chose it deliberately for its associations with John Calvin, the predestinarian, and his gloomy, doom-ridden work ethic. Not at all! I was merely trying to introduce a minimal change in Caldwell, for the reasons I explained.

Ten.
FAMOUS FICTION

[March 17, 1941] Campbell had an idea of his own. I don't know if he was saving it specifically for me, or if I just happened to be the first author to walk in after the idea had occurred to him.

He had come across a quotation from an eight-chapter work by Ralph Waldo Emerson called *Nature*. In the first chapter, Emerson said, "If the stars should appear one night in a thousand years, how would men believe and adore, and preserve for many generations the remembrance of the city of God. . . ."

Campbell asked me to read it and said, "What do you think would happen, Asimov, if men were to see the stars for the first time in a thousand years?"

I thought, and drew a blank. I said, "I don't know."

Campbell said, "I think they would go mad. I want you to write a story about that."

We talked about various things, thereafter, with Campbell seeming to circle the idea and occasionally asking me questions such as "Why should the stars be invisible at other times?" and listened to me as I tried to improvise answers. Finally, he shooed me out with, "Go home and write the story."

In my diary for that day I said, "I'll get started on it soon, as I think the idea is swell, and I even envisage making a lead novelette out of it; but I don't delude myself into thinking it will be an easy story to write. It will require hard work."

[Isaac's footnote] Here and elsewhere I have always spoken with complete candor about the role of others in the genesis and development of my stories—particularly Campbell's role. Nevertheless, I am a little sensitive when people overestimate the importance of such contributions. It is one thing to say, "I think people would go crazy if they see the stars for the first time in a thousand years. Go home and write the story." It is quite another to go home and actually write the story. Campbell might suggest but it was *I* who then had to go home and face the empty sheet of paper in the typewriter.

On the evening of March 18, 1941, I began the story.

It was a crucial moment for me. I had as yet, in almost three years of selling, failed to do anything outstanding. [Of my] thirty-one stories, published and unpublished, sold and unsold, only three were what I would now consider as three stars or better on my old zero-to-five star scale, and they were my three positronic robot stories: "Robbie," "Reason," and "Liar."

I put a piece of paper in the typewriter, typed the title, which Campbell and I had agreed should be "Nightfall," typed the Emerson quotation, then began the story.

I remember that evening very well; my own room, just next to the living room, my desk facing the southern wall, with the bed behind me and to the right, the window on the other side of the bed, looking out westward on Windsor Place, with the candy store across the street.

Did I have any notion that . . . I was going to write the best science-fiction story of all time? How could I?

Yet some people think exactly that of "Nightfall" [which has] come to be considered a classic. [But] My own three favorite short stories are, in order, (1) "The Last Question," (2) "The Bicentennial Man," and (3) "The Ugly Little Boy."

Still, ["Nightfall"] was a turning point, even if I can't figure out the reason. After "Nightfall" was published, the rejections stopped. I simply wrote and sold, and within a year or two, I had reached the Heinlein/van Vogt level, or almost.

When, forty years after the story was published, I got around to establishing a corporation, I had no choice. I called that corporation Nightfall, Inc.

[1941—with the war going badly in Europe—and after a future-historical story called "Pilgrimage" had been rejected several times] I still wanted to write a future-historical.

I love historical novels (if they contain neither too much violence nor too much sleazy sex). . . . Naturally, just as loving science fiction led me to the desire to write science fiction, the love of historical novels led me to the desire to write historical novels.

To write a historical novel was, however, impractical for me. It would require an enormous amount of reading and research and I just couldn't spend all that time at it. [He was in graduate school]. . . . It occurred to me that I could write a historical novel if I made up my own history . . . a science-fiction story that *read* like a historical novel.

Now, I won't pretend that I made up the idea of writing histories of the future. It had been done numerous times, most effectively and star-tlingly by the British writer Olaf Stapledon, who wrote *First and Last Men* and *The Star Makers*. These books, however, read like histories and I wanted to write a historical *novel*, a story with conversation and action just like any other science-fiction story except that it would deal not only with technology but with political and sociological problems.

Why shouldn't I write of the fall of the Galactic Empire and the return of feudalism, written from the viewpoint of someone in the secure days of the Second Galactic Empire? I thought I knew how to do it for I had read Edward Gibbon's *Decline and Fall of the Roman Empire* from first page to last at least twice, and I had only to make use of that.

I was bubbling over by the time I got to Campbell's, and my enthusiasm was catching. It was perhaps too catching, for Campbell blazed up as I had never seen him do. "That's too large a theme for a short story," he said.

"I was thinking of a novelette," I said, quickly, adjusting my thoughts.

"Or a novelette. It will have to be an open-ended series of stories."

"What?" I said, weakly.

"Short stories, novelettes, serials, all fitting into a particular future history, involving the fall of the First Galactic Empire, the period of feudalism that follows, and the rise of the Second Galactic Empire."

"What?" I said, even more weakly.

"Yes, I want you to write an outline of the future history. Go home and write the outline."

There Campbell had made a mistake. Robert Heinlein was writing what he called the "Future History Series." He was writing various stories that fitted into one niche or another of the series, and he wasn't writing them in order. Therefore he had prepared a Future History outline that was very detailed and complicated, so that he would keep everything straight. Now Campbell wanted me to do the same.

I went home, dutifully, and began preparing an outline that got longer and longer and stupider and stupider until I finally tore it up. It was quite plain that I couldn't work with an outline. (To this day I cannot—for any of my stories, articles, or books, whether fiction or nonfiction.) . . .

On August 11, therefore, I started the story I had originally intended to write (with modifications that resulted from my discussions with Campbell), and the heck with possible future stories. I'd worry about them when the time came—and *if* the time came.

Since the First Galactic Empire was breaking down (in my story), certain scientists had set up a Foundation on a world at the rim of the Galaxy, purportedly to prepare a vast encyclopedia of human knowledge, but actually to cut down the period of feudalism and hasten the rise of the Second Empire. I called my story, "Foundation" (and the stories to which it gave rise have been lumped together, consequently, as "the Foundation series").

The Foundation series proved to be the most popular and successful of all my writings, and my continuation of these stories in the

1980s after a long hiatus proved even more popular and successful. These stories contributed more than any others to making me more nearly rich and famous than I could have imagined. Most of the Foundation series was being written even while I was a complete failure at the NAES [wartime work at the Naval Air Experimental Station in Philadelphia, in the early years of his first marriage].

Of course, I had no way of knowing what was to come while I was working as a chemist during World War II, but looking back on it, I note that chemistry, my profession, continued to fail and to do so more drastically with time. Not only didn't I get along with my superiors but I was not a particularly good chemist and never would be.

But *history*, which I had discarded [as a profession], made its appearance in the most unlikely form, as a series of science-fiction historical novels of the future, and lifted me to the heights.

[My addition—he did love chemistry. Here's what he said to his Columbia professor who asked] "Why the hell do you sing in lab, Asimov?" . . .

I said, earnestly, "Because I'm not in chemistry to make a living, sir. It's not my bread-and-butter. I'm going to make money writing. I'm in chemistry because I love it. It's my cakes-and-ale, and I can't help singing when I'm working. I'll try to stop, sir, but it will be an effort. It's no effort not to sing for those who complain. I don't imagine they like their work."

It was a little exaggerated, but not really far off. It was also a calculated gamble, and it worked. [Professor] Thomas was impressed, and from that moment on we were buddies . . . Just the same, I cut out most of the singing in lab . . .

Eleven.
DURING THE WAR

[Summer 1942] The world news continued depressing in the extreme. To be sure . . . the United States had won the Battle of Midway, which marked the turning point in the war with Japan, but I didn't know it was the turning point. . . . On land, the Nazi armies were pouring toward the Don River and southward toward the Caucasus. (In the fighting in the Caucasus, my Uncle Ephraim was killed in action. He was my father's favorite brother—at least my father mentioned him more than he did the other two.)

On July 25, 1942 (my brother Stanley's thirteenth birthday), I took the train to New York in order to keep my wedding date.

The matter of my wedding was heavily distorted by the fact of war. The [NAES] Navy Yard gave me exactly eight days for a honeymoon, from Sunday to Sunday, inclusive. I couldn't exactly complain of this, considering the war crisis, but neither did I want to waste an hour of the period if I could help it. For that reason, I could not have a civil wedding since that would have meant waiting to be married on Monday.

Since neither my family nor Gertrude's family had any religion, we had no rabbis of our own, and it proved difficult to get one out of the Yellow Pages. I would have settled for a practitioner of any religion, asking only that the marriage be a legal one in the eyes of the government, but the old folks weren't quite that easygoing.

We found a rabbi. I don't remember his name. I never saw him again. . . . It was a difficult and embarrassing session. The rabbi chanted Hebrew over us in a cracked voice, which I suffered in resignation, while Gertrude tried hard (and not entirely successfully) not to giggle.

Nor did it go entirely smoothly. The rabbi demanded a witness and it turned out that it had to be someone who was not a member of either family.

No such creature existed within the walls of the apartment and Mr. Blugerman was forced to go into the hall and commandeer the first innocent bystander who passed. The bystander was dragged into the apartment, rather confused, and then it turned out that to fulfill his official function he had to wear a hat and he had none on him since it wasn't raining in the hall. The rabbi therefore seized my father's hat, which happened to be resting on some piece of furniture, and planted it firmly on the stranger's head.

My father, whose ideas on hygiene were complicated and, in some ways, senseless—but very firm—rose in horror to protest, remembered where he was and what was happening, and sank back in frustration. I suspect he never wore that hat again.

At another point, the rabbi raised a glass from which Gertrude and I had drunk and was going to smash it under his heel for some complicated symbolic reason and Mr. Blugerman snatched it from his hand.

But eventually, at 5:30 P.M. on July 26, 1942, Gertrude and I were man and wife (or with equal validity, woman and husband). The marriage took place five and a half months after we had met at our St. Valentine's Day blind date, and I was twenty-two and a half years old at the time.

[During the honeymoon at a Catskill resort] A quiz was held during the afternoon, and guests were invited to volunteer. I raised my hand, of course, and became one of the contestants. . . . I was third in line, and when I rose to field my question in the first round, spontaneous laughter broke out from the audience. They had laughed at no one else.

The trouble was that I looked anxious, and when I look anxious I look even more stupid than usual. The reason I was anxious was that I wanted to shine and I feared I would not. I knew that I was neither handsome, self-assured, athletic, wealthy, nor sophisticated. The only thing I had going for me was that I was clever and I wanted to show off to Gertrude. And I was afraid of failing and spelling "weigh" "WIEGH."

I ignored the laughter as best I could, and tried to concentrate. The master of ceremonies, trying not to grin and failing, said, "Use the word 'pitch' in sentences in such a way as to demonstrate five different meanings of the word." (Heaven only knows where he got his questions.)

More laughter, as I paused for a moment to collect my thoughts. I then said, "John pitched the pitch-covered ball as intensely as though he were fighting a pitched battle, while Mary, singing in a high-pitched voice, pitched a tent."

The laughter stopped as though someone had pulled a plug out of the socket. The master of ceremonies had me repeat it, counted the pitches, considered them, and pronounced me correct. Naturally, by the time the quiz was over, I had won. . . . I noticed, though, that winning the quiz did not make me popular at the resort. Many people resented having wasted their laughter. The thought apparently was that I had no right to look stupid without being stupid; that, by doing so, I had cheated.

[Life at the Philadelphia Navy Yard] The Jews at the Navy Yard did not feel themselves to be in an enviable position. It seemed to some of us that there were strong feelings among some of the Gentiles that the war was being fought to "save the Jews" and that Pearl Harbor was a put-up job somehow arranged by Roosevelt and his Jewish friends. It seemed reasonable for us Jews to fear that continued reverses in the war would cause a vast increase of anti-Semitism in the United States.

In fact, some of my fellow Jews spoke to me about my effervescence in the lab. They hinted that I ought to keep a low profile, since if I made myself annoying and unpopular that would reflect on the Jews generally.

I told them to go to the devil. It was quite clear that anti-Semitism in the world of 1942 could not be blunted by the "good behavior" of individual Jews any more than the lynching of blacks could be stopped if some of them behaved like cringing Uncle Toms. So I stayed myself. Being myself did me no particular good, but I don't think it harmed the Jewish cause particularly.

A kind of crisis arose in September, however, as the first High Holiday season of post–Pearl Harbor approached. Before Pearl Harbor, Jewish employees at the Navy Yard were routinely given time off for Rosh Hashanah (the New Year) and Yom Kippur (the Day of Atonement). The new rules after Pearl Harbor, however, made it quite clear that the only day off other than Sundays was to be Christmas. No exceptions.

Some of the Jewish employees felt very strongly that they oughtn't to work on Yom Kippur, even if they worked on all the other Jewish holidays. It occurred to someone that perhaps a deal could be made. If the Jewish employees were allowed to take Yom Kippur off, they would work on Christmas.

. . . I said, quite flatly, that I never observed [the Jewish holidays] and that I had no objection to working on them. [I was told] what was being planned, the switchover of Christmas for Yom Kippur, and it wouldn't work unless the petition was signed by all Jews without exception. Otherwise the attitude would be that if some Jews could work, all could . . .

So I signed. It was against my principles but I couldn't bring myself to interfere with the concerns of many people for the sake of my principles.

The next day, Bob Heinlein [who worked at the Navy Yard too] stopped in to see me. "What's this I hear about your not working on Yom Kippur, Isaac?"

"I signed a petition about working on Christmas instead, " I said.

"You're not religious, are you?"

"No, I'm not."

"You're not going to temple on Yom Kippur, are you?"

"No, I'm not."

"Then why are you planning to take off on Yom Kippur?"

By now I imagine I was flushing with annoyance. "I won't go to church on Christmas, either," I said, "so what difference does it make which day I take for nonreligious purposes?"

"It doesn't. So why not take off Christmas with everyone else?"

I said, "Because it would look bad if I didn't go. They explained to me that . . ."

Heinlein said, "Are you telling me that they *forced* you to sign?"

It seemed to me that I was going to be used as a stick to beat down the petition.

"No," I said strenuously, "I was not *forced* to sign it. I signed it voluntarily because I wanted to. But since I freely admit that I intend no religious observances I will agree to work on Yom Kippur if I am told to, provided that does not prejudice the petition."

And that's the way it was. On September 19, the Navy Yard announced that Jewish employees would be allowed to take off Yom Kippur with pay, and without having to work Christmas—and because of Heinlein's encounter with me, I had ended up volunteering to work on Yom Kippur.

On Monday, September 21, 1942, I was therefore the only Jewish employee at the Navy Yard (I believe) to show up at work. It was no great hardship, but I must admit that I resented Heinlein's having put me on the spot. He meant well, I'm sure, and we stayed good friends, but I have never been able to erase the memory of his having backed me into a corner.

[Games in the Navy Yard's cafeteria] What irritated me most was (a) the food and (b) Heinlein's patriotic refusal to recognize that anything prepared for noble war workers could possibly be inedible. When . . . I spoke eloquently of cardboard potatoes and wilted lettuce and middle-aged roast beef, Heinlein passed a ukase to the effect that from then on anyone who complained about the food would have to put a nickel in the kitty. (When enough had accumulated, I think he was going to buy a war bond.)

I objected bitterly for I knew it was aimed at me. I said, "Well, then, suppose I figure out a way of complaining about the food that isn't complaining. Will you call it off?"

"Yes," he said.

After that, I had a mission in luncheon life that took my mind off the food, at least. I was going to find a way of complaining that couldn't be objected to. My best solo attempt, I think, was one time when I pretended to be sawing away ineffectually at a dead slab of haddock and asked with an innocent air of curiosity. "Is there such a thing as tough fish?"

"That will be five cents, Isaac," said Heinlein.

"It's only a point of information, Bob."

"That will be five cents, Isaac. The implication is clear."

Since Bob was judge, jury, and executioner, that was that.

But then someone new joined the table who did not know the game that was going on. He took one mouthful of some ham that had been pickled in formaldehyde and said, "Boy, this food is awful."

Whereupon I rose to my feet, lifted one arm dramatically, and said, "Gentlemen, I disagree with every word my friend here has said, but I will defend with my life his right to say it."

And the game of fine came to an end.

[On September 25, 1943] The Soviets announced that they had recaptured Smolensk and Roslavl, and on September 27, among the many places recorded in the Soviet war communique as having been recaptured was Petrovichi—or at least the ground on which Petrovichi had stood—after it had remained twenty-six months in German hands.

Bob Heinlein shook my hand and solemnly congratulated me.

The siege of Leningrad was lifted that January [1944]. My Uncle Boris had survived the nine-hundred-day ordeal and was among those who were taken eastward for recovery and rehabilitation. He sent letters to my parents, who responded with packages containing food and other useful items.

[February 1944—having to write a Navy Yard report on seam-sealing compounds] The chief problem for me, I knew, would be the actual writing of the report. Writing was not a simple procedure in the Navy Yard, even for an illiterate—let alone someone like myself who was an expert at writing and would therefore violate all official illiteracy rules.

Early in my Navy Yard career, I had been asked to write a letter and it was promptly brought back to me. It was not written in Navy style.

"What is Navy style?" I asked, blankly.

They took me to a large filing cabinet containing all kinds of letters written in a formal, convoluted fashion. There had to be a heading of a certain kind, and then an "in re" with a coded letter-number entry. Each paragraph had to be numbered. Every sentence had to be in the passive.

The safest thing, they said, would be to find some paragraph in some previous letter that was approximately what I wanted to say and then make use of it with minimum changes.

I could see the purpose of that. Clear, literate writers could be trusted to use their ingenuity—but what of the average employee? By using fixed paragraphs, no idiot (however deeply immersed in idiocy) could go far wrong. It was like painting with numbers. It was a little hard on the few literates in the place, but that is a small price to pay for the privilege of avoiding rapid and total collapse, so I learned how to write Navy style.

Specifications had to be written Navy style also. Every paragraph had to be numbered; so did every subparagraph and every subsubparagraph. The main paragraphs were listed as I, II, III, and so on. If anything under a particular paragraph had to be enumerated it was A, B, C. . . . If A included enumerated items it was 1, 2, 3. . . . Under any of these was a, b, c . . . , and under these (1), (2), (3) . . . , and so on.

Furthermore, if in any one sentence you have to refer to another sentence, you located the referred sentence in its position in the specification, as, for instance, II, C, 3, a, (1).

Generally, there weren't too many indentations, or too many references back and forth, and the specifications, while rather tortuous, could be understood—given several hours of close study.

When it finally came my time to prepare the specification of the seam-sealing compounds, a certain Puckishness overtook me. Writing with absolute clarity, I nevertheless managed to break everything down into enumerations, getting all the way down to [(l)] and even [(a)]. [These brackets are Isaac's.] I further managed in almost every sentence to refer to some other sentence for which I duly listed a complete identification.

The result was that no one on earth could have plunged into it and come out unscathed. Brain coagulation would have set in by page 2.

Solemnly, I handed in the specification. I had done nothing wrong, so I could not be scolded or disciplined. All they could do would be to come back with some embarrassment and ask for simplification—and, of course, the joke would be over and I would simplify. I just hoped that none of my supervisors would require hospitalization. I didn't really intend things to go that far.

But the joke was on me. My supervisors were wreathed in smiles at this product of the satirist's art. They took it straight and swallowed it whole. . . . Years later, I was told that that specification was still preserved (under nitrogen, do you suppose?) and handed out to new employees as an example of how specifications ought to be written.

I worried, sometimes, in looking back on it, just how much, in my eagerness to play a harmless little joke, I had set back the war effort.

I was tiring of the Foundation series . . . I wanted a chance to make use of the other writing I was doing—the Navy style—which, unless I exorcised it somehow, might well corrode my vitals.

When I handed in "Dead Hand" [the fifth Foundation story], I suggested to Campbell that I do a short story I planned to call "Blind

Alley," in which I made use of my Navy Yard experience. The story was to involve red tape, and part of it was to be told in the form of letters between bureaucrats in the Navy style, with the thesis being that it protected against stupidity but could not protect against ingenuity— if there was enough of that.

Campbell laughed and agreed, and on September 2, I began it. It was set in the Foundation universe, at the height of the Galactic Empire, before the fall of that Empire and the beginning of the Foundation. I did that because it was easier to do than to make up a completely new background.

It was the one story written in the Foundation universe (whether part of the Foundation series or not) in which there were extraterrestrial intelligences. In all the other stories, a purely human Galaxy is described, with no other intelligent beings present and with no unusual or monstrous animals either.

The device of an all-human Galaxy had apparently never been used before. Stories of interstellar travel prior to the Foundation, notably those of E. E. Smith and by Campbell himself, had always presupposed numerous intelligences and had used these intelligences as devices wherewith to drive the plot.

The multi-intelligence Galaxy is, to my way of thinking, more probable than the all-human one. However, I was concentrating on political and social forces in the Foundation series and I would have complicated these unbearably if I had introduced other intelligences. Even more important, it was my fixed intention not to allow Campbell to foist upon me his notions of the superiority and inferiority of races, and the surest way of doing that was to have an all-human Galaxy.

In "Blind Alley" the plot, as it worked itself out in my head, was to have a clever bureaucrat use Navy style to help save an extraterrestrial intelligence that would otherwise be destroyed. I knew that Campbell would interpret this as a superior humanity helping an inferior race and he would have no objection to it, and as long as he didn't interfere to introduce a heavy-handed indication of this interpretation,

I would be satisfied. I mailed the story to him on October 10, and a check for $148.75 was in my hands on October 20 [1944].

[Lots of war news in his diary and his full autobiography] On the January 8 visit, we discussed the next Foundation story, and Campbell said he wanted to upset the Seldon Plan, which was the connecting backbone of the series. I was horrified. No, I said, no, no, no. But Campbell said, Yes, yes, yes, yes, and I knew I wasn't going to sell him a no, no.

I made up my mind, rather sulkily . . . to follow orders, but to get my own back by making the new Foundation story the longest and biggest and widest yet. On January 26, 1945, then, I began "The Mule."

On that day, I had been married two and a half years, and that may have influenced me, for the heroine, Bayta, was modeled on Gertrude—certainly in appearance. Toran, her husband, was modeled on myself, though his appearance wasn't described as similar to mine.

Bayta was, of course, the key to the whole story and was the person who defeated the Mule at the end, while Toran was definitely subsidiary and bumbled about in Bayta's wake. I suppose that was the way I viewed the family situation. I was clever academically and I had writing talent. For the rest, I never felt that I was particularly bright in anything that had to do with ordinary living and with human interrelationships.

As for the Mule himself, his personal appearance was based on my friend Leonard Meisel, who by then was the only person at the Navy Yard with whom I could completely relax.

I worked rapidly, more rapidly than I had at any other time during the war. To be sure, the story took me some three and a half months to complete, but it ended being fifty thousand words long, approaching novel length. It was the very first story I had ever written that was so long, that had so intricate a plot, and that had so lengthy a cast of characters. And with Gertrude to inspire me, I think that Bayta was the first successful, well-rounded female character I ever had in any of my stories. (I loved Susan Calvin of the robot stories passionately, but she could scarcely be considered well-rounded.)

It helped the progress of the writing that news in the world outside looked so good. With the new year, the Soviets opened another offensive in the East and swooped into Germany proper. By the time I was working on "The Mule," the Soviet Army was within striking distance of Berlin, and I felt that every day I was taking a giant stride toward New York and my return to research.

The month of April ended with the Germans in collapse, with the Soviets in Berlin, and with Adolf Hitler a suicide. In the first week of May, in which I excitedly waited for the end of the war in Europe and the end of the long nightmare of Nazism . . . the only black spot was that Roosevelt had not survived a little longer to see the end of Hitler.

I kept racing ahead in the last stages of "The Mule." It was almost as though the Mule's ambitions were collapsing in time to Hitler's. (The Mule was in no way a Hitlerian character, however. The story line worked out as it did, in fact, precisely because the Mule was not a complete villain.)

On May 8, 1945, the war in Europe was over. . . . For me, on a much smaller scale, the month had its victory, too. I finished "The Mule" on May 15, brought it to Campbell on May 21, and received the acceptance on May 29 in the form of a check for $875—50,000 words at $.0175 per word.

It was an incredible sum. That one check was only a little less than I had made in the first three years after my first visit to Campbell. It represented a quarter of my annual salary at the Navy Yard. Yet my comment in the diary was, "Falls flat somehow, however. Guess I'm so sure of sales these days, the thrill is gone."

Certain success evicts one from the paradise of winning against the odds.

On July 27, I received a new classification from the draft board—1AB. The added B was a bow of recognition to my nearsightedness, but it meant nothing. Anyone in 1AB was draft material, and I still had five months to go to the safety of my twenty-sixth birthday. So I requested a hearing with the local draft board, which was granted and set for August 7. I made ready to leave on the afternoon of the sixth.

We were getting ready to go, and I remember exactly what happened.

I was reading a copy of Will Durant's *Caesar and Christ*, the third volume of his history of civilization, and Gertrude was ironing some clothes.

The radio stopped its regular programming for an emergency bulletin: The United States had dropped an atomic bomb on Hiroshima.

I was not surprised, mind you. I had known it was in the works since 1941. Therefore my original comment was not one of shock or awe or horror or anything like that.

Besides, something else was on my mind. Therefore, my first words when I heard the dramatic announcement were a thoughtful, "Hmm, I wonder how that will affect my draft status?" . . .

On August 14, Japan surrendered, and draft quotas were cut at once, and I felt myself hoping a bit. . . . Just as soon as I knew I would *not* be drafted, I would . . . return to Columbia.

Twelve.

POSTWAR, AND THE ARMY

On September 7, 1945 . . . my draft board greetings had come. . . . It did not escape my notice that if, in the third grade, I had kept my mouth shut and let my mother's lie stand, and had not insisted on a change in my birth date, then September 7, 1945, would have been my twenty-sixth birthday and I could not have been drafted. As it was, I was four months short of my twenty-sixth birthday.

It also did not escape my notice that the war was over, that millions of Americans had been drafted over the past few years and had had to face bombs and bullets while I had been safe at home; that many thousands of them had been wounded or killed while I had been safe at home; and that now I would be going off to face no more danger than the ordinary risks of ordinary life.

I was aware of all this and I did my best not to view the event as more tragic than it was. The fact remained, however, that I didn't want to go into the army; I wanted to go back to Columbia. And I didn't want to leave Gertrude; I wanted to stay with her. So I felt terrible.

[But he was drafted.]

[After months of being a poor soldier but not being reprimanded] a friendly lieutenant told me that the commanding officer, before basic had begun, had gone over the soldiers with his subordinates and had said concerning me, something as follows:

"Now this guy Asimov you might as well leave alone. He's got a 160 AGCT score and they ain't going to use him anywhere except behind a desk so don't waste time on him. He's the kind of stupe that's okay on those shit tests, but he don't know his right foot from his left and there ain't no use trying to teach him because he ain't got any sense. I been watching and I can see that."

After that I was ignored by every officer and noncom in the place.

When I found this out, I was indignant beyond words. Not, you understand, that I quarreled with the commanding officer's opinion of me, which I thought was accurate enough and a credit to his perspicacity. What graveled me was that no one was kind enough to whisper the news to me so that I could relax. I would gladly have agreed to have continued to do my best to make beds, clean rifles, and march, but why should I not have done it with a song in my heart? . . .

I did manage to write one story while I was in the army. During basic training, I persuaded the librarian to lock me in the library when it closed for lunch and to allow me to use the typewriter. After a few sessions, I had completed a robot story, which I mailed to Campbell. It was called "Evidence" and it appeared in the September 1946 *ASF* [*Astounding Science Fiction*].

The interesting thing about the story is that when I reread it recently because it was appearing in a collection and I had to check it for typographical errors, I realized that it was the first story I wrote that sounded as though I might have written it forty years later.

The worst of the pulpishness was suddenly gone and from "Evidence" onward I wrote much more rationally (at least so it seems to me). Why my writing should have suddenly matured while I was in the army, I don't know. I have brooded about it but have no answer. . . .

After I got back from my fourth weekend pass on February 4, I was given a temporary assignment as a typist in the orderly room.

I discovered that being a typist was equivalent to being an aristocrat. You wore a regular uniform at all times (never fatigues) and you never pulled KP. After this, I did everything I could to get a typist's position.

The best trick, when in a new place, was to walk into the orderly room and say to the master sergeant as politely as possible, "Sarge, could I possibly use the typewriter for just a little while to type a letter to my wife?"

Naturally, I wouldn't ask this unless I saw the orderly room was empty and the typewriter unused. Writing letters to a wife was a noble occupation for a soldier, and a master sergeant was not likely to discourage that. He would therefore say (with what is for a master sergeant the quintessence of courtly politeness), "Go ahead, soldier, but get your ass in gear and make it snappy."

I would then sit down, make sure the sergeant was not particularly occupied, and would begin typing with machine-gun rapidity. I would not get far before a fat forefinger would tap my shoulder. "Hey, soldier, how would you like to be a typist?"

There were never enough soldier-typists to meet the demand, and none who could type as quickly as I could or (as sergeants quickly discovered) were as reliable as I was.

It was time to explode an atom bomb in such a way that its effects could be carefully studied. This was slated to happen at Bikini, an atoll in the Pacific. The experiment was named "Operation Crossroads," I suppose because the atomic bomb placed humanity on a crossroads to death and destruction or to life and prosperity, depending on how nuclear energy was used . . .

Among the army personnel were to be a number of "critically needed specialists" designed to lend flavor and importance to the army's role, and I was to be one of those critically needed specialists. For this I had my AGCT score to thank.

[After being sent to Hawaii to await Operation Crossroads] Sometime during my stay in Hawaii, I underwent a turning point in my personality. Until then, I had always been eager and willing to display my intelligence and learning—even insistent on it. It wearied people and made me disliked and, in my saner moments, I knew it wearied people and made me disliked—but I couldn't resist.

Then, one day, I was the only critically needed specialist in the barracks, idly reading something or other, while at the other end of the room, three soldiers were talking to each other.

They were "nonspecialists" (the kind I always dismissed in my mind as "farmboys") and they were talking about the atom bomb since that was very much in the minds of all on Operation Crossroads. One of the three took it upon himself to explain how the atom bomb worked and, needless to say, he got it all wrong.

Wearily, I put down my book and began to get to my feet so I could go over and assume "the smart man's burden" and educate them.

Halfway to my feet, I thought: Who appointed you their educator? Is it going to hurt them to be wrong about the atom bomb? And I returned, contentedly, to my book.

This does not mean I turned with knife-edge suddenness and became another man. It's just that I was a generally disliked know-it-all earlier in my life, and I am a generally liked person (I believe) who is genial and a nonpusher later in my life. Looking back to try to see where the change began, I find it in this incident in the barracks outside Honolulu.

Why? I'm not sure I know. Perhaps it was my surrender of the child-prodigy status. Perhaps it was my feeling that I had grown up, I had proved myself, and I no longer had to give everyone a headache convincing them that I was, too, smart. (Of course, I backslide now and then, but not often.)

[One of the backsliding moments, in 1967] It seems that I had once read in *The Historians' History of the World* that Abd er-Rahman III, the greatest King of Muslim Spain, who had reigned fifty years with great success and prosperity, had confessed that in all that time, he had had only fourteen happy days. It seemed a remarkable commentary on the human condition, and I remembered it—especially since I myself had had far more than fourteen happy days.

A couple of weeks before my lunch with [editors] Tim [Seldes] and Wendy [Weil], I had bought a paperback book of quotations edited by George Seldes, Tim's uncle. I like books of quotations and tend to buy them when I see them. This one, however, was filled with quotations that were expressed in such turgid and unmemorable prose that (even though I agreed with virtually all the liberal sentiments) I threw the book away.

It did, however, have the Abd er-Rahman III quotation under "Happiness." It went something like this: "I have reigned fifty years at the height of prosperity and power, loved by my friends, respected by my subjects, and feared by my enemies, yet in all that time I have known but fourteen completely happy days." I noticed that quote because until that time I had thought I was the only person in the world who knew it.

At the lunch I said to Tim, "I just bought your uncle's book of quotations."

"Really," said Tim, "and did you notice the mistake in the very first item?"

Well, I hadn't. I knew that Tim asked me that only to puncture the rumor that I had a photographic memory, and the fact was that I hadn't the faintest idea what the first item in the book was. Thinking rapidly, however, I recalled that in the introduction to the book (I read introductions) it stated that the paperback (which I had bought) differed from the hardcover edition in listing quotes alphabetically by subject rather than by author. If in the hardcover the listing were alphabetically by author, then the Abd er-Rahman III quote was probably first.

Thinking that through took only a few seconds, so when I said, calmly, "Yes, I did," it sounded as though there had been no pause at all.

Tim said, disdainfully, "You're bluffing. You don't even know what the first quotation was."

"Yes, I do," I said. "It was Abd er-Rahman III's statement, "I have reigned fifty year. . . ." and I completed it with reasonable accuracy.

Both Tim and Wendy were now staring at me, and Tim said, "And what was the error?"

"Although Abd er-Rahman III is quoted as saying he reigned fifty years, they give his dates of his reign, and he died after reigning only

49 years," I said (having happened to notice everything about that fascinating quotation). "That's not really a mistake, however. He was counting the years by the Mohammedan lunar calendar, in which there are only 354 days to the year." I then went on (remembering another item I had noticed), "The quotation is only first in the hardcover, of course. In the softcover it is on page 441 and under. . . ."

Tim could stand no more. He leaned across the table, seized my lapel, bunched it, drew me toward him, and said loudly, "Asimov, to choose a phrase at random—you're a *prick*."

I couldn't have done it for any other quotation in the book, and it was sheerest luck that Tim had picked on it.

[April 1946—about to go by ship to Hawaii] I had completed my first half year in the army, and I was rather astonished I had survived it as well as I had. I hadn't even gotten into trouble with any of the officers except—nearly—once.

I was walking down the street near the barracks one morning, with my cap shoved back on my head, my hands in my pockets, whistling cheerfully—quite as though I were a teenager back in Brooklyn—and I passed a colonel.

The trouble was that I passed him without seeing him, as I used to pass the candy store's customers once.

"Soldier!" came the call.

I stiffened, stopped whistling, withdrew my hands from my pockets, adjusted my cap, and stepped up briskly. "Sir?" I said, saluting.

He returned the salute. "Do you know who I am?"

"I don't know your name, sir, but you're a colonel in the United States Army."

"Did you salute me when you passed me just now?"

"No, sir."

"Why not?"

"I was thinking of something, sir, and I didn't see you. I'm sorry, sir."

He asked me if I knew the reason for military courtesy and I was able to give him a reasoned exposition. He asked me to whom I was assigned and I told him. He asked me what I was doing, and I explained my position as critically needed specialist on Operation Crossroads.

"And your qualifications for that job?"

"Two degrees in chemistry from Columbia University, sir."

Up to that point, I was sure I was going to be reported and disciplined, but now he sighed. I guess the thought of a private with two degrees in chemistry broke his heart. He said, "I've been in the army for thirty years, and I'll just never get used to these new ways."

He left me in discouragement and I waited till he was out of sight, then went my way.

[Due to a snafu—situation normal, all fucked up—Isaac's allotment was stopped because somewhere in the army it was assumed he'd been discharged.] [A colonel] who impressed me as a rather good-natured, long suffering fellow, said, "You never applied for discharge, did you?"

"Yes, I did, sir. On February 11, I applied for a research discharge under Order 363."

He spread his arms. "Well, it's probably some mixup but it's against Crossroads policy to send anyone to Bikini who may be subject to discharge. I may have to take you off the project."

I returned to the ship and must have set a world record for holding my breath, for the *Cortland* was due to leave for Bikini three days later, on May 17. . . .

I left for Camp Lee [to straighten out the snafu] the day before the ship left Hawaii for Bikini. This meant that I never saw a nuclear bomb explosion close up. It also meant that, perhaps, I did not die of leukemia at a comparatively early age.

On July 11, I finally had my discharge hearing. I went in with many a pat on the back and many a grinning remark that no one at Camp Lee had ever been discharged at his own request. . . . The interview lasted fifteen minutes, during which I did my best to appear quiet and reserved. I explained the nature of my research at Columbia, why

I had ceased doing research (there was no question that at the Navy Yard I was helping the war effort), and how certain I was that I would go back to research the instant I was discharged.

Finally, one of them asked me why I had not tried out for officers' candidate school. I suggested that my eyes would not meet the required standards, but he said that objection could be met. Was there any other reason?

This question, I knew, was the jackpot, win or lose. If I expressed disdain for officer status, then I could stay in the army for life, as far as they were concerned, and be a private every day of it. If I expressed enthusiasm for officer status, they would have me sign an application for officer training. Neither alternative was bearable and I had to find something that was neither disdain nor enthusiasm and I had to do it without perceptible pause. . . .

"If my eyes do not disqualify me, sirs, then I don't think that there is anything in my intelligence or in my educational background that could possibly disqualify me. However, as I am certain you all know, it takes far more than intelligence and education to make a good officer. It takes initiative, courage, and a stability of character, which, to my regret, I don't think I possess. It is embarrassing to have to admit it, but if I lied on the subject in order to become an officer, the army would discover the lie quickly enough."

They didn't ask me anything more, and I was relieved. I didn't want to be an officer under any conditions and that in itself was a character trait that disqualified me, so that my statement was true enough. I had phrased it in such a way, however, as to leave them flattered to ecstasy.

[He was promoted to corporal, and on July 18 his discharge was approved.] On Sunday the twenty-eighth I took the train to Windsor Place. I was in civilian clothes again (hurrah) and at the station, and an Army major inadvertently stepped on my foot.

"Pardon me," he said, automatically.

I waved a lordly hand. "That's all right, bub," I said, and with that, I knew I was out of the army.

Thirteen.
BECOMING A PH.D.

On Monday, September 23, 1946, I registered at Columbia again, just as though the four-and-a-half-year lapse had never been. I had left a young man just twenty-two; I came back nearly twenty-seven. Had I not been interrupted, I might conceivably have earned my doctorate at the age of twenty-four, which would have been more in accord with my child-prodigy status, but now that could never be. Tens of millions of people had suffered far worse than I did in the course of World War II—but when no one was looking, I sometimes mourned the four-year delay . . .

I discovered, rather ruefully, that in the war years, Linus Pauling's theory of resonance had taken over organic chemistry completely so that I was virtually a beginner again and would have to learn the subject afresh.

For once I was getting along with a superior. Professor Dawson and I were soulmates. This was not because I had ceased to be me. It was entirely because Dawson didn't mind my peculiarities. Indeed, he was amused by them.

For one thing, I was always running into him with excited ideas, or comments, or results. "Phenomenon-a-minute Asimov" he used to refer to me in speaking to others.

One time, for instance, I reported to him that a sample of enzyme wasn't working no matter what I did. I was very gloomy about it for I couldn't understand what I had done wrong. And then I became aware of the fact that I was not using a 2-milliliter pipette, but a 0.2 milliliter one—one that had only one-tenth the capacity of the former, though it had the same outward dimensions. Therefore I was always adding just one-tenth the amount of enzyme I thought I was adding.

This was a terribly stupid mistake for a chemist to make. A good chemist should be able to tell the capacity of a pipette in the dark just by the feel of it.

Of course, I was far too excited to think about the stupidity of the matter and, therefore, to hide the fact so that no one would know how stupid I was. After all, I had solved the problem of the nonworking enzyme. I therefore rushed into Dawson's office (quite disregarding the fact that he was talking to someone) and said, "I've got the answer to the enzyme problem, Dr. Dawson. I was using a 0.2-milliliter pipette instead of a 2-milliliter pipette."

Another research professor might have kicked me out of the laboratory for aggravated stupidity in the first degree, but Professor Dawson chose to regard it as an example of honesty. In fact, he was quoted to me as using the term "absolute integrity" in reference to myself, and I didn't quite have the absolute integrity to tell him it was only stupidity.

As a matter of fact, Dawson had lots of opportunity to observe my stupidity/integrity. According to a system he had himself worked up, all students entered all experimental results each day in a notebook in which every page was backed by carbon paper and an identical copy page. At the end of each day, the carbons were handed to Dawson.

(The idea was, I think, that no student could then hocus the observations, though that notion didn't occur to me for years. I thought Dawson just wanted to look at the observations. Eventually, when it finally occurred to me that some people considered it conceivable that observations could be altered, I wrote a mystery novel about it.)

I handed in my carbons dutifully each day, and every week Dawson and I would go over them together. Since I was always undeft enough to have some experiments that went stupidly awry, Dawson had many occasions to laugh.

It turned out, as a matter of fact, that he had saved a particular set of experimental results I had recorded in early 1942 before I left for the Navy Yard. I had conducted the experiment with such incredible lack of skill that my results came out all over the place. I made a mark for each observation on the graph paper, and they covered the paper in almost random fashion. It looked as though the paper had been hit by shotgun pellets, a point I incautiously mentioned, so that everyone called it "Asimov's shotgun curve" after I had drawn a curve of the proper shape cavalierly through the midst of the marks.

Every once in a while, then, when Dawson wanted to boast about me to someone, he would pull out that shotgun curve. Apparently, the logical thing for any student of normal intelligence to do was to record their observations on scrap paper *before* entering it in the book and then enter them only if they looked good—and it never occurred to me to do that. That was just compounded stupidity, again, but Dawson chose to consider it absolute integrity.

Of course, he knew very well that I was a hopeless mess in the laboratory. At one time he said to me, "Don't worry, Isaac. We've got plenty of hands and if you can't run the experiments we'll hire someone to run them for you. You just keep getting the ideas; that's what we need."

On the other hand, he could speak frankly, too. I once told him of my futile attempts to enter medical school, for he was now serving as the premedical adviser, and he said to me, "It's a good thing you didn't get in, Isaac."

"Oh? Why is that, Dr. Dawson?" I smirked, for I expected him to tell me what a great chemist I was and how the world of chemistry couldn't have endured the loss of me.

"Because you would have made a lousy doctor, Isaac."

Well, it was true.

I owe a great deal to Dawson and I am selfish enough to wish it were true that (as he keeps telling me in recent years) his greatest claim to fame now is the fact that he was my research professor. If it were true, it would be a pleasant way of returning, even if only inadequately, his faith in me and his kindness to me.

Part of my duties as a research student was to prepare a seminar on my research. I had to explain the nature of the problem, then go on to explain what I was doing and why, what I hoped to accomplish, and so on. When I was done, I expected to field searching questions from the floor. Other people in the department were supposed to attend, and the idea was that no one was to become too ingrown, that each student should be exposed to all the other currents permeating the Columbia chemistry department.

That was the theory, but many people found seminars frustrating. Those who lectured on the problem seemed never to grasp the level of ignorance of those not working on it—or were afraid to show anything less than complete erudition. In five minutes, usually, the lecturer had left his audience behind and completed his presentation talking only to himself and his research professor.

I did not intend to do this in *my* seminar, which was slated for December 17. I lacked intellectual insecurity and I did not feel it necessary to be erudite. Besides, I had my fiction-writing experience, in which one has to assume the reader begins by knowing nothing of the story one is going to tell.

I prepared my talk meticulously, therefore, from first principles. I went into the seminar room some hours before the talk, and covered all the boards with equations and chemical formulas. One student, stumbling into the room as I was finishing, looked at the mass of hieroglyphics with dismay and said, "I'll never understand this."

I said, soothingly, "Nonsense. Just listen to everything I say and all will be clear as a mountain pool."

What made me so sure of that, I don't know, but that's how it was. I gave the talk from the beginning and moved slowly along all the equations and formulas, without having to suffer the distraction and interruption of having to write them down as I talked.

In the end the audience seemed enthusiastic and Professor Dawson told someone (who promptly passed it on to me) that it was the clearest presentation he had ever heard. It happened to be the first time I ever presented a formal hour-long talk to an audience in my life.

[February 1947] I was still collecting my notes for the book on World War II I wanted to write. Looking back on it now, I grow impatient with myself. How ridiculous it was. . . . I found that I had . . . in excess of two million words of notes altogether. I started indexing the notes toward the end of February, and that was the giveaway. It was clear that the indexing was an impossible job, and the whole project suddenly faded and died. I doubt that I ever wasted so much time on so futile a project in my life—but at least I learned how *not* to write a nonfiction book, so perhaps it wasn't all that futile after all.

[May 1947] In running my chronometric experiments, I put my enzyme solution into the vessel first and then quickly dumped the catechol solution into it. The enzyme reaction starts at once. First, of course, I had to prepare the catechol solution fresh, for it would undergo spontaneous changes that would make the experiment meaningless if it were allowed to stand around too long.

At the beginning of each day, therefore, I would prepare the catechol solution. I would weigh out a fixed quantity of solid catechol, which comes as white, very fluffy, needlelike crystals, and then I would dump it little by little into a beaker of distilled water.

Catechol, as it happens, is very readily soluble, especially when it exists as fluffy crystals that present a large surface to the water. The result is that as soon as the catechol touches the surface of the water it dissolves. It just seems to vanish without ever penetrating the water's skin.

As I watched it one morning I thought idly: What if it dissolves just *before* it hits the water?

That, I thought at once, might make the basis for a science-fiction story.

But then I thought again. It would not be long now before I would have to write up my research observations in the form of a long and complicated dissertation. That dissertation would have to be written in a convoluted and stylized fashion or it would never pass.

I dreaded that. I had spent nine years now trying to learn to write clearly and well, and now I would have to write a dissertation turgidly and sloppily. It would be even worse than doing a Navy Yard specification, and I didn't know how I could bear it.

Well, then, instead of writing a story about a compound that dissolved before it hit the water, why not write a mock dissertation about it? Why not deliberately write turgidly and sloppily and in this way draw the fangs of the monster?

I suggested such a thing to Campbell and he laughed and said, "Go try it."

Before I visited Campbell that day, I had dropped in to see the editor of *Thrilling Wonder*. . . . Sam Merwin Jr. (his father and namesake had been a well-known author and editor). . . . Not only did he want a story from me but also he wanted a 40,000-word lead novel for *Startling Stories*, the sister magazine. *Startling* featured such a lead novel in every issue, and good ones were hard to come by. I was enamored with the notion myself, since 40,000 words at $.02 a word came to $800, so I agreed to try.

I got to work on the story for Merwin on June 2. I called it "Grow Old with Me." This was supposed to be a quotation from Robert Browning's "Rabbi ben Ezra" and should have been "Grow Old Along with Me," but I remembered the line incorrectly and didn't bother checking.

It dealt with an old tailor who managed to get transferred into a future in which old people underwent euthanasia unless they could prove themselves useful to society. The problem was to work out a way in which an old tailor from the past could prove useful enough to a society of the future to be kept alive. I was so excited at the thought of $800 that I did ten pages that first day and five the day after.

Then, on June 5, unable to resist the other project, I began writing my mock dissertation, which I called, in true dissertation form, "The Endochronic Properties of Resublimated Thiotimoline." (I had intended a still longer title but it would have to fit into the *Astounding* table of contents and I would have to be realistic about it.) I finished it on June 8, complete with tables, graphs, and with references to nonexistent journals, and then took it to Campbell. [Who took it, for $60.]

In addition to taking a course on advanced organic theory. . . . I spent the summer of 1947 making endless calculations concerning my chronometric observations. I was trying to find the most satisfactory theories, the clearest explanations of what was happening—in short, the best possible way of arranging my forthcoming dissertation.

And I also spent it on "Grow Old with Me." . . . By August 27, I had quite a bit of it in final copy and took it in to Merwin for an interim report, so to speak. . . . I called him the next day and again found he liked it. He urged me to continue at full speed.

I was certain that sometime in 1948 I would complete my research, get my degree, and be out in the cold world. It meant I would need a job, for nothing in my nine years' career as a professional writer gave me any cause to suppose that I could ever support myself with my typewriter.

[At] the annual convention of the American Chemical Society. . . . I registered with the employment clearinghouse. With my usual Asimovian flare for relying on lofty principles when that was not advisable, I added to the card on which I listed my vital statistics and my qualifications the totally unnecessary note: "Not interested in any work having any connection with the atomic bomb."

This was stupid, since no one was likely to offer me such work, and if anyone did, I could always have turned it down. As it was, I made myself seem like a trouble-making radical, and you can guess the result. Throughout the entire five days of the convention, I received not one call to an interview. . . .

The utter failure at the convention put me under a dank blanket of apprehension concerning the future. I had for quite a while been totally absorbed in the gathering success of my research—the clear indication that I would have an interesting dissertation and therefore my degree. I couldn't help but view that as the climax of my education and my life, almost as though I were envisaging a cartoon in which I stood on a podium with light radiating from my head, stars going on and off, and the caption reading, "Success!"

Except that that's not how life is. It goes on, and by the time I had my degree, I must also have a job, and how was I going to get that? Aside from the lack of interest at the convention, the fact was that the job market had been declining steadily since the war, and as a Jew who spoke with a Brooklyn accent and, as anyone could tell at a single glance, lacked sophistication and poise, I was scarcely in the first rank of candidates for any job.

[After big revisions were demanded of "Grow Old with Me"] For the first and only time in my life, I openly lost my temper with an editor. I snatched up the manuscript, said, "Go to hell," and stalked angrily out of the office.

It was wrong of me to do that. An editor is entirely within his rights to reject a story, even a story he has ordered.

As I progressed in my dissertation, I went over it with Dawson, who insisted on considering each sentence at length and deciding how it could be made more accurate.

It was a chore for me because I was used to writing quickly and to consider only my own judgment in such matters. However, I wasn't writing for an editor but for a committee of professors, and Professor Dawson knew better than I how to appease them. I therefore consistently followed his suggestions, although I moaned now and then.

The greatest difficulty arose over my use of the constant M. I had introduced it at the appropriate time to indicate how the well-known chronometric equation, which had appeared in a number of papers emerging from Professor Dawson's group, could be corrected and, by use made of it, made more nearly a straight-line function.

After a while, Dawson put down his pen and said, "What is M?"

I was surprised. "Why, you know what it is, Dr. Dawson. It's mixing time."

"Why don't you say so?"

Now I was really surprised. "But Dr. Dawson, if I say so *now*, I'll kill the suspense." I couldn't believe that I had to explain this.

"Isaac," he said, "I hate to break the news to you, but you're not writing one of your science-fiction stories."

I was horrified. "You mean I have to define *M*?"

"The instant you first use it."

I did so, though I muttered something about "ruining the whole thing."

It really did spoil my fun and erased any pleasure I could have had in the dissertation. Nor did it really help. Once it was all done and under consideration, one professor was reported to have said, "It reads like a mystery story." And he didn't say it with approval.

February 17, 1948, was the silver anniversary of the family's arrival in the United States.

Quite independently, it was also the day the March 1948 *Astounding* reached the stands. It contained "Endochronic Properties of Resublimated Thiotimoline."

The previous June, when I had sold it to Campbell, I had feared it might come out not long before I was slated to be up for my doctorate and that it might be used to prove that I lacked the proper gravity of character to make a good chemist. . . . So I asked Campbell to run the article under a pseudonym. Campbell agreed. . . .

Now came February 17. [One of the other research students] said, "Hey, that was a funny satire on chemistry by you in the new *Astounding*, Isaac."

I grinned foolishly and beamed with pride, as I always do on such occasions, and said, "Thanks."

And then, after a goodish time, I suddenly remembered the pseudonym and said, rather stiffly, "What makes you think the article was by me?"

. . . "Well, when I noticed your name on it, I thought, 'Gee, I'll bet he wrote it.' "

[Another student said] "Don't tell me you put your own name on a satire on chemistry when your dissertation is coming up?"

Since that was precisely the thought that flashed through my mind, I went off and called Campbell.

Campbell remembered I had asked him to use a pseudonym, but he had an explanation for failing to do so. "I forgot," he said. Perhaps Campbell forgot out of an instinctive feeling that forgetting was the proper thing to do. He had a number of infallible instincts.

For one thing, as I found out from Campbell a few weeks later, the article proved to be a howling success with the readers. He received a flood of letters from them and, as a matter of fact, interest in the article has never died down.

Campbell said that some readers had even fallen for it and thought thiotimoline was a real compound. They flooded the New York Public Library (he said) demanding to see the journals I had quoted and were reluctant to believe the librarians who assured them there were no such journals.

Then, too, the thiotimoline article seemed to tickle the fancy of every chemist who happened to be a science-fiction fan. By word of mouth, it spread to chemists who never read science fiction. I began to get requests to have it printed in obscure little periodicals put out by chemical associations. I got letters from chemists who clearly did not know I had ever written anything else.

The thiotimoline article was, in fact, the first thing I had ever written that made any mark at all outside the closed circle of science fictiondom—and I owed it to Campbell's forgetfulness.

But that still left me in trouble at home, and if I thought it would escape the eyes of the Columbia scientists, I was crazy. The very day after its appearance, Professor William von Doering, a young organic chemist who was already making his mark in the world and who was himself the kind of eccentric who wore bow ties in a world of four-in-hands, stopped me in the hall to make humorous references to it. I also found out that another member of the department was a rabid science-fiction fan, so he couldn't possibly have missed it. And if two members knew, then there was no hope of secrecy—everyone would know.

I was sunk in misery and decided that I would never pass my oral examinations.

[After more problems with the research] I finished the dissertation, all seventy-four pages of it (enough length to make a good Foundation novelette, but with infinitely more sweating and less enjoyment) on April 3, and went over the whole thing, proofreading it with Stanley's help. (Stanley had managed to get the money to go to NYU, was finishing his freshman year, and was doing well.)

The title is "The Kinetics of the Reaction Inactivation of Tyrosinase During Its Catalysis of the Aerobic Oxidation of Catechol," a far worse title than that of my thiotimoline satire. What's more, I achieved a far more involuted and turgid academese than I had dared put into my satire. Here is a sentence taken at random from my dissertation: "It will be recalled that an analysis of the Chronometric Equation (see Section: The Q-t RELATIONSHIP) led to the conclusion that if the equation satisfactorily expressed the entire reaction course, the time required for half the original enzyme to be inactivated was independent of the initial enzyme concentration (see Equ. 8) and that the overall rate of enzyme inactivation was proportional to the 1.5 power of the concentration of active enzyme present in the system at any time (see Equ.12)."

That's one sentence and it's enough. No need to risk coagulation of the brain by going any farther.

There are, generally, two types of responses to a doctor's orals. One is paralysis which, at its extreme, leaves you unable to answer any question, including "What is your name?" The other is hysteria, which at its extreme leads you to respond to "What is your name?" with a long, jolly peal of laughter. . . .

It was clear that I was going to react in the second fashion: not paralysis, but hysteria. I was laughing as I went in.

I got up and gave my speech with only an occasional giggle, and then the questioning began. . . .

One fellow asked me how I knew the potassium iodide I used was indeed potassium iodide. My impulse was to answer truthfully that I never questioned it. It said, "Potassium iodide" on the label and that was enough for me.

Some dim instinct warned me that that was the wrong answer. I thought desperately and quickly and said, "Well, sir, it dissolves as potassium iodide does, and yields iodine as potassium iodide does, and it gives me my end point as potassium iodide would, so it doesn't matter what it really is, does it?"

That was a good answer.

One fellow asked me how I knew that the enzyme I used was indeed derived from the mushroom species I said it was. I said it came from mushrooms bought at the grocery store.

"So what?" said he.

"So *Agaricus campestris* is the only species sold in the grocery store."

"How can you be sure of that?"

Again I had to think rapidly. "If I had any doubts, sir, I would have referred to a text on mushrooms."

"Whose?" he said.

I said, shrewdly, "Yours." That was a bad answer. He hadn't written any such text.

At one point, I muffed questions I ought not to have muffed . . . at another point when I didn't know the answer, I hesitantly guessed and Dawson, who sat opposite me at the other end of the table, leaned back so that no one would see him (they were all looking at me, of course) and shook his head slightly from side to side.

Whereupon I said, despondently, "But I see that Dr. Dawson is shaking his head at me, so I guess I'm all wrong."

That was surely one time that Dawson had reason to disapprove of my "absolute integrity" for he turned a distinct pink and said, "You were not supposed to say that, Isaac," and everyone turned to him and made mock-serious comments about helping his student unethically.

No one was really unkind to me, however, and after an hour and twenty minutes, Professor Ralph S. Halford asked me the final question.

He said, "What can you tell us, Mr. Asimov, about the thermodynamic properties of the compound known as thiotimoline?"

For just an instant I was thunderstruck, and then the hysteria I had been fighting off all this time washed over me and I broke into peal after peal of helpless laughter and had to be led from the room.

I had reason to laugh. It didn't seem conceivable to me that they would tease me in that fashion if they had not by then decided to pass me. Apparently, thank goodness, they had read the thiotimoline article and had taken it in the spirit in which it was meant.

I was right. In five minutes they had come out and, as was traditional in the case of a pass, each held out his hand and said, "Congratulations, Dr. Asimov!"

I had made it. I was Isaac Asimov, Ph.D.

Fourteen.
POSTDOC

The next day, June 3, 1948, I officially started my post-doctoral stint with [Robert C.] Elderfield. . . . The Columbia Appointments Office had issued a handout to the newspapers saying that the *average* Ph.D. salary, fresh after graduation, was $5,400 a year. Since I was only going to get $4,500 from Elderfield, it was clear that I was considerably below par. . . .

Now that I was through with my doctoral effort, I felt it possible to begin new things. For one thing, I bought a copy of Glasstone's *Textbook of Physical Chemistry* . . . the first scientific book I ever bought of my own volition and not because it was a class requirement. It served as the nucleus of my personal library of science which, as the years passed, was to grow larger and larger and more and more important to me.

Second, it was time, at last, to begin a new science-fiction story. It was now a full year since I had made my last sale—the thiotimoline piece. Since then, I had written only "Grow Old Along with Me," which, of course, had been a fiasco. On June 3, 1948, therefore, I began "The Red Queen's Race," a tale involving time-travel paradox. . . . It featured a tough-guy detective as hero—quite unusual for me. . . .

My postdoctoral work was going on unimpressively. I was running tests on all kinds of antimalarials, making observations, preparing graphs, trying to find out what happened to it in living tissue in order to decide whether it was changed into some intermediate form that was itself more active. Then, perhaps, the intermediate could be isolated, analyzed, synthesized, and used directly.

The trouble was that I didn't see anything coming out of my efforts. I was constantly terrified that Elderfield would say so and kick me out—not that I was afraid either of him or of being kicked out in themselves—but the specter of unemployment was a very fearful one for anyone who had spent his second decade of life in the Great Depression.

On September 7, however, the Segals [friends met on a Catskills vacation] dropped in and Jack asked me what kind of work I was doing. They knew I was doing chemical research at Columbia but knew no details. My mind was full of it at the time so I explained the importance of antimalarials, the nature of quinine, atabrine, and quinacrine, using my hands and fingers to represent chemical formulas. I explained that what we wanted to know was what happened to these substances in the human body to see if these were changed into the real antimalarial and what that might be.

They listened in apparent absorption, and, at the end, Jack said to me, "You're a very good explainer. I wouldn't have thought anyone could have made that clear to me."

I laughed, and was pleased, and we went on to other things, and eventually the Segals went home.

The effect on me, however, was similar to the one that had followed young Emmanuel Bershadsky's praise of *The Greenville Chums at College.* I had on that earlier occasion begun to think of myself as a writer; now, as a result of Jack's remark, I began to think of myself as an explainer. I never forgot, and the desire to explain began to grow on me from that day. What's more, I stopped worrying about Elderfield and his opinion of me. I decided I was good at my work.

Thank you, Jack Segal, wherever you are.

[1949] Despite Elderfield's offer of a second year, I felt no great security in my job . . . nor could I find any security in my writing.

Books of my own . . . seemed an utter will-o'-the-wisp. . . . It was at this crucial moment of uncertainty that I received a phone call from Bill Boyd of Boston University School of Medicine.

[He was offered] only an instructorship . . . for a year only with no guarantee of continuation or advancement (although, of course, both would be in the cards if I gave satisfaction), and the salary was $4,500. It seemed little, if at all, better than what I had with Elderfield, and I wasn't going to move to Boston for that. I turned it down out of hand.

[But Boyd's boss, Burnham S. Walker, read Isaac's dissertation and wrote Isaac that he was "particularly impressed" with it.] I promptly sent off a pleasant reply, trying to indicate that I didn't consider the job offer dead . . .

[He was asked to Boston for an interview.] The ante had gone up. I was still only being offered an instructorship, but the salary was going to be $5,000, and a one-month vacation with pay was to be included.

[After various interviews] Walker told me I would be expected to help teach the medical school freshmen and asked if I could teach biochemistry.

"Certainly," I said.

Since he didn't ask me if I had ever taken any course in biochemistry, or if I knew anything about biochemistry, I felt it would be impolite to force upon him the information that the answer to both those possible questions was "No." The course wouldn't start 'til February and by then I should know enough to get along.

I asked him to send me a letter formally offering me the position and then I went home wondering if I ought to accept it. Back in New York, everyone at Columbia told me to jump at the offer, and if the school had been located in New York I would have.

I love New York. I had never felt at home in Philadelphia and I don't know that I would ever feel at home in Boston. And yet I didn't love New York to the point of wanting to starve in it.

[In the meantime, he gave the revised manuscript of "Grow Old Along with Me"—he had learned the correct quote—to his friend and then agent Fred Pohl, who took it to Doubleday.]

Doubleday . . . was willing to publish it as a *book*, provided I rewrote it and lengthened it from its 40,000 words to the full novel-length 70,000 . . . on March 31, Pohl handed me a check for $135 [for the option on the book]. He kept $15 as agent's fee on the option . . .

Finally, on April 4, I received a formal notification . . . that I had been appointed an instructor in biochemistry at Boston University School of Medicine as of May 1, 1949.

Well, what could I do? I had been looking for a job madly for two months, and this was the only one that turned up and, except for the fact that it was in Boston, was a satisfactory one. On April 5, I accepted officially and that meant farewell to [Manhattan's] Stuyvesant Town [where he lived then] and, far worse, farewell to New York . . .

In making this decision, I completely ignored the potential earning power of my writing. Looking back on it now it might seem amazing that I did so, but *at that time* it would have been madness to do anything else.

During my eleven years as a professional science-fiction writer who for seven years had been at the top of the tree, I had made a total of $7,593, or just about $700 a year. To be sure, I hadn't been a full-time writer at all, but my best year, 1944, had only brought in $1,100, and as a full-time writer I would do well to double that, and $2,200 a year would not support me.

In fact, could I even double the rate at which I earned money if I spent full time at the typewriter? It wasn't writing time that was the bottleneck. You might remain at a typewriter hour after hour after hour, and yet produce very little. What one needs is *thinking* time, and that can't be rushed. You have to think up your plots and your complications and your resolutions, so that most of your time is going to be spent thinking and not typing.

[He was also worried that, without *Astounding* and Campbell, he would not sell much.] And yet if Campbell represented a dead end to me, was there any way of branching out? If I couldn't follow [Robert] Heinlein into the slicks, was there anyplace else I could forge a path for myself?

On March 21, 1949, I had attended a lecture given by Linus Pauling. It was the best lecture I had ever heard. Even Gertrude, who was present, and who did not understand a word, enjoyed it. It was possible, then, to make science attractive to anyone.

Inspired by Pauling's speech, and remembering Jack Segal's remark months before about what a good explainer I was, I decided to write a piece of nonfiction. I called it "Detective Story for Non-Chemists" (a title based on Tarpley's [the fellow researcher who had noticed the thiotimoline article] remark, once, that a good chemist had to have a detective instinct). It dealt with the manner in which chemists had worked out the chemical structure of the molecule of biotin, one of the B vitamins.

[Campbell rejected it as being too dull and detailed as a nonfiction piece for *Astounding*.] I did not, however, forget it, or my general desire to write nonfiction.

[May 29, 1949] . . . Doubleday was taking the revised "Grow Old Along with Me" and it would be out as a book the next January . . . I was delighted. It seemed a happy send-off. But it was difficult to be altogether happy. I was leaving Columbia at last nearly fourteen years after I had first entered it, and although I had longed often enough to be through with it, now that I was really going to leave, it was hard to forget that I had spent half my life associated with it. Then, too, I was leaving New York City for the second time, nearly three years after having gotten out of the army and returned, and this time it was not "for the duration"; it might be for all my life . . .

I remember I met old Professor Thomas on the Columbia campus on Friday, May 27, my last full day on campus. He was getting on in years now and walked with a cane.

I said to him, "Well, Professor Thomas, I'm leaving Columbia today after fourteen years."

I thought that the least he could do would be to break into tears, but he only banged his cane against the brick walk and said, "About time! About time!" turned, and tramped off.

Fifteen.
TEACHING, WRITING, AND SPEAKING

On June 1, 1949, I showed up at the medical school and spent my first day at the job. It wasn't encouraging. I discovered that Bill Boyd, a full professor, was making $6,000. I seemed, financially, to be already near the top for an academic job. I doubted if I would ever make, even in a good writing year, as much as $10,000.

Oh well—so I would never be rich. My salary would do for a childless couple, especially since my savings had been slowly accumulating as a result of cautious and frugal living in the past and now stood at $6,200.

If, that is, the job continued. The trouble was it lacked security. My salary did not come out of Boston University funds. It was out of funds from government grants . . . and each year those grants would have to be renewed or I would face the sudden kickout.

In Boston, I felt as much an exile at first as I had felt in Philadelphia. Boston, however, was a livelier city than Philadelphia had been, and my surroundings were academic rather than bureaucratic, which meant they were more stimulating.

As time went on, I rapidly grew to like Boston and New England generally. I found a liberal newspaper, the *Boston Globe*, and I discovered there was no shortage of eating places or science-fiction fans.

Eventually, when mobility increased, I discovered that the New England countryside was delightful.

Walter Bradbury [Doubleday editor] . . . wrote to ask me for a different title . . . since *Grow Old Along with Me* did not sound like science fiction and, indeed, carried romantic implications. He was quite right. I decided to change the title to *Pebble in the Sky* . . .

On November 9, there came the news [of a grant renewal], so I was assured of a salary for a second year. [Furthermore] I now made the discovery that books, unlike magazine stories, made money for themselves while the authors slept or dallied or twiddled their fingers.

That same day, I got a telegram from Fred Pohl to the effect that Unicorn Press, a small book club specializing in mysteries, had taken *Pebble in the Sky* for an advance of $1,000. Such earnings were split half and half between publisher and author, with Fred taking his agent's 10 percent of my half, but that still meant $450 for me eventually when it came to statement time (Book publishers pay accumulated earnings twice a year). Well, goodness, that was half a year's rent and I hadn't had to do any work for it at all.

This is not to say that this new variety of writing success didn't bring some problems in its wake. At about this time, I received a copy of the book jacket for the forthcoming *Pebble in the Sky*. I was delighted, especially with my own handsome dream-prince of a photograph.

The back cover, in addition to the photo, had a biographical sketch, and the last sentence was, "Dr. Asimov lives in Boston, where he is engaged in cancer research at Boston University School of Medicine."

It had never occurred to me that the medical school might be mentioned and now I wondered if the school might be offended by this. It was too late to change the jacket and I was not of a mind to hang by my thumbs and wait for an explosion. I thought I would have to confront the issue now and I already knew that I could not give up my writing. If it came to a choice . . .

I asked for an appointment with Dean Faulkner, and when I kept that appointment, I put it to him frankly. I was a science-fiction writer, I said, had been for years, and the people who hired me knew that was so at the time they hired me.

My first book was coming out in a month or two, under my own name, of course, and my association with the medical school was mentioned on the back cover. I hadn't known it would be, but there it was. Did he want my resignation?

The dean considered thoughtfully (he was a true Boston Brahmin with a long face and an easy smile) and said, "Is it a good book?"

Cautiously, I said, "The publishers think so."

He said, "In that case the medical school will be glad to be identified with it."

That took care of that.

[Walter Bradbury] was less than encouraging concerning my new novel, *The Stars, like Dust*—. No contract. He would give me an option for $250 to keep me working, but he would have to see six or seven chapters now before a contract would be possible, and the six or seven would not include the first two chapters—which he was throwing out.

I had apparently committed the customary sin of the sophomore novel. The first novel was fine since I was writing as a novice and had no reputation to uphold. Once it was accepted, however, I was a "novelist" and had to write the second novel while keeping that reputation secure, which meant I had to write deeply and poetically and wittily and so on.

Bradbury got my error across to me very easily.

He said, "Do you know how Hemingway says, 'The sun rose the next morning'?"

I had never read Hemingway, but I had heard of him, of course. I said, "No. How does he say it?"

"He says, 'The sun rose the next morning.'"

I got it. From that day to this, I labored to make my style a spare one. I eschewed all ornamentation for its own sake, and if ever my style seems to depart from the starkly straightforward and simple, it is only to achieve humor.

[His first encounter with med students in the biochemistry lab] I stood there in my white lab coat feeling very superior and professorial with all the students deferentially calling me "Doctor."

Then one student came over and with no trace of wise-guyishness at all, said, "Pardon me, Dr. Asimov, are you a Ph.D. or a real doctor?"

It put me in my place. A Ph.D. is the highest academic degree there is, and is awarded only for original research. An M.D., on the contrary, is given out on satisfactory completion of schoolwork and is, academically, of no greater value than a Bachelor of Arts. Nevertheless, in a medical school, those with no more than a Ph.D. are second-class citizens. [Janet can't help adding "that's not how it was in MY medical school."] I knew that, but the student's question brought it home, and the value of my academic career in my own eyes, at least as long as I was in the medical school, declined.

Then, on February 7 [1950], I gave my first lecture—on simple lipids—and survived.

Dr. Walker was surer of my talents in this direction than I was. He had been invited to give a talk at Bates College in Lewiston, Maine. He couldn't go, but suggested they invite me, telling them I was "an interesting speaker" and "quite a colorful character." . . .

I spoke to perhaps sixty people, and they sufficed to fill the room. I don't remember what I talked about and I didn't note it in my diary, but I did speak extemporaneously, something I have done ever since. I did say in my diary that the talk "met with roaring approval. Applause! Laughter! I laid them in the aisles."

I'm sure I did. I always have since (well, nearly always). Talking that successfully, off-the-cuff, to an audience of strangers, cured me of my panic at lecturing.

Thus . . . just before the Bates lecture, I had gone to Dr. Walker with a certain worry.

"Dr. Walker," I said, "last night I dreamed I got up before the class to give my lecture and I couldn't think of a thing to say. Do you think there's something ominous in that?"

"I think there's something normal in that," he said. "We all have dreams like that. Wait till you dream that you not only can't think of a thing to say but you're standing there naked."

After the Bates College talk, however, I no longer had dreams like that.

[In March, the short version of his dissertation was published.] It was not only my first scientific publication, it also was my longest and my best. Over the next three years I was to publish six papers on research work done in my Boston University laboratory. All of them were in collaboration with others who did the actual work, though I did the supervision and the actual writing. All those papers were unimportant and I enjoyed none of them. After 1953, I never again published a scientific paper involving research.

The trouble was that . . . even while I still thought of myself as a researcher, I scorned and detested the writing end of it. Writing a research paper is a tedious and stylized job. You cannot write as you wish; you cannot use English; you cannot have fun. It was even worse than being back in the Navy Yard making certain that no paragraph in a report was anything but a repetition of a paragraph in some earlier Navy Yard report.

Preparing my dissertation with Dawson had been an unsettling experience, but I found that writing papers on my own was no better. Such papers had to pass the eagle eyes of Walker and Lemon and then, on being submitted to a journal, had to undergo the dour glances of nameless reviewers. In the end, nothing got through but well-chewed cud.

I might not have minded, but I felt myself to be a writer, and I hated having my name on such limp and bedraggled material.

[Visiting Campbell in New York] He would talk of nothing but dianetics. I didn't argue much; I just remained impervious and said I didn't believe it. Finally Campbell said, half in anger and half in jest, "Damn it, Asimov, you have a built-in doubter."

"Thank goodness I do, Mr. Campbell," said I.

My clipping service had been sending me all kinds of reviews of *Pebble in the Sky*, and I had bought a scrapbook and had been carefully pasting them up. On June 24, when the Newmans and Bersons [friends] were visiting our apartment, I brought out the book and went over the reviews very pridefully for them.

During the course of that, I heard Roger [Newman] say in a very low voice, to himself rather than to anyone else, "The old lady shows her medals." (That was, of course, the name of a play by James M. Barrie.)

I pretended I hadn't heard, closed the book as soon as I decently could, and put it away. From that day on, I have never showed my reviews to anyone nor, as far as is humanly possible, done anything that could be construed as showing my medals. (Of course, you might construe this autobiography as a case of showing my medals, but I'm doing my level best to show my boobie prizes as well.) Thank you, Roger Newman, wherever you are.

[On October 3, 1950, Isaac attended a lecture on science fiction by Gotthard Guenther.] I took a seat well in the back without making myself known, and I had not yet reached the stage where I could be recognized offhand. I could therefore listen in welcome anonymity.

Guenther . . . had a peculiarly Teutonic notion of the mystical value of soil. He felt that civilization was a product of the Old World and could not flourish indigenously in the New. (When someone raised the question of the Incas and the Mayas, he dismissed them with a wave of his hand.)

Therefore, he maintained, when Old World civilization was transplanted to the New World, a distortion was introduced and one of the ways in which this distortion was evidenced was by the peculiar American invention of science fiction, which was not to be confused with earlier European ventures in the field (Jules Verne, for instance). American science fiction turned Old World values upside down.

Take, for instance, he said, the story "Nightfall" by Isaac Asimov. (At this point I shrank lower in my seat.) It dealt with stars as instruments of madness, whereas in all Old World views of the universe, the stars were seen as gentle, benign, and friendly.

He continued to describe the manner in which "Nightfall" reversed or distorted common views and, in general, built up an interpretation of the story that had me gasping.

When the lecture was over, members of the audience flocked around him, and I waited patiently. When I was the only one left, I said, "Dr. Guenther, your analysis of 'Nightfall' is all wrong."

"Well, that is a matter of opinion," said Dr. Guenther, smiling gently.

"No, it is not," I said, forcefully. "I am *certain* you are wrong. Nothing of what you said was in the author's mind."

"And how can you know that?"

That was when I let the guillotine blade fall. "Because, Dr. Guenther, *I* am the author."

His face lit up, "You are Isaac Asimov?"

"Yes, sir."

"How pleased I am to meet you." Then he said, "But tell me, what makes you think, just because you are the author of 'Nightfall,' that you have the slightest inkling of what is in it?"

And of course I couldn't answer that question because it suddenly became clear to me that there might well be more in a story than an author was aware of.

Dr. Guenther and I became good friends after that, and on October 17, I gave a guest lecture to his class.

By the end of the year [1950], my earnings had just topped the $4,700 mark . . . almost as much as the $5,000 stipend I earned at

Boston University. . . . For the *first* time, the thought flickered across my mind that I might conceivably make a living as a writer if I chose to.

In a way it was exceedingly fortunate that this had happened when it did and not two years sooner. Had I reason to think the thought at the end of 1948, rather than at the end of 1950, I would never have been persuaded to move to Boston in search of a livelihood. I would have been content to remain in New York and take a job there, anywhere.

And that would have been bad, I think. My academic position at Boston University School of Medicine was valuable to me; the prestige it brought was useful; the background it supplied for writing other than science fiction was indispensible. No, my literary poverty lasted just exactly long enough. It served to deposit me in the medical school, and then it rose sharply so that I would not be stranded there for life.

[Isaac worked on a textbook with two colleagues, and then] the galleys of *Biochemistry and Human Metabolism* began to come in in three copies plus a master. . . . Each of us—[Burnham] Walker, [Bill] Boyd, and I—searched our own copies for mistakes. We then foregathered. The author of that chapter would list the corrections and they would be entered in the master. Each of the other two would then add any other corrections he had found . . . on a surprising number of occasions, there were mistakes none of us found.

The publisher's proofreader himself searched for mistakes and would point out inconsistencies in capitalization, hyphenation, and so on. It was a dreadful chore to try to decide on consistency, especially when the three of us never agreed. Finally Bill Boyd said, "According to Emerson, 'A foolish consistency is the hobgoblin of little minds.' "

After that, whenever we came to a trivial inconsistency, we would chorus "Emerson!" and let it stand.

[The Asimov's had a new baby, son David, born in 1951. Their customary movie-going diminished in frequency.] I can't say my taste in movies testified to any deeply intellectual instincts, by the way. I liked adventure movies and would see, with pleasure, almost anything with swordplay or with a chase sequence. And I liked comedy, the more slapstick the better, and musical comedies, too . . .

Oddly enough, or not so oddly perhaps, I didn't like what were called "science-fiction" movies, with rare exceptions, such as *The Shape of Things to Come.*

For the most part, science-fiction movies seemed to be innocent of science and, for that matter, of acting, and I found them acutely embarrassing. *The Thing,* for example, was unbearably bad, and I was disgusted at the fact that it was made, and ruined, from Campbell's classic story "Who Goes There?"

[Writing began to conflict with research.] I found the feeling of being a research chemist (or biochemist) fading away. I had worked so hard for it, I had achieved a doctorate and even, finally, professorial status, and now, suddenly, it was leaving me—because I had found something else, something I had been doing for years before I started my research, yet which till 1952, I had never clearly thought of as my life's work.

I was beginning to think of myself as a writer and that was crucial. . . . As research steadily lost its glamour for me, writing grew steadily more attractive. And as writing grew more attractive, research steadily lost its glamour. Either tendency reinforced the other in a spiral that made me, with each month that passed, more of a writer and less of a researcher.

[He got into trouble with the school over not doing research.] Let me make it clear that I was turning against research and not against teaching. I loved teaching, and the textbook was a form of teaching. I particularly loved lecturing.

There could be no question but that my teaching was satisfactory. I had improved steadily in the organization, drama, and interest in my lecture presentations. (This would seem to be my own estimate of the situation, but I know the students agreed with me.)

On April 15, 1952, I gave my final lecture of the third teaching semester in which I had been involved. It was "Heat and Work," and somewhere in the middle, I delivered a ringing sentence on the concept of the "heat death" of the universe, and there followed a wild and enthusiastic peal of applause that did not allow me to continue for quite a while.

A story reached me once that on another floor, a member of the Physiology Department said, "What was that?" at the sound of distant laughter and applause.

Another member said, "Probably Asimov lecturing."

And it was.

[On a visit to science-fiction editor Horace Gold] He suggested a robot novel and I demurred. I had only written robot short stories and didn't know if I could carry a whole novel based on the robot idea.

"Sure you can," he said. "How about an overpopulated world in which robots are taking over human jobs?"

"Too depressing," I said. "I'm not sure I want to handle a heavy sociological story."

"Do it your way. You like mysteries. Put a murder in such a world and have a detective solve it with a robot partner. If the detective doesn't solve it, the robot will replace him."

That was the germ of a new novel I called *The Caves of Steel*. When I wrote it, I did my best to ignore this business of robots replacing human beings. That was typically Gold and not at all Asimov—but Horace kept pushing, and in the end, some of it was forced in, though not nearly as much as Horace wanted.

What pleased me most about *The Caves of Steel* when I came to write it was that it was a pure mystery story set against a science-fiction background. As far as I was concerned it was a perfect fusion of the two genre, and the first such perfect fusion. A number of people agree with me in this.

The year 1952 saw McCarthyism at its peak in the United States. At no time did it affect me directly in any way, but the spectacle sickened me. My liberal friends and I denounced Senator Joseph R. McCarthy to each other and if we were representative samples of American public opinion he wouldn't have lasted five minutes. The fact is we weren't. The average American was all for McCarthy and his simple-minded and destructive "patriotism."

I remembered what Ted Sturgeon had once said at a [science-fiction] convention—that science fiction was the last bastion of freedom of speech. The censor minds did not read science fiction, could not understand science fiction, and would not know what to suppress if they did read it. If censorship ever got so sophisticated that even science fiction fell prey to it, then all was over. Every vestige of democracy would be gone.

So I set about giving my opinion of McCarthyism in a science-fiction story. I called it "A Piece of Ocean" at first, then changed the name to "The Martian Way." It dealt with Martian colonists with a problem, who were victimized out of a solution by a McCarthy-style politician and who were in this way forced to find a still better solution. I finished it on June 10. I did the 18,000 words in four weeks.

In this story, by the way, I described a "space walk" in euphoric terms, over a decade before space walks actually took place and apparently *did* induce euphoria.

The November 1952 *Galaxy* included "The Martian Way," which got the cover—with my name misspelled.

Somehow I thought that the story would elicit a mass of mail denouncing my own portrayal of McCarthyism, or supporting it, but I got nothing either one way or the other. It may be that my satire of McCarthy was so subtle that everyone missed it.

[Jumping ahead to 1954] Every once in a while the television set proved to be more than a medium of entertainment and also became a method for involving one's self with the world in a way that would have been impossible before television.

In 1954, Senator Joseph R. McCarthy, who was all-powerful

because so many Americans were dupes and so many others were cowards (and who had easily survived my own satire of him in "The Martian Way"), tangled with the army. The army, backed up against the wall and trembling with fear, had no choice, at last, but to fight back, accusing McCarthy of attacking the army out of revenge for their having inducted a protégé of his.

Considering that McCarthy was destroying the United States (and one can easily argue that it was his legacy that led to a number of wrongheaded decisions on the part of the American government, including those that involved us in the disastrous Vietnam War), it was in the highest degree ironic that the point at which the line was drawn was over whether McCarthy was trying to pull strings to get some pampered youngster out of the army or not. That, however, was the point over which the army dared fight.

The hearings that resulted were on every day, and there were summaries every night. I watched them during the day when I could and I never missed the summaries at night. It seemed to me that surely there was no way on earth that any sane person could fail to see McCarthy's gangsterism, and I trembled over the possibility that Americans would prove obstinately irrational and cling to the monster. Fortunately, McCarthy was, unwittingly, on my side. Through his own persistent and unbelievable display of unpalatability and the smooth work of Attorney Joseph Welch, McCarthy was destroyed.

January 2, 1953, saw me thirty-three years old, and I had a pleasant birthday present . . . a Doubleday contract for *The Caves of Steel*, a contract which called for a $1,000 advance. Still, if Doubleday's stock was going up with me, Campbell's was going down. Now that he had broken with dianetics, he grew increasingly interested in parapsychology or, as it is also called, psionics, or, simply, psi. Increasingly, the stories in *Astounding* involved telepathy, precognition, and other wild talents.

It bothered me that Campbell's predilections should be so reflected in the magazine. It bothered me that I should see so many of his editorial comments so quickly translated into stories by overcooperative authors. What's more, Campbell's editorials, which had grown to be four thousand to six thousand words long in each issue, began to infuriate me with their ultraconservative and antiscientific standpoint.

I was having a stronger and stronger impulse to stay away from him, but the ties of love, and the memory of all he had done for me, kept me from ever breaking with him. On my visit to New York toward the end of 1952, Campbell talked to me about a story idea he was thinking of. It was about someone who could levitate (a wild talent, see) but could not get anyone to believe him. Campbell wanted to call it "Upsy-daisy."

I hesitated, decided I could do it my way, and wrote it during the first half of January. I called it "Belief." I mailed it off to Campbell on January 12 and when I hadn't heard from him in ten days, I called and found there was a three-page letter on its way to me. As might have been predicted, I didn't have *enough* psi in the story; I had made it too rational.

I changed it as much as I could bring myself to, but not as much as Campbell would have liked and, in the end, he took it.

Science fiction was becoming important enough to have books written *about* it. One of the first of these was Sprague de Camp's *Science Fiction Handbook* . . . a marvelous book . . . in Sprague's gentle and courteous style. He included a brief biography of me, which contained no mistakes, and in it he had this to say: "Asimov is a stoutish, youngish-looking man with wavy brown hair, blue eyes, and a bouncing, jovial, effervescent manner, much esteemed among his friends for his generous warm-hearted nature. Extremely sociable, articulate, and witty, he is a perfect toastmaster."

Well, I could argue with that, but I certainly don't intend to. . . . He also said, "Asimov writes a brisk, smooth, straightforward style with keen logic and human understanding." I don't intend to quarrel with that, either.

Later in the book he said, "Simak's stories may be compared with Asimov's," which is perceptive of Sprague, since I consciously tried to imitate Cliff's style. . . .

[Isaac wrote an introduction to a collection of de Camp's stories.] I was at least as complimentary to him as he was to me. We always had a real love feast going—but then we each meant it. . . . [It was] the first Introduction I ever wrote to someone else's book. (It wasn't the last. Indeed, I have by now written so many that I honestly think it is possible that if all of them were counted it might turn out I have written more introductions to other people's books than anyone else in history.) . . .

My writing became ever more direct and spare, and I think it was *The Caves of Steel* that lifted me a notch higher in my own estimation. I used it as a model for myself thereafter, and it was to be decades before I surpassed that book in my own eyes.

Yet even as *The Caves of Steel* was raising my science fiction to a new level of expertise, something new was beginning.

A certain publisher, Henry Schuman, was interested in putting out a line of science books. . . . [He] was talking not of textbooks, not of books for the general public even, but of books for teenagers. That was a new wrinkle. I agreed to give it serious thought, but I kept my enthusiasm low . . . yet I thought about it . . .

On June 12, I had dinner with him and he introduced me to a Dr. Washton, who was his science advisor . . . [and who] gave me a short lecture on how to write for the early teenage audience. He told me, for instance, that no sentence must be longer than twenty-five words. (I followed instructions very carefully in this book [on the chemicals of life], with the result that I didn't like it very well when it was completed. It was the only book in which I accepted supervision of this kind. Afterward, I put the lecture out of my mind and just let the words flow naturally. Things went much better that way.)

[Years later, Isaac did many books for children and for teenagers.] It is not very difficult to write for teenagers if you avoid thinking of them as children. I do *not* simplify my vocabulary for them, though I often add the pronunciations of the technical terms, merely to reduce the terror they inspire visually. I do avoid sentences that are too long and complex and I do not indulge in obscure allusions. What is lacking in a teenager is not intelligence or reasoning ability, but merely experience.

[At the 1953 World Science-Fiction Convention in Philadelphia he met Randall Garrett, James Gunn, Philip Farmer, and] another personage, not a professional author yet, but destined to become one, and a more colorful one, perhaps, than anyone else in science fiction, even myself. He was just a boy then, perhaps no more than eighteen . . . [with] the livest eyes I ever saw, filled with an explosive concentration of intelligence.

Those live eyes were now focused on me with something that I can only describe as worship.

He said, "Are you Isaac Asimov?" And in his voice was awe and wonder and amazement.

I was rather pleased, but I struggled hard to retain a modest demeanor. "Yes, I am," I said.

"You're not kidding? You're really *Isaac Asimov*?" The words have not yet been invented that would describe the ardor and reverence with which his tongue caressed the syllables of my name.

I felt as though the least I could do would be to rest my hand upon his head and bless him, but I controlled myself. "Yes, I am," I said, and by now my smile was a fatuous thing, nauseating to behold. "*Really*, I am."

"Well, I think you're . . ." he began, still in the same tone of voice, and for a split second he paused, while I listened and everyone within earshot held his breath. The youngster's face shifted in that split second into an expression of utter contempt and he finished the sentence with supreme indifference "—*nothing!*"

The effect, for me, was that of tumbling over a cliff I had not known was there, and landing flat on my back. I could only blink foolishly while everyone present roared with laughter.

The youngster was Harlan Ellison, you see, and I had never met him before and didn't know his utter irreverence. (Harlan insists he said, "You aren't so much," but I think well of my memory and I'll stand by my version.) . . .

It was all good clean fun, and ever since then Harlan and I have loved each other deeply and truly. . . . The fan world tends to think there's a deadly feud between us, but they're quite wrong. It's just our way of honing our wise-guyishness against each other's sensibilities.

[Harlan came to New York City to speak at Isaac's memorial service. He was wonderful.]

[Recounting many sales] One sale I made, which pleased me enormously, was a parody of a poem by William S. Gilbert. In *Patience*, the poet, Bunthorne, sings a very effective solo that begins, "If you're anxious for to shine in the high aesthetic line . . ."

I parodied this with a poem I called "the Foundation of S.F. Success," which began, "If you ask me how to shine in the science-fiction line . . ."

It was a parody of myself and of the Foundation series, in which I openly admitted my debt to Roman history in the second verse, which goes:

"So success is not a mystery, just brush up on your
    history, and borrow day by day.
"Take an Empire that was Roman and you'll find it is at
    home in all the starry Milky Way.
"With a drive that's hyperspatial, through the parsecs you
    will race, and you'll find that plotting is a breeze,
"With a tiny bit of cribbin' from the works of Edward
    Gibbon, and that Greek, Thucydides."

F & SF [*The Magazine of Fantasy and Science Fiction*] occasionally published poetry, and it was Tony Boucher who bought the parody. He was delighted and wrote to tell me he thought it the cleverest bit of self-parody since Swinburne. He paid me $15 for it—not much, but it was the first poetry I'd ever sold.

To be sure, it was not really poetry, but only comic verse; but then, comic verse is the limit of my poetic muse. Fortunate is the man who knows his own limitations.

Sixteen.
BEYOND LIMITATIONS

[Isaac began to write science articles, not just for scientific journals, but for other magazines.] I had by now [1954] published five articles in the *Journal of Chemical Education* [*JCE*]. All were trivial, but amusing. The fifth was entitled "Potentialities of Protein Isomerism," and . . . it dealt with the number of possible ways in which the amino acids in various protein molecules could be lined up. The possibilities were absolutely flabbergasting, since the 539 amino acids in the horse hemoglobin molecule could be arranged in a number of different ways equal to a 4 followed by 619 zeros.

It occurred to me that this was amazing enough to be of science-fictional interest, and, after all, the *JCE* did not pay for an article, while *Astounding* would.

I therefore wrote up my protein isomerism article in an entirely different style and shape, made it 5,000 words long, entitled it "Hemoglobin and the Universe," and sent it off to Campbell on July 19, 1954. He accepted it and paid me $150 for it.

My thiotimoline articles were fiction pieces written in nonfiction style. "Hemoglobin and the Universe" was the first true nonfiction article I had ever sold to a science-fiction magazine.

It excited me enormously. Writing nonfiction for the science-fiction audience meant I did not have to keep either my science or my vocabulary to the early teenage level, as in *The Chemicals of Life*, nor did I have to adopt the stylized turgidity of a textbook. In "Hemoglobin and the Universe" I wrote about science in a friendly, bouncy way, and I could tell at once that I had come home. That was the way I *wanted* to write nonfiction, and from then on I sought out every possible opportunity to do so. Not only friendly and bouncy but, even more so, *personal*.

[Later] In fiction, every story has to be different, no matter what. Not so in nonfiction. I could write an article for the *Journal of Chemical Education*, expand and popularize it for *Analog,* shorten and simplify it for *Science World.* Though it remained essentially the same article, the changes were useful and did not represent "cheating," since each article was aimed at a different audience and had to be tailored to suit.

It also became apparent that I could write all these different nonfiction articles much more rapidly and with less mental turmoil than I could write fiction. Then, too, although a nonfiction article could be rejected, it simply *was* rejected. Never did I have the long, complicated arguments for revision that I received from Campbell, or the short, brutal ones that I received from Horace Gold. As a matter of fact, the percentage of rejections was less in the case of nonfiction.

Insensibly, I found myself increasingly drawn to nonfiction.

Despite my sale of "Hemoglobin and the Universe," I did not totally abandon the *JCE*, for which I wrote another small paper, entitled "The Radioactivity of the Human Body." In it, I discussed the radioactive atoms that occurred naturally in the human body and pointed out that by far the most important of these and the one that was absolutely bound to have crucial effects upon the body was carbon-14 . . . it was published in the February 1955 issue.

As far as I knew at the time, this was the first occasion on which anyone had pointed out the importance of carbon-14 in this respect. It was an original idea of mine, although I believe Willard Libby, the Nobel Prize–winning specialist in carbon-14, may have had the idea at the same time . . .

Nearly four years later, Linus Pauling published a paper in the November 14, 1958, *Science* that discussed the dangers of carbon-14 in a careful and systematic way.

I'm sure Pauling's article played its part in the eventual agreement on the part of the three chief nuclear powers to suspend atmospheric testing, for Pauling was one of the most prominent and influential critics of such tests, and he used the production of carbon-14 in such tests as one of its chief long-term dangers.

I do not in any way want to dispute priorities with Pauling. I merely had an idea, which I did not develop. Pauling developed it thoroughly on the basis of the work done by Libby.

Still, I did work up the courage to send Pauling a reprint of my *JCE* article by way of a mutual friend, carefully stating that I was not disputing priorities.

Pauling was kind enough to send me the following letter, dated February 11, 1959:

Dear Professor Asimov,

I am pleased that . . . should have sent on to me the copy of your carbon-14 paper . . . I now remember that I had read that paper when it appeared (I always read the *Journal of Chemical Education*) but I had forgotten about it, except that without doubt the principal argument remained in my mind. I am sorry that I did not mention it in the carbon-14 paper that I published recently, a copy of which is enclosed.

> Sincerely yours,
>
> s/ Linus Pauling /s

I don't want to arrogate to myself too much importance, of course, but I think it is fair to say that I may indeed have influenced Professor Pauling, and through him I therefore played a very small part in bringing about the nuclear-test ban—and I'm delighted.

Of all my science-fiction shorts, I enjoy my robot stories most. I almost feel as though I have the patent on the robots. When other writers produce robot stories in which the robots follow the Three Laws (though no one is allowed to quote them except myself), I feel benign about it. When, however, some other writer dares to have his robots defy and disobey the Three Laws, I can't help but feel it is a case of patent infringement.

I was learning that to a writer, all is useful raw material. I had gone through a student-nurse textbook of chemistry, and two editions of a medical-student textbook of biochemistry, and was working desultorily on a third edition of the latter. The experience, looking back on it, had been a dreary one, but it had its comic parts, and it could be made interesting to a science-fiction audience. I began an article for Campbell, therefore, that I called "The Sound of Panting." (That was the sound that resulted from trying to keep up with the literature.)

[In 1954] I had, as yet, no inkling that the time was to come when what was most interesting about me as a writer was the number of books I had done.

After my parents sold the candy story, my mother decided to go to night school and learn how to write. She knew, of course, how to write Yiddish perfectly and Russian just as perfectly, but neither used the Latin script. She had to learn that to write English.

She learned quickly and in a very short time was able to send me short letters in painstakingly formed English writing. One of the teachers at the night school finally nerved himself to ask The Question [as the Asimov family referred to it].

"Pardon me, Mrs. Asimov," he said, stopping her in the hall, "are you by any chance a relation of Isaac Asimov?"

My mother, who was four feet, ten inches tall, drew herself up to her full height and said, proudly, "Yes. He is my dear son."

"Aha," said the teacher, "no wonder you are such a good writer."

"I beg your pardon," said my mother, freezingly, "no wonder *he* is such a good writer."

[In 1954, he and Gertrude had a daughter named Robyn Joan.] The "y" in Robyn was at my insistence, for I didn't want people to think she was a boy, and the Joan was added as a very plain alternative in case when she grew up she decided she disliked Robyn. Fortunately, she did not. She took to Robyn as I had taken to Isaac, and any other name for her is inconceivable.

[1956] Campbell . . . proudly showed me his newest toy. It was called the "Hieronymus machine" after its inventor, and it was a device of surpassing idiocy. It contained a meaningless electric circuit inside, one that could (Campbell seriously claimed) even be replaced by a paper diagram of the circuit without impairing its efficiency. (Which is true, I suppose, since you can't impair zero efficiency.)

To work the machine, you turned a dial while stroking a plastic surface, and at some reading of the dial there would be a change in the feel of the surface. It would become stickier. From the dial reading at this point one could diagnose diseases and so on.

Campbell insisted I try the machine. Ordinarily, I would have refused, since I lack any desire at all to lend myself to such folly. On this occasion, though, I was delivering a manuscript [*The Naked Sun*] on which thousands of dollars would rest on Campbell's decision and, frankly, since the dianetics thing, I no longer trusted the rigidity and integrity of his judgment.

So I agreed to play. Naturally, no matter how I turned the dial I felt no change in the feel of the plate; there was no onset of stickiness and I certainly wasn't going to lie to Campbell and say there was so that he could then use me as evidence of the working of the Hieronymus machine.

So I twisted and stroked, and stroked and twisted, while my fingers grew sweaty with anxiety and began to slip more easily along the plate.

"Mr. Campbell," I said, hesitantly, but truthfully, "the plate feels slippery."

"Aha," said Campbell, triumphantly, as he carefully took the reading. "Negative stickiness!"

And that's how great nonsense discoveries are made.

I was thinking about writing another story about Multivac ("Franchise," which had been the first, had been written as a direct consequence of my introduction to Univac in the 1952 election).

I had worked out ever greater developments of Multivac, and eventually I was bound to consider how far I could go; how far the human mind (or, anyway, *my* human mind) could reach . . .

I sat down to write "The Last Question," which was only forty-seven hundred words long, but in which I detailed the history of ten trillion years with respect to human beings, computers, and the universe. . . . I wrote the whole thing in two sittings, without a sentence's hesitation . . . I knew at the instant of writing it that I had become involved in something special. When I finished it, I said, in my diary, that it was "the computer story to end all computer stories, or, who knows, the science-fiction story to end all science-fiction stories." Of course, it may well be that no one else agrees with me, but it was my opinion at the time, and it still is today.

[Seeing one of the planetarium versions of "The Last Question," in 1972] I was astonished at my own reaction to it. Though I knew the story (of course) and though the narration and dialog suffered by not being handled by professional actors, the effect built and pyramided.

I didn't write the story with clever attention to technique; my stories work themselves out with no conscious interference from me. Just the same, the six episodes of the story were successively briefer, more sweeping, and more chilling, just as though I had deliberately planned them that way for effect. Then the final episode slows and waits—and the planetarium grew dark and stayed dark for over two minutes while the last paragraphs of the story were recited in a quiet increase of tension, and the audience was absolutely silent.

Even I, who knew what was coming, waited, scarcely able to breathe, and for the others the final, sudden creation of the universe must have done everything but stop the heart.

It was a terrific show; in fact, it was that show that finally convinced me that "The Last Question" was the best story I had ever done and (my private conviction) the best science-fiction story anyone had ever done.

[See appendix for "THE LAST QUESTION"]

Seventeen.
LIMITATIONS CAME

My history, well into middle age, was marked by my inability to get along with my fellows and my superiors. . . . I suspect I was not popular with much of the [medical school] faculty and perhaps couldn't be no matter how sweet I might try to be. Being the best lecturer in the place might please me and please the students [Janet's note: my brother, at the medical school, told me I.A. was the best lecturer.], but it would not necessarily win me medals from the other lecturers.

Furthermore, it was impossible for me to hide the fact that I had an outside career and that I made money out of it. That was another reason for struggling faculty members not to love me. Nor was the range of my writing something to be approved of. . . . Finally, I had completely abandoned any pretense of doing research and spent all my spare school time writing nonfiction, which could not help but displease the administration.

I tried to make up for my outside income by never asking for a raise. (It would be ridiculous for me to scramble after a few more school dollars when my writing earnings were steadily increasing.) . . . This, which I considered, in my innocence, to be ethical behavior on my part, proved to be another point against me. To be paid so little was interpreted as meaning that that was all I deserved.

Worse than any of this, of course, was the offense I had given [one member of the administration] . . . in abandoning his research. He dedicated himself to the task of getting rid of me.

[But Isaac had been made an associate professor, which gave him tenure. He was told, however, that he had to do research.] I finally grew angry enough to say, "... as a science writer, I am extraordinary. I plan to be the best science writer in the world and I will shed luster on the medical school. As a researcher, I am simply mediocre and ... if there's one thing this school does *not* need, it is one more merely mediocre researcher."

[He was told] "This school cannot afford to pay a science writer. Your appointment will come to an end as of June 30, 1958."

I was ready for that, too. I said, "Very well ... you may refuse to pay me a salary." (With heroic self-control I refrained from telling him where he could put my salary.) "In return, I will do no teaching for the school. However, there is no way you can take away my title. I have tenure."

[One faculty member complimented him on his bravery in fighting for academic freedom.] I shrugged, "There's no bravery about it. I *have* academic freedom and I can give it to you in two words."

"What's that?" he asked.

"Outside income," I said.

After two years, it finally came to a vote by the faculty senate (or whatever the group was that had to approve the decision). ... I kept my title. ... In fact, on October 18, 1979, I was promoted to full professor.

Eighteen.
GOING ON

As I ended my school career, I was making five times as much money in my writing as in my teaching. What's more, I had now reached the stage of mass production that has characterized my literary life ever since . . . in fact, had [the B.U. Medical School officials] been willing to let things be as they were, I would have had to quit on my own within the space of a year or so, or watch my literary career be aborted.

Indeed, my freedom from the bonds of my teaching position seemed to be joined by a freedom from the bonds of chemistry as the subject of my nonfiction. . . . [On] the very first day of my new jobless status, I began *The Clock We Live On*, which was to be entirely on astronomy and chronometry. These were subjects in which I had never taken a single course at any stage in my school career.

You might say that, having cut free, I could now afford to take my chances. I had no formal academic standing to endanger, no colleagues to offend.

However, I was not being foolhardy either. I was not blithely launching myself onto a sea of ignorance. The fact is that I had now been reading science fiction for nearly thirty years and had been writing it for twenty. One cannot be a *serious* reader and writer of science fiction without getting a broad smattering of many aspects of science and a surprisingly deep understanding of some. And astronomy is, preeminently, *the* science most clearly associated with science fiction.

The fact, therefore, that I had never taken any courses in astronomy merely meant that I was weak on some of the mathematical aspects of celestial mechanics and on the nuts and bolts of telescopes and other instrumentation.

On the descriptive and conceptual aspects of astronomy and even on some of the celestial mechanics, I had an iron-bound grip, so that I began work on *The Clock We Live On* with absolute assurance.

And, as I went on to discover, each time I wrote a book on some subject outside my immediate field it gave me courage and incentive to do another one that was perhaps even farther outside the narrow range of my training. . . . I advanced from chemical writer to science writer, and, eventually, I took all of learning for my subject (or at least all that I could cram into my head—which, alas, had a sharply limited capacity despite all I could do).

As I did so, of course, I found that I had to educate myself. I had to read books on physics to reverse my unhappy experiences in school on the subject and to learn at home what I had failed to learn in the classroom—at least up to the point where my limited knowledge of mathematics prevented me from going farther.

When the time came, I read biology, medicine, and geology. I collected commentaries on the Bible and on Shakespeare. I read history books. Everything led to something else. I became a generalist by encouraging myself to be generally interested in all matters.

Fortunately, I didn't have to approach anything (or almost anything) completely fresh. My avid and generalized reading as a youngster came to my aid, for as the years passed, I discovered (with a great deal of pleasure) that I simply never forgot the trivia I had read. It was all there in my head and required only the slightest jog to spring to the surface.

This is not to say I wasn't capable of making mistakes through carelessness or through writing overhurriedly or through being misled by my sources—but none of those mistakes (as far as I know) ever betrayed ignorance of the subject. I grew more casually confident of my polymath abilities with each year, and it was that, even more than my prolificity, that has impressed people and led to my gaining a rather unusual reputation for "knowing everything."

As I look back on it, it seems quite possible that none of this would have happened if I had stayed at school and had continued to think of myself as, primarily, a biochemist . . . [so] I was forced along the path I ought to have taken of my own accord if I had had the necessary insight into my own character and abilities.

[Writing a science column at the suggestion of Bob Mills, first editor of *Venture* and then of *Fantasy and Science Fiction*] At the very beginning, Bob made some suggestions, but that stopped very quickly, and it came to be understood that I was to write what I wanted, exactly how I wanted, and that I was to get galleys of each column so I could see to it that it was set in print just as I wanted it to be.

It was an ideal arrangement. Bob Mills was the first to call me "The Good Doctor" in blurbing my articles . . . it was in these articles, in fact, that I first developed my leisurely and personal style of talking to the readers directly.

[1958] The death of Cyril Kornbluth . . . had a peculiar effect on me . . . I remember his death having made the first page of the *New York Times* in a box in the lower left-hand corner—though perhaps it was only on the obituary page.

A queer kind of envy overcame me, a feeling that I might not get equal billing when it came my time to die, and a frustration at never knowing whether I had or not.

I recognized the feeling to be a silly one and I decided to exorcise it by writing a story about it. . . . I called the story "Obituary," and actually it was more a thriller than a science-fiction story, but it was a thriller in which the villain used time travel to see his own obituary.

One of the few depressing lunches I have had with Austin Olney [Houghton Mifflin editor] came on July 7, 1959. I incautiously told him of the various books I had in progress, and he advised me strongly not to write so busily. He said my books would compete with each other, interfere with each other's sales, and do less well per book if there were many.

The one thing I had learned in my ill-fated class in economics in high school was "the law of diminishing returns," whereby working ten times as hard or investing ten times as much or producing ten times the quantity does *not* yield ten times the return.

I was rather glum that meal and gave the matter much thought afterward.

What I decided was that I wasn't writing ten times as many books in order to get ten times the monetary returns, but in order to have ten times the pleasure . . .

I found a letter waiting for me at school that asked me to come to Cornell University on November 10 to give a talk . . . [for] five hundred dollars. I had never heard or conceived of anyone being paid that much to talk, and I was convinced it was a misprint for fifty dollars . . . to write and say, "Surely you meant fifty dollars" was somehow unthinkable. It would expose my low opinion of myself . . . after considerable hesitation . . . I wrote an answer that said, very formally, "In return for your offered fee of Five Hundred Dollars ($500), I will gladly agree to . . ." If they answered me with happy outcries, I was all set. If they came back with pained explanations, it was all off.

They answered me with happy outcries.

[At a dinner with fellow science-fiction writer Poul Anderson and his wife, Karen, he said] I tried to keep my library small . . . there were times when an empty space was the most valuable item in the bookshelves.

Poul turned to Karen and said, "Listen to this man. He speaks pearls."

I wish it were easy to stick to this view, however. No matter how I try, books keep adding themselves to my library—and throwing away a book, or just giving it away, is so hard. After all, when I think of the long years in which I never so much as had a book . . .

[At the 1959 World Science-Fiction Convention in Detroit] I met Avram Davidson for the first time . . . he had a full beard, a keen intelligence, and was a practicing Orthodox Jew. I didn't meet many . . . during a discussion in which he had stressed his orthodoxy just a little too hard for my comfort, I said, when asked my stand on the matter, "I'm an atheist."

"Yes," said Avram, without batting an eye, "but what kind of atheist? A Baptist atheist? A Hindu atheist? A Seventh-day Adventist atheist?"

I got the idea. "A Jewish atheist," I said, "which means I have to fight the irrational elements in Judaism particularly."

[By the way] Science-fiction conventions have a serious purpose, one that is primarily aimed at the science-fiction reader who is given his chance to participate in a subculture that is important to him. That is why the conventions shift their site from year to year. This gives the average fan of a particular region, one who has perhaps little in the way of pocket money, a chance to attend, now and then, without having to travel far.

Most of the fans attending are young people, many of them in their teens. It is a great opportunity for them to meet those writers who are, in their eyes, legendary heroes. There are celebrity introductions for the readers, and autographing sessions . . .

In one way, autographing became an increasing problem for me, since it supplied me with more and more work; partly because the number of my books was increasing steadily, and partly because those books were individually popular. In another sense, they were not a problem, because I loved autographing. . . . (There is the occasional joker who hands me a blank check. I just sign it along with everything else, but when the joker gets it back he finds I have signed it "Harlan Ellison.") . . .

When I am feeling particularly suave during the autographing sessions, which is almost all the time, I kiss each young woman who wants an autograph and have found, to my delight, that they tend to cooperate enthusiastically in that particular activity.

The conventions include talks and panel discussions on every aspect of the writer's/artist's/editor's/agent's life; on the problems of writing and publishing; and on all the fringe areas, too, from Hollywood to comic books. Readers are fascinated by this, since so many of them are aspiring writers.

[His Houghton Mifflin book, *Realm of Numbers*, had his name misspelled on the cover—it was corrected.] The other thing I remember about that book was that my father read it (he read a number of my books). When he was partway through, he said to me, during one of our phone conversations, that he was enjoying the suspense.

"Suspense?" I said, astonished. "What suspense?"

He said, "Well, I'm just beginning about the square root of two. Tell me, *do* they ever find an exact solution for it?"

[At a party] . . . someone asked the company generally if they knew what troilism was.

I said, "Sure—sex with three people participating."

The questioner looked disappointed and said, "Ah, but do you know the derivation of the word?"

I thought I might as well be polite and let him have a turn, so I said, "What?"

"Well," he said, "in *Troilus and Cressida*, Troilus watched Cressida making out with Diomed."

"In the first place," I said, "he didn't watch with any pleasure; he was brokenhearted, and he certainly didn't participate. In the second place, Ulysses was also there watching, which would make if a foursome. And in the third place, it is much simpler to suppose that 'troilism' is derived from the French word *trois*, meaning 'three.' "

This was an example of reversion to type. When I was young, I used to show off in that snotty fashion all the time. Since the war I had stopped doing it, which I think was the chief reason I changed from a disliked youngster to a well-regarded fellow of mature years. But even now, sometimes—I forget.

Nineteen.
MAJOR NONFICTION

 The 1950s [were] the decade of my greatest science-fictional triumphs, [but as] the 1950s ended, I [ended] most of my involvement with the field.

Even as I was writing "The Ugly Little Boy," the Soviet Union sent up the first artificial satellite and the United States went into a panic, feeling it would be left behind in the technology race. It seemed to me that it was necessary for me to write science books for the general public and help educate Americans.

[Letter] You have no idea how responsible I feel as a science writer. Every one of my library copies of my science books is margined with notes, bringing it up to date, correcting or extending it. Even if no additional edition is ever called for, I still must do this for myself.

[Isaac and I had met in 1959 at a Mystery Writers of America dinner, hearing Eleanor Roosevelt speak, and had exchanged a few letters. Then he was asked by an editor at Basic Books to write a summary of twentieth-century science, for adults.]

I did have some fears that my career as a science writer might be aborted by publishers who would dismiss me as "just a science-fiction writer." This was unnecessary because the problem never arose. My reputation as *both* kept rising and never interfered with each other. My Ph.D. and my professorial position may have helped and I have always been glad I fought to keep the latter title.

The result is that I have never found it necessary to hide my science fiction. When asked by people who don't know me just exactly what it is that I write, I answer, "All sorts of things, but I am best known for my science fiction."

[He was, nevertheless, nervous about signing the contract for this particular book. Since I knew both science and science-fiction writing, he wrote to me about the book's possibility.] I did not actually ask for advice since I have always had a reluctance to load anyone else with responsibility for my decisions, but in this case I did not have to ask. She replied that of *course* I could do it, and I *must* do it. I could not turn down a challenge like that and expect to rise in my profession.

She was perfectly right, so I signed . . . I tore into the book with a fury and in a period of eight months had written and put into final form half a million words—remarkable even for me.

[The book] gave me a chance to present a logical unfolding of a field of knowledge, to make an exciting story out of it, with the scientist as hero and with ignorance as the villain.

[The editor, without consulting Isaac, sent chapters of the book to different experts.] In one chapter I discussed the matter of overpopulation and hoisted my usual warning signals of alarm. The "expert" who read that particular chapter actually had the incredible audacity-*cum*-ignorance to write in the margin, "I'd say this was God's problem, wouldn't you?"

It was the work of a moment to write underneath, "God helps those who help themselves" and to place an enormous STET over the entire passage. I was particularly watchful, come galleys time, to make sure the passage remained, too.

[It] was published in 1960 under the title of *The Intelligent Man's Guide to Science.*

I objected to the title on the ground that "man" seemed unduly restrictive . . . [the editor] would have none of it. He was intent on imitating the title of George Bernard Shaw's book *The Intelligent Woman's Guide to Socialism and Capitalism.* Naturally, there were protests from woman and all I could do was smile wryly and say, "by 'intelligent man' I am referring to the writer, not the reader."

George Gaylord Simpson gave it the best review of any I have ever received. He called me a "natural wonder and a national resource"—a phrase you won't blame me for remembering.

[Letter] Someone pointed out a horrible geographic error . . . I placed Lake Michigan between Lake Huron and Lake Erie instead of between Lake Huron and Lake Superior.

It is so embarrassing to pull a bad blooper in public. I risk it constantly . . . and considering the volume I turn out, the number of subjects I cover and the speed with which I do it, I make amazingly few bloopers (if I do say so myself) but that does not in the least diminish my embarrassment and horror when a blooper is discovered.

[The editor] writes to me to say that just because I am a natural resource doesn't give me the right to switch geography.

[Letter] I am working away at my articles for *The Book of Knowledge.* When I was a little boy I knew some people who had *The Book of Knowledge* but my family, of course, was far too poor ever to buy me one. Occasionally I would be in the house of the lucky people who had it and invariably I would sneak over to the bookcase and—if no one were looking—I would take out one of the volumes and leaf through it. As I think back on it, now, I realize that nobody would possibly have minded and that I could probably have received permission to come there and read through it at leisure if I had only asked. Unfortunately, it never occurred to me to ask, because it seemed patent on the face of it that these wonderful books were not meant to be touched by little children.

Anyway, when I was asked to do a couple of article for *The Book of Knowledge*, my first impulse was to refuse because they gave me a very short deadline and God knows I have enough work as is. However, the thought of myself at the age of ten came sharply back to me as though the little boy were someone else with whom I could maintain contact. I was overwhelmed with the thought that somewhere the little boy existed and somehow he would know that the man he grew into was going to write articles for *The Book of Knowledge* and that he would be very pleased and excited by it. So I agreed to do it.

[Letter] I'm doing a section on Einstein's Relativity and my system for writing about something I have only the vaguest notion of is to close my eyes and type VERY VERY FAST.

Twenty.
WRITING AND THINKING ABOUT WRITING

On January 2, 1960, I was forty years old, and middle-aged. There is no possibility of pretending to youth at forty. To be sure, there's nothing wrong with middle age, but it comes hard to a person who is a child prodigy by profession.

I was finally finishing up the definition cards for *Stedman's Medical Dictionary*, on which I had been working, on and off, for two years. It was just one of a number of little miscellaneous jobs that constantly plagued me. I would write entries for various encyclopedias . . . there was also the ongoing bimonthly column of reviews for *Hornbook*.

These little jobs were never as pleasurable as books or stories, since they were so restrictive. They were invariably closely bounded as to subject matter and length and, for that matter, deadline.

I might have routinely refused all such tasks, but they had their usefulness, too. They managed to force me into what might otherwise have been neglected byways of knowledge, which I could then incorporate into my various books.

Nothing goes really to waste, if you're determined to learn.

I had already learned, for instance, that although I was one of the most overeducated people I knew, I couldn't possibly write the variety of books I manage to do out of the knowledge I had gained in school alone. I had to keep a program of self-education in process.

My library of reference books grew and I found I had to sweat over them in my constant fear that I might misunderstand a point that to someone knowledgeable in the subject would be a ludicrously simple one.

Sometimes I really do make an egregious error, and I can always count on letters from my readers to correct me.

[In 1964] I received a letter from Linus Pauling with reference to [a science article by Isaac]. He himself, said Pauling, had frequently been caught in one mistake or another, but never in his entire career had he made a mistake of twenty-three orders of magnitude, as I had in this article. That's all he said; he didn't say where the mistake was.

I started rereading the article in a fever of panic. If I couldn't find the error, not only would I be humiliated, but also I would not be able to reprint the article in the collection *Of Time and Space and Other Things*.

I found it. I had made use of Avogadro's constant (the number of protons making up a gram . . .) and had multiplied by it once instead of twice (or possibly twice instead of once—I forget). I corrected the error for the collection, and didn't know whether to be proud of Pauling's confidence that I could find the error without help, or annoyed with him for not having helped anyway.

[While working on putting the illustrations to the text of *The Human Body*, with a middle-aged female editor at Houghton Mifflin] We were working in a room that was not truly closed off but had walls that did not reach to the ceiling and that had a gap where the door should be. That meant that the full office noise of the rest of the floor reached us, but it didn't bother me. I'm a strainer; I strain out what I don't want to pay attention to. Apparently Helen could, too, so we worked on, oblivious to the noise.

Finally, when we hit the cross section of the male genitalia, I thought about it and said, "I tell you what, Helen, let's tackle this little by little starting with the easy parts. For instance, let's place the penis right here. (I was referring to the label.)

I spoke, as I always do, in my ordinary speaking voice, which *does* tend to rattle distant windows, and I had no sooner delivered that line when every bit of noise on the floor stopped. It was as though it were all some giant television set that had been turned off with a snap. In that sudden enormous silence, I sat, puzzled and waiting.

Finally, very slowly, as though dreading what there might be to see, a head began to appear at one side of the door, more and more and more, until an eye could be seen—and it was Austin [Olney—head of the Juvenile Division at Houghton Mifflin].

"Wouldn't you know? It's Isaac," he shouted, and everyone rushed in.

"It was business," I yelled. "It was strictly business. We were labeling diagrams. I tell you it was perfectly innocent."

But everyone pretended that they had interrupted an act of fornication and I grew scarlet with frustration. Helen, I noticed, wasn't in the least put out. She smiled demurely and was completely in control.

As the number of books increased, I had to make a numbered list of dedications, which I had to study more and more closely to see if some deserving person had been omitted, or whether enough time had elapsed for a repeat.

It is questionable, of course, as to whether a dedication is necessarily to be considered an honor. Consider the case of nineteenth-century English wit Douglas W. Jerrold. He was told that a friend of his, a prolific but third-rate writer, was dedicating the next of his numerous books to him. Jerrold sighed, shook his head, and said, "Ah, that's a fearful weapon that man has."

[In 1960 *Playboy* poked fun at science fiction, using material from *Marvel*, a 1938–1941 magazine which] had tried (and failed) . . . to make a go by introducing the sex motif. The stories dealt very heavily with the hot passion of alien monsters for Earthwomen. Clothes were always getting ripped off and breasts were described in a variety of elliptical phrases—and these were the events and phrases quoted in the *Playboy* article.

Cele Goldsmith, then editor of *Amazing*, read the article and called me at once. She suggested I write a story entitled "Playboy and the Slime God" satirizing the satire. I was strongly tempted to do so for several reasons:

1. Cele was a beautiful woman and I happen to be aesthetically affected by beautiful women.
2. I take science fiction seriously, and I was annoyed at the satire.
3. I just happened to think up a plot.

So I wrote "Playboy and the Slime God," using some of the same quotes that *Playboy* had used and trying to show what an encounter between sex-interested aliens and an Earthwoman might *really* be like.

[Later] When Groff Conklin was considering the story for one of his collections, he asked, rather piteously, if I could come up with an alternate title.

"You bet," I said, "how about, 'What Is This Thing Called Love?'"

He was delighted, and so was I, because it fit the story perfectly.

[The first time Robyn read one of his books] She came to me, one time, with the sad announcement that she had nothing to read.

"Read one of my stories," I said.

"Your stories aren't for kids," she said.

"I have a story about a little boy," I said. "How about that?"

"Where?"

I got a copy of *Nine Tomorrows* for her, opened it to the story "The Ugly Little Boy" and said, "Here, Robyn, read this."

Off she went to her room, from which she emerged on several occasions to tell me that she was on page so-and-so and it was great. Then there was quite a long lapse, and when she finally emerged, her face was red and swollen and tear-streaked, and she fixed me with a woeful look and said, "You didn't tell me the ending was sa-a-a-ad!"

As a father, I hugged her and consoled her, but as a writer I was delighted.

Twenty-One.
ON PROLIFICITY

My favorite kind of day (provided I don't have an unbreakable appointment that is going to force me out into it) is a cold, dreary, gusty, sleety day, when I can sit at my typewriter or word processor in peace and security . . .

A compulsive writer must be always ready to write. Sprague de Camp once stated that anyone wishing to write must block out four hours of uninterrupted solitude, because it takes a long time to get started, and if you are interrupted, you would have to start all over again from the beginning.

Maybe so, but anyone who can't write unless he can count on four uninterrupted hours is not likely to be prolific. It is important to be able to begin writing at any time. If there are fifteen minutes in which I have nothing to do, that's enough to write a page or so. Nor do I have to sit around and waste long periods of time arranging my thoughts in order to write.

I was once asked by someone what I did in order to start writing. I said, blankly, "What do you mean?"

"Well, do you do setting-up exercises first, or sharpen all your pencils, or do a crossword puzzle—you know, something to get yourself into the mood."

"Oh," I said, enlightened, "I see what you mean. Yes! Before I can possibly begin writing, it is always necessary for me to turn on my electric typewriter and to get close enough to it so that my fingers can reach the keys."

Why is this? What is the secret of the instant start?

For one thing, I don't write only when I'm writing. Whenever I'm away from my typewriter—eating, falling asleep, performing my ablutions—my mind keeps working. On occasion, I can hear bits of dialogue running through my thoughts, or passages of exposition. Usually, it deals with whatever I am writing or am about to write. Even when I don't hear the actual words, I know that my mind is working on it unconsciously.

That's why I'm always ready to write. Everything is, in a sense, already written. I can just sit down and type it all out, at up to a hundred words a minute, at my mind's dictation. Furthermore, I can be interrupted and it doesn't affect me. After the interruption, I simply return to the business at hand and continue typing under mental dictation.

It means, of course, that what enters your mind must stay in your mind. I always take that for granted, so that I never make notes. When Janet and I were first married, I would sometimes say, during a few wakeful moments at night, "I know what I ought to do in the novel."

She would say, anxiously, "Get up and write it down."

But I would say, "I don't have to," turn over, and let myself drift off to sleep.

And the next morning I would remember it, of course. Janet used to say that it drove her crazy at first but she got used to it.

The ordinary writer is bound to be assailed by insecurities as he writes. Is the sentence he has just created a sensible one? Is it expressed as well as it might be? Would it sound better if it were written differently? The ordinary writer is therefore always revising, always chopping and changing, always trying on different ways of expressing himself, and, for all I know, never being entirely satisfied. That is certainly no way to be prolific.

A prolific writer, therefore, has to have self-assurance. He can't sit around doubting the quality of his writing. Rather, he has to *love* his own writing.

I do. I can pick up any one of my books, start reading it anywhere, and immediately be lost in it and keep on reading until I am shaken out of the spell by some external event. Janet finds this amusing, but I think it's natural. If I didn't enjoy my writing so much, how on earth could I stand all the writing I do? . . .

I do edit the first draft and make changes that usually amount to not more than 5 percent of the total, and *then* I send it off.

One reason for my self-assurance, perhaps, is that I see a story or an article or a book as a *pattern* and not just as a succession of words. I know exactly how to fit each item in the piece into the pattern, so that it is never necessary for me to work from an outline. Even the most complicated plot, or the most intricate exposition, comes out properly, with everything in the right order.

I rather imagine that a grand master in chess sees a chess game as a pattern, rather than as a succession of moves. A good baseball manager probably sees the game as a pattern rather than as a succession of plays. Well, I see patterns too in my specialty, but I don't know how I do it. I simply have the knack and had it even as a kid.

Of course, it helps if you don't try to be too literary in your writing. If you try to turn out a prose poem, that takes time . . . I have therefore deliberately cultivated a very plain style, even a colloquial one, which can be turned out rapidly and with which very little can go wrong. Of course, some critics, with crania that are more bone than mind, interpret this as my having "no style." If anyone thinks, however, that it is easy to write with absolute clarity and no frills, I recommend that he try it.

Being a prolific writer has its disadvantages, of course. It complicates the writer's social and family life, for a prolific writer has to be self-absorbed. He *must* be. He has to be either writing or thinking about writing virtually all the time, and has no time for anything else . . .

I imagine it does weary a family to have a husband and father who never wants to travel, who never wants to go on an outing or to parties or to the theater, who never wants to do anything but sit in his room and write. I daresay that the failure of my first marriage was partly the result of this.

Twenty-Two.
ON WRITERS' PROBLEMS

The writer's life is inherently an insecure one. Each project is a new start and may be a failure. The fact that a previous item has been successful is no guard against failure this time.

What's more, as has often been pointed out, writing is a very lonely occupation. You can talk about what you write, and discuss it with family, friends, or editors, but when you sit down at that typewriter, you are alone with it and no one can possibly help. You must extract every word from your own suffering mind.

It's no wonder writers so often turn misanthrope or are driven to drink to dull the agony. I've heard it said that alcoholism is an occupational disease with writers.

[When an interviewer, on the phone, asked about his drinking, and he said he didn't drink] There was a short pause, then she said, "Are you Isaac Asimov?"

"Yes," I said.

"The writer?"

"Yes," I said.

"And you've written hundreds of books?"

"Yes," I said, "and I've written every one of them cold sober."

She hung up, muttering. I seemed to have disillusioned her.

The most serious problem a writer can face, however, is "writer's block." . . .

When a writer has it he finds himself staring at a blank sheet of paper in the typewriter (or a blank screen on the word processor) and can't do anything to unblank it. The words don't come. Or if they do, they are clearly unsuitable and are quickly torn up or erased.

What's more . . . the longer the inability to write continues, the more certain it is that it will continue to continue . . .

In real life, some science-fiction writers, and very good ones too, have had serious episodes of writer's block that sometimes extend for years.

It may be, therefore, that a writer's block is unavoidable and that at best a writer must pause every once in a while, for a shorter or longer interval, to let his mind fill up again.

In that case, how have I avoided writer's block, considering that I never stop? If I were engaged in only one writing project at a time I suppose I wouldn't avoid it. Frequently, when I am at work on a science-fiction novel (the hardest to do of all the different things I write), I find myself heartily sick of it and unable to write another word. But I don't let that drive me crazy. I don't stare at blank sheets of paper. I don't spend days and nights cudgeling a head that is empty of ideas.

Instead, I simply leave the novel and go on to any of the dozen other projects that are on tap. I write an editorial, or an essay, or a short story, or work on one of my nonfiction books. By the time I've grown tired of these things, my mind has been able to do its proper work and fill up again. I return to my novel and find myself able to write easily once more.

This periodic difficulty of getting the mind to deliver ideas reminds me of how irritating that perennial question is: "Where do you get your ideas?"

I suppose that all writers of fiction are asked that, but for writers of science fiction, the question is usually phrased, "Where do you get your crazy ideas?"

I don't know what answer they expect, but Harlan Ellison answers,

"From Schenectady. They have an idea factory and I subscribe to it, so every month they ship me a new idea."

I wonder how many people believe him.

I was asked the question a few months ago by a top-notch science-fiction writer, whose work I admire greatly. I gathered that he was suffering from writer's block, and phoned me as one notoriously immune to it. "Where do you get your ideas?" he wanted to know.

I said, "By thinking and thinking and thinking till I'm ready to kill myself."

He said, with enormous relief, "You too?"

"Of course," I said, "did you ever think it was easy to get a good idea?"

[Letter] I couldn't sleep last night so I lay awake thinking of an article to write and I'd think and think and cry at the sad parts. I had a wonderful night.

Twenty-Three.
MISCELLANEOUS OPINIONS AND QUIRKS

[Letter] To me it seems to be important to believe people to be good even if they tend to be bad, because your own joy and happiness in life is increased that way, and the pleasures of the belief outweigh the occasional disappointments. To be a cynic about people works just the other way around and makes you incapable of enjoying the good things.

[Letter] Every nation in the world should agree that in any battle fought, the losing general should be instantly executed. In the event of threatened war, the military services of either side will claim they're not ready because the generals can't risk losing a battle.

[Writing of the years of worry during Hitler's racism] I also tried to avoid becoming uncomfortably hooked on anti-Semitism as the main problem of the world. Many Jews I knew divided the world into Jews and anti-Semites, nothing else. Many Jews I knew recognized no problem anywhere, at any time, but that of anti-Semitism.

It struck me, however, that prejudice was universal and that all groups who were not dominant, who were not actually at the top of the status chain, were potential victims. In Europe, in the 1930s, it was the Jews who were being spectacularly victimized, but in the United States it was not the Jews who were worst treated. Here, as anyone could see who did not deliberately keep his eyes shut, it was the African Americans.

For two centuries they had actually been enslaved. Since that slavery had come to a formal end, the African Americans remained in a position of near-slavery in most segments of American society. They were deprived of ordinary rights, treated with contempt, and kept out of any chance of participation in what is called the American Dream.

I, though Jewish, and poor besides, eventually received a first-class American education at a top American university, and I wondered how many African Americans would have the chance. It constantly bothered me to have to denounce anti-Semitism unless I denounced the cruelty of man to man in general.

I once listened to a woman grow eloquent over the terrible way in which Gentiles did nothing to save the Jews of Europe. "You can't trust Gentiles," she said. I let some time elapse and then asked suddenly, "What are you doing to help the blacks in their fight for civil rights?" "Listen," she said, "I have my own problems." And I said, "So did the Gentiles." But she only stared at me blankly. She didn't get the point at all . . .

The whole world seems to live under the banner: "Freedom is wonderful—but only for me."

[Sharing a platform with a famous Holocaust survivor] He said that he did not trust scientists and engineers because scientists and engineers had been involved in conducting the Holocaust.

What a generalization! It was precisely the sort of thing an anti-Semite says. "I don't trust Jews because once certain Jews crucified my Savior."

I brooded about that on the platform and finally, unable to keep quiet, I said, ". . . it is a mistake to think that because a group has suffered extreme persecution that is a sign that they are virtuous and innocent. They might be, of course, but the persecution process is no proof of that. The persecution merely shows that the persecuted group is weak. Had they been strong, then, for all we know, they might have been the persecutors."

Isaac at the 1966 Lunacon—the New York Science Fiction Society convention. (*Courtesy Jay Kay Klein*)

Isaac at Boskone 11—the New England Science Fiction Association convention—in 1974. (*Courtesy Jay Kay Klein*)

Isaac congratulating Clifford Simak in 1971. *(Courtesy Jay Kay Klein)*

Janet, Harlan Ellison, and Isaac at a science-fiction convention in 1972. *(Courtesy Jay Kay Klein)*

John Campbell, Janet, and Isaac in a science-fiction convention hotel room. *(Courtesy Jay Kay Klein)*

Isaac in 1973, with his hair at its longest. *(Courtesy Jay Kay Klein)*

Isaac and his good friend Lester del Rey. *(Courtesy Jay Kay Klein)*

Isaac with his friend Marty Greenburg at the 1980 Noreascon II World Science Fiction Convention. *(Courtesy Jay Kay Klein)*

Isaac with a collection of some of the books he wrote. *(Courtesy Jay Kay Klein)*

Isaac and Janet at Lunacon '88. *(Courtesy Jay Kay Klein)*

Isaac and Robyn. (*Courtesy Jay Kay Klein*)

Ben Bova and Harlan Ellison at Isaac's memorial service. *(Courtesy New York Society for Ethical Culture)*

Isaac answering questions. He believed that it was important to be able to say, "I don't know." *(Courtesy Jay Kay Klein)*

[The famous man] said, "Give me one example of the Jews ever persecuting anyone."

Of course, I was ready for him. I said, "Under the Maccabean kingdom in the second century B.C.E., John Hyrcanus of Judea conquered Edom and gave the Edomites a choice—conversion to Judaism or the sword. The Edomites, being sensible, converted, but, thereafter, they were in any case treated as an inferior group, for though they were Jews, they were also Edomites."

[The famous man] said, "That was the only time."

I said, "That was the only time the Jews had the power. One out of one isn't bad."

That ended the discussion, but I might add that the audience was heart and soul with [the famous man].

The Bible says that those who have experienced persecution should *not* in their turn persecute: "Thou shalt neither vex a stranger, nor oppress him; for ye were strangers in the land of Egypt" (Exod. 22:21). Yet who follows that text?

[Isaac gave a talk at a book fair] . . . with my usual indifference to such matters, I didn't realize it was Rosh Hashanah. It wouldn't have mattered at all except that a couple of days later I received a phone call from a young man, who was a stranger to me but who had apparently seen a notice in the *Globe* that I had spoken at the book fair and who felt he had a right to ask me why I had spoken on Rosh Hashanah.

I explained politely that I hadn't known it was Rosh Hashanah, but that if I had, I would still have spoken, because I was a nonobserving Jew. The young man, himself Jewish, flung himself into a self-righteous lecture in which he told me my duties as a Jew, observant or not, and ended by accusing me of trying to conceal my Jewishness.

I felt annoyed. I thought I had caught his name when he started the conversation, but wasn't sure. I had caught enough, however, to feel confident of my next move. I said, "You have the advantage of me, sir. You know my name. I didn't get yours. To whom am I speaking?"

He said, "My name is Jackson Davenport." (not his real name, but his real name was just as Anglo-Saxon, I assure you.)

"Really? Well, my name, as you know, is Isaac Asimov, and if I were really trying to conceal my Jewishness as you claim I am trying to do, my very first move would be to change my name to Jackson Davenport."

That ended the conversation with a crash.

[Being on a panel with Wernher von Braun] I was not an admirer of Wernher von Braun. He had worked under Hitler and would have won the war for the Nazis if he could. I know, of course, that it might be said that he was just being patriotic or that he would have been thrown into a concentration camp if he had refused or that he had to work on rockets whatever the purpose—and for those reasons I was prepared to remain neutral where he was concerned. I did not have to be friendly.

When we all got onto the platform, therefore, I studiously remained at the end opposite from that occupied by von Braun and did my best to be unaware of his existence.

It didn't help. The moderator, anxious to introduce everyone to everyone, brought von Braun to me and began performing the introduction. There were eight hundred people in the audience watching and I had two seconds to decide what to do. I couldn't make a scene; he was holding out his hand.

I had to take it and hold it as briefly as possible—but I did shake hands. Ever since then, I have had the queasy feeling that I have shaken a hand that shook the hand of Adolf Hitler.

The panel itself went by without incident. I spoke last and perforce went beyond the speculations of the others by speaking of the possibilities of interstellar travel.

Afterward several people, including some panelists, met with the press. I was among them. In the fifteen minutes that followed, however, no reporter bothered to address a single question to me, since I was only a science-fiction writer.

Then they took our names to make sure they were all spelled right. Finally, one reporter, addressing us en masse, asked, "Should any of you be referred to as 'Doctor'?"

I waited for someone else to speak, and when no one did, I said, dryly, "I have a Ph.D. so you can call me 'Doctor.' I'm the science-fiction writer."

[He'd been persuaded to join Mensa, but was getting disenchanted] In a way, I was a marked man at the meetings. A certain percentage of the members, especially the younger and newer ones, seemed to feel that the way to establish their credentials was to take me on in a battle of wits and shoot me down.

I didn't feel the same endless necessity to take on new competitors, and I was in no mood to be an old gunfighter forever compelled to shoot it out with any challenger who could say, "All right, Ringo. Reach!" . . .

It struck me that I did not particularly want to associate with people on the sole ground that they were like me in whatever quality it is that makes one do well on an intelligence test. I wanted people who more or less shared my common assumptions and universe outlook so that there could be a reasonable dialog.

I met astronomer Carl Sagan, then of Harvard, and had lunch with him. We had already corresponded and I had received some of his papers. He was an ardent science-fiction reader.

I visualized him as an elderly person (the stereotype of the astronomer at his telescope), but what I found him to be was a twenty-seven-year-old, handsome young man; tall, dark, articulate, and absolutely incredibly intelligent.

I had to add him to Marvin Minsky [of MIT] and thereafter I would say that there were *two* people I would readily admit were more intelligent than I was. We have been very good friends ever since.

[About a talk to a pharmaceutical company, which videotaped it] The young man in charge of the TV cameras told me he would signal me when the time came to bring the talk to a halt because the film was running out. There would be signal cards telling me how much time remained.

When I was done, he told me ebulliently, "I don't know how you did it, Dr. Asimov. You never seemed the least bit concerned as the signal cards went up. You didn't hurry, you weren't rattled, and you finished in the most natural way with just twenty-two seconds to spare."

Once again, as on so many previous occasions in my life, I missed my chance to be suavely sophisticated. I should merely have smiled and murmured, "We old-timers have no trouble with this sort of thing."

Instead, I goggled at the young man and said, "What signal cards?"

"Didn't you see them?" he said, disbelievingly.

I shook my head. "I forgot all about them."

He staggered away. People never realize how nonvisual I am.

[Letter] I'm pretty temperamental about sounding untemperamental. I've thrown many a fit at any editorial suggestion that I'm the kind of author who throws fits. [Isaac, you are a very stubborn man. Are you sure you're not part Swede?] Well, I'm Russian, and you know about Rurik . . .

[Letter] There is no orgastic pleasure whatever in reading galley proof on a bus . . . the galleys kept slipping this way and that and the motion of the bus kept lulling me to sleep. The worst moment I had was when I went to the rear to visit the rest room . . . I took my galleys with me being too paranoid to leave it on my seat. There is a handhold on the side of the rest room so that you don't get killed while the bus careens. I grabbed hold of it with the same hand that held the galleys. Then I waited for something to happen (the mad swaying of the bus back and forth and the certainty of imminent death inhibited the natural urinary process.) As I waited I noticed that my galleys were swinging back and forth with the bus's motion as I held them with two fingers and that if they shook loose they would go RIGHT INTO THE HOPPER. It took me a tenth of a second to put the galleys down in a safe place, but during that tenth of a second, the vision of those galleys in the hopper seared my soul. I still haven't quite recovered.

When I hear music that makes me feel happy, I know it's Tschaikovsky. When I hear music that makes me feel awed, I know it's Beethoven. . . . Odd, isn't it, how Sousa and Strauss had the trick of writing original compositions that you already know?

[Letter] History is the best thing to reread—and to write. I know history so well that Earth's past is like a rich tapestry to me. . . . In history, everything's one piece. You pick up history by any strand and the whole thing comes up . . .

I suppose history books are mainly written by liberals because most conservatives can't write.

[Letter about a review of *King Lear*] The reviewer complained about the play itself and I was most indignant. He thought that King Lear was a miserable human being. OF COURSE he was . . . all through the first half of the play, Lear was unreasonable, autocratic . . . so rotten that one actually ought to sympathize with Goneril and Regan, if one didn't know the end of the play to begin with. The point is not where the people started, but where they ended. Goneril and Regan grow more frozen in villainy steadily to the very end. Lear, however, CHANGES. That is the heartbreak and the glory of the play; that at the age of eighty, he is still capable of redemption through suffering. It is the only play I have ever read that makes it clear and understandable that suffering can be a good thing if through it you attain a new view of the universe and of yourself, EVEN IF ONLY FOR A FEW HOURS.

[Letter] To learn is to broaden, to experience more, to snatch new aspects of life for yourself. To refuse to learn or to be relieved at not having to learn is to commit a form of suicide; in the long run, a more meaningful type of suicide than the mere ending of physical life.

Knowledge is not only power; it is happiness, and being taught is the intellectual analog of being loved.

Twenty-Four.
SEXISM AND LOVE

[At a New York University session on creativity] Someone read a paper which listed the criteria of creativity in scientists. Criterion after criterion began "The scientist expects his wife to be . . ." or "The scientist chooses a wife who . . ."

Finally I could stand it no more and broke in and said, "The scientist might choose a husband, you know."

There was a sharp intake of breath all around the table, and as I stared in surprise from one to another, I realized that they thought I was implying homosexuality.

Well, even if I were, so what! But I wasn't! I said, irritably, "For God's sake, the scientist could be a woman, couldn't she?"

And everyone exhaled in relief. What amused and irritated me was that two of the scientists sitting around the table were women, and they had been just as shocked at the thought of scientists choosing a husband as the men were. It was 1963, and I was still alone in my feminism. Women's Liberation had not yet arisen to join me.

[Letter] Bright women learn to measure their responses to avoid seeming brighter than their male companions. Some learn to do it so automatically they forget how not to do it. Those women who resent the necessity feel such relief at meeting a man so secure as to not require the measuring of response that they are apt to fall in love on the spot. What such women sometimes fail to realize is that to the man

167

the relief is equal. To any decently intelligent man, it is ruinous to sexual attraction to have to talk down always and forever.

All my life I have been a great believer in equality of the sexes (arguing with Campbell bitterly on this point) and I think a woman should NOT submerge herself in a man (biologically, the reverse seems appropriate, but let me eschew ribaldry). However, this feminist viewpoint breaks down in the case of true love. TRUE love can't be very common, it suddenly seems to me; particularly when combined with sensitivity, articulateness, and philosophic seeking after truth. Submergence of the woman is all right then, for the man submerges too and a greater unit DOES exist . . .

[After going to a party where a striptease film was shown] The striptease is obviously the acting out of an exaggerated bout of sex in public, vertical instead of horizontal, and without a man. I tried hard to overcome a sense of prudish shock. It seemed so pathetic that a woman should have to make a living in this fashion and equally pathetic that an audience should have to watch for default of anything better—and I was a little indignant that something which I prize very highly should be exposed in this undignified manner. I frequently have the feeling that I have invented sex and patented it and that any infringement on the patent is to be strongly resented . . .

[Letter] I would not want to live in a weather paradise like southern California or Hawaii. [In the northeast] the change in rotten weather from one kind of rotten to another kind of rotten is very stimulating and keeps you on the move and the thoughts racing. To live in a salubrious climate justs gets you lying under palm trees while coconut milk is dribbled into your mouth by a native girl and nothing GETS DONE. Well, nothing ELSE gets done.

[Letter] . . . I love to be told that I am good. Why? Not because it convinces me that I am, in any absolute sense. But because it convinces me that I impress another in such a way that that person thinks I am good. For that person, I AM good. . . . That is a very wonderful thing, for intelligence you are born with and cannot help, and many very horrible and disgusting people have been luminously intelligent. Ditto, good looks; ditto good health; ditto musical talent or writing ability; ditto, almost everything.

But the capacity to be good, to make someone happy, is a creation of yourself; a very difficult thing to create; a very rewarding thing.

Twenty-Five.
LIFE WHILE FAMOUS

[In 1964] Boston University expressed a wish to collect my papers. Dr. Howard Gotlieb, the head of special collections, wrote to ask me for them and I thought he was joking . . .

Gotlieb assured me solemnly that he was serious, and so I dragged out what manuscripts and papers I had, together with some spare copies of various books in various editions, and took them down [to B.U.] . . .

"Is this all?" asked Gotlieb.

"I'm afraid so."

"But what have you done with all the rest?"

"Lately, I've been giving some of the stuff to the Newton Public Library, but mostly I've been burning them."

Gotlieb turned a pretty shade of mauve. "*Burning* them?"

"You know, when they crowd up my filing cabinets, and I don't need them anymore, I get rid of them. They're just junk."

I then received an emotional lecture on the value of a writer's papers to the cause of future research . . . I didn't have the heart to argue. I faithfully promised to bring in all material and not burn anything. It took a while, though, to educate me . . .

"Holographic corrections!" he said. "How valuable that makes this!"

"What are holographic corrections?" I asked.

"I mean you've made corrections in writing."

I laughed. "That's nothing. I make many more corrections in first draft."

"Where's the first draft?"

"Oh, I tear up each page as I finish with it."

Gotlieb frowned fearfully. "Didn't you promise to bring in everything?"

"First drafts, too?" I said, thunderstruck.

Then, on a still later visit, it turned out that he wanted the fan mail also. He wanted *everything*.

"You won't have room," I protested.

"We'll *make* room," he answered firmly.

So in the years since then, I have been periodically flooding the Special Collections Division of Boston University Library . . . All of it has their storage vault under severe internal pressure, and the explosion, when it comes someday, will probably wreck a half-mile stretch of Commonwealth Avenue, but my conscience is clear. I've warned them.

[After Isaac died, his brother Stan went through all the huge quantity of letters stored at B.U. He put together and edited a lovely book of excerpts—*Yours, Isaac Asimov, A Lifetime of Letters*, published by Doubleday just before Stan died in August 1995.]

[Isaac never had e-mail.]

I might say, in passing, that the postcard is a noble invention. It saves enormous amounts of time and postage. It sacrifices privacy, but I have never written a postcard I haven't been willing to have the postman read.

Of course, there is the case of the jovial woman editor with whom I carried on a genial mock flirtation. (In my younger days, I flirted almost indiscriminately with every woman in sight and not one of them ever took me seriously—which may not be exactly complimentary, now that I think of it.) In any case, I wrote her a brief card and, out of sheer habit, ended with a double entendre.

Back came a letter: "Dear Isaac. I have been propositioned before—but never on a postcard."

[He was persuaded to novelize the movie *Fantastic Voyage*.]

One thing bothered me. The ending, as it was to appear in the movie, was fatally flawed. The crew had to get out of the body within an hour because the miniaturization would only last that long. Expansion to normal size would kill the patient, of course. The crew did manage to get out at the very last second, but . . . I told [the editor] I would have to change the ending . . .

"It leaves the submarine inside," I said. "The sub will expand and kill the patient."

"But the submarine is eaten by a white cell."

"So it expands inside the white cell."

"But the submarine is digested."

"A white cell can't digest metal, and if it could, that would only rearrange the atoms and . . . trust me, that submarine has to get out . . . and there has to be an understanding that the Hollywood people won't change the ending back, or interfere with any other changes I make."

It was a lucky thing I made that stipulation, for there were numerous inadmissible points in the movie as it was made. There was no consideration of surface tension or even of the fact that air was made up of atoms and molecules and wasn't a continuous fluid.

I did my best to correct the worst of the flaws, but there were some that were intrinsic in the whole notion of miniaturization, which is, of course, basically impossible even in theory, in my opinion.

[Isaac's novelization came out before the movie was released. Without discussing the scientific flaws with his family, he took them to the movie preview.]

I got my first look at Raquel Welch . . . [and] wondered if I had been entirely wise [in refusing to fly to Hollywood]. There are worse things than being in an airplane, I thought, and not meeting Raquel Welch was surely one of them.

I was particularly impressed by the scene in which Raquel was attacked by antibodies. Those antibodies had to be stripped from her body before they killed her, and four pairs of male hands moved instantly to her breasts to begin the stripping—and there was room there (it appeared to my fevered vision) for all eight hands.

When the movie ended, the spaceship had been left behind, inside the white cell, and Robyn turned to me and said at once, "Won't the ship expand now and kill the man, Daddy?"

"Yes, Robyn," I explained, "but *you* see that because you're smarter than the average Hollywood producer. After all, you're eleven."

[He won a Hugo—the prestigious award given at the World Science-Fiction Convention—first in 1963 for his science essays in *Fantasy & Science Fiction*.]

[During the Hugo awards ceremonies at the Cleveland World Convention in 1966] I considered [Tolkien] a shoo-in, whatever the competition [for the best novel series containing three or more novels]. . . . Other series were nominated just to make it look legitimate . . . I was pretty sure that Foundation would end in last place, but just being nominated was a great honor, so I went . . .

I was the winner over Tolkien, Heinlein, Smith, and Burroughs . . . that was my second Hugo, and the most valuable ever handed out.

[He won four more, including one posthumously.]

[In 1966 his first humorous piece on television science fiction appeared in *TV Guide*.]

I said [*Star Trek*] "seems to have the best technical assistance of the current crop," but I did wax a little jovial over one particular blooper. That was when I ran into the *Star Trek* phenomenon. The viewers of the other shows didn't mind my comments (it may be they didn't know how to read), but the "Trekkies" were heard from at once. Even Janet Jeppson wrote me an angry letter.

Surprised, I watched the program and could see that it had its points. It was certainly the most intelligent science fiction I had seen yet on any of the visual media.

I began to feel that I had worked to harm something I should have labored to save, and for the first time I approached *TV Guide* and asked to do an article. They agreed . . .

I turned out "Mr. Spock Is Dreamy," in which I was funny, but in which I managed to say a lot of nice things about *Star Trek*. . . .

Janet sent me a mollified letter. It also established my friendship with Gene Roddenberry, the producer of the show, and I felt enormously better.

At the end of the first year, those who make such decisions decided to cancel [*Star Trek*]. This decision was greeted by instant and massive protest from the fans, which caught the decision makers by surprise. The poor half-wits didn't know just how articulate and impassioned science-fiction fans could be. The decision was withdrawn and [the show] continued for two more years before it finally went off the air.

However, it never died. Reruns went on forever, and they still go on. There were . . . motion pictures made with the old cast . . . and a new TV series . . . [and more] . . .

[And Isaac was often a guest speaker at the huge *Star Trek* conventions.]

[In 1976] Two young women, who had met me casually at one of the *Star Trek* conventions, happened to share the same birthday. It occurred to one of them that a good birthday present for the other would be a luncheon with myself as guest. I let myself be talked into it . . .

We had a very animated luncheon and I put myself out to be charming and amusing, since both of the young women were attractive and obviously pleased with me. Finally, since the girls had ordered a birthday cake, the waiter brought one with great éclat and put it in front of me, assuming naturally that it was my birthday and that my young granddaughters were helping me celebrate.

Whereupon I said, haughtily, "Waiter, place that cake in front of the girls. It is their birthday. *I* am the birthday present."

It was a pleasure to watch the waiter give the old-man-with-the-white-sideburns that look of sudden awed respect.

[*Photosynthesis* was written for Basic Books—publisher Arthur Rosenthal.]

Somehow I took it for granted that by the time the book rolled off the presses, it would be called *The Green Miracle* or *The Food Factory* or something like that. It wasn't . . .

"Arthur," I said uneasily, "how can the book sell well with that ridiculous title?"

Arthur said . . ." If you'll look under the photograph [of the Sun], you'll see your name printed very clearly—and spelled correctly."

It was nice to have a publisher's confidence, and, indeed, the book did moderately well.

I taped a show with Walter Cronkite, who was narrating a program on the future, one called "The Twenty-first Century." I was rather excited about this, for I admired Cronkite extravagantly.

I sat down in a chair across a low, round table from him, and while the technicians fiddled with the light, I wondered whether I could say, "My father will be very thrilled, Mr. Cronkite, when he finds out you've interviewed me."

It seemed so childish a remark that I didn't dare make it. I was afraid Cronkite would call off the whole thing in disgust.

My hesitation gave him the chance to speak first. He said, "Well, Dr. Asimov, my father will be very thrilled when he finds out I've interviewed you."

[At a panel discussion] One of the panelists . . . was Kurt Vonnegut, whom I now met for the first time. Over a glass of beer that evening (I had ginger ale) he said to me, "How does it feel to know everything?"

I said, "I only know how it feels to have the reputation of knowing everything. Uneasy."

[Comment after one of his talks to librarians] "Dr. Asimov," she said, "I just want you to know that in our branch, your books are the most frequently stolen."

There was widespread laughter and I said that this seemed to indicate that either my readers were particularly dishonest, which I doubted, or that once having one of my books in their possession they couldn't bear to give it up on any account—something for which I couldn't blame them.

Twenty-Six.
THE BIBLE

[In 1965 he wrote a book he called *It's Mentioned in the Bible*, but it came out as *Asimov's Guide to the Bible*.]

I have always been interested in the Bible, though I can't recall ever having had any religious feelings even as a youngster. There's a swing to biblical language that impresses the ear and the mind. I assume that the Bible is great literature in the original Hebrew or, in the case of the New Testament, Greek, but there is no question that the Authorized Version (that is, the King James Bible) is, along with the plays of William Shakespeare, the supreme achievement of English literature.

I also take a kind of perverse pleasure in the thought that the most important and influential book ever written is the product of Jewish thought. (No, I don't think it was written down at God's dictation any more than the *Iliad* was.) I call it "perverse" because it is an instance of national pride which I don't want to feel and which I fight against constantly. I refuse to consider myself to be anything more sharply defined than "human being," and I feel that aside from overpopulation the most intractable problem we face in trying to avoid the destruction of civilization and humanity is the diabolical habit of people dividing themselves into tiny groups, with each group extolling itself and denouncing its neighbors.

I remember once a fellow Jew remarking with satisfaction on the high percentage of Nobel Prize winners who were Jewish.

I said, "Does that make you feel superior?"

"Of course," he said.

"What if I told you that 60 percent of the pornographers and 80 percent of the crooked Wall Street manipulators were Jewish?"

He was startled. "Is that true?

"I don't know. I made up the figures. But what if it were true? Would it make you feel inferior?"

He had to think about that. It's much easier to find reasons to consider oneself superior than inferior. But one is just the mirror image of the other. The same line of argument that takes individual credit for the real or imaginary achievement of an artificially defined group can be used to justify the subjection and humiliation of individuals for the real or imagined delinquencies of the same group.

My father received [the Bible book] in Florida. (I always gave him a copy of every book I wrote, and he would show it to everyone he knew but would not allow them to touch the books. They had to look at it while he held it. He must have made himself, and me, so unpopular.)

He telephoned me to tell me he had read only seven pages and had then closed the book because it didn't reflect the Orthodox viewpoint. This was the period [in his father's retirement] when he had returned to Orthodoxy so he could have something to do. I felt bad about that, because it was the clearest evidence of his backsliding, and I disapproved.

Having spent so much time on *Asimov's Guide to the Bible* . . . I went to Brandeis to see a magnificent collection of old Bibles.

At one point we were looking at a Jewish Bible published in Spain before the expulsion of the Jews. It was open to the seventh chapter of Isaiah, and was in Spanish, except for one word that was in Hebrew and stood out like a sore thumb amid the rest.

My friend said to me, "Why do they have one word in Hebrew?"

Having spent some time on that very point in my Bible book, I said, "That's the verse that, in the King James, goes 'Behold a virgin shall conceive, and bear a son.' The only trouble is that the Hebrew word is *almah*, which does not mean 'virgin' but 'young woman.' If the Jewish publishers were to translate the word correctly they would seem to be denying the divinity of Jesus and they would be in serious trouble with the Inquisition. Rather than do that, or translate it incorrectly, they leave that word in Hebrew."

I said all this in my usual speaking voice and in very much the manner in which I would have delivered a lecture at school. While I was talking (at somewhat greater length than I report it here), the nearest security guard approached and listened curiously.

I didn't notice that, but my friend did, and (like most of my friends) he overestimated the importance of my name. He therefore said to the guard . . . "Do you know who he is?"

And the guard said, "God?"

My friend needn't have laughed *that* hard.

Twenty-Seven.
CHANGES

[On August 3, 1969] the Sunday *New York Times* . . . interview of me . . . took up a full page in the Book Review section and was very good. What particularly pleased me was that toward the end he included a tribute I had paid my father for buying me a new typewriter even before I had made my first sale, as his evidence of faith in my perseverance and ability.

I promptly called my parents in Florida to ask if they had seen the *Times* yet. They hadn't, and my mother, who answered the phone, said my father wasn't feeling well. I asked to speak to him and he seemed annoyed at my mother for having overdramatized the situation.

He said, "So I have pains. I have pains all the time now; and I've had it for years. Sometimes it's a little worse, sometimes a little better, and finally I die. So what? When I die, I die."

"Yes, Pappa," I said, "but how do you feel *now*?"

"Not so bad. She's just making a fuss. I'll send her out for the *Times*. That will give her something to do."

Later on in the day, he called me . . . very pleased. Of course, he did his best not to be sickening about it, since he always prided himself on his stoical approach to life, but he rarely fooled me.

Some years before, I heard Shelley Berman do a comic routine on *The Ed Sullivan Show*. He played his own father, whose accent, intonations, idioms, personality, and retail store were exactly like my own father's . . . I called my father long-distance . . .

"Hello, Pappa. It's Isaac. Did you hear Shelley Berman on the TV just now?"

"Yes," said my father, and nothing more.

Rather at a loss for words, I waited, and then finally said, "I heard him, too, so—so—so I thought I'd call and ask how you are."

There was another pause, and my mother said, "He's fine."

I was astonished. "Mamma!" I said, "what are you doing on the phone? Where's Pappa?"

My mother said, "He's in the corner, crying. What did you say to him?"

So much for my father and his stoicism.

On Monday, August 4, 1969, things fell apart.

At 8:45 P.M. that evening I was on the phone and the operator broke in to tell me that someone else was trying to reach me on a life-and-death emergency. . . . Stupidly, turning cold all over, I said, "Life and death?"

I heard my brother's voice break in. "Tell him it's Stanley calling." . . .

I broke off my conversation, was connected to Stanley, and I said, "What's the matter?"

It was a useless question. I knew what had happened.

That afternoon, my father had died, a little less than a year after he had gone to Florida . . .

At least I had spoken to him the day before. He had indeed felt poorly then. He felt worse on the morning of the fourth, was taken to the hospital, and died there in a matter of hours.

He was seventy-two years and seven months old at the time of death, and had survived the onset of his angina pectoris by thirty-one years. He had remained mentally alert to the very end and was never bedridden till the last day. It was a source of great solace to me that on the last full day of his life I had spoken to him (and so had Stanley, in connection with the *Times* article) and that he himself had read the article and had seen that I had appreciated what he had done for me and that I had let the world know.

[Isaac died at seventy-two and approximately three months, but he was not so lucky to avoid being bedridden many times before that.]

The death of my father seemed to sensitize me to the manner in which my life seemed to be falling apart. Gertrude and I had been talking divorce . . .

[In the spring of 1970] Divorce had come close enough to make it seem advisable to me to find an apartment for myself, one small enough for me to handle and yet large enough to hold my library. I found such an apartment in Wellesley . . . I would be no more than five miles from the house, so that I could see the kids and be available for emergencies . . .

[But separation plans did not work out, and his lawyers told him] I would have to go to another state where no-fault proceedings could be instituted and where I could set up a legitimate residency. California and New York were the only two possibilities and, of the two, I chose New York. New York would be closer to my children; it was the place I was brought up; it was where all my major publishers (except Houghton Mifflin) were based.

[He moved to Manhattan to an apartment hotel and began to work again. It took three years to get a divorce.]

Twenty-Eight.
SHAKESPEARE

 After I had handed in *Asimov's Guide to the Bible*, I felt bereft. I had worked on it so long and enjoyed it so much, I resented having to stop. I wondered if there were anything else I could do that would be comparable in pleasure, and what is the only part of English literature to compare with the Bible? Of course—the plays of William Shakespeare . . .

I therefore began to write *Asimov's Guide to Shakespeare*, intending to go over every one of his plays carefully, explaining all the allusions and archaisms, and discussing all his references involving history, geography, mythology, or anything else I thought could use discussion.

The most fun I've ever had, writing, was when I wrote my autobiographies. After all, what more interesting subject can I have than myself? Leaving this out of account, however, *Asimov's Guide to Shakespeare* was the most pleasant work I had ever done. I have loved Shakespeare since I was a young boy, and reading him painstakingly, line by line, and then writing at length about everything I read was such a joy.

[After moving to New York] I received galleys of the book—a *lot* of galleys, for the book was half a million words long. That gave me something to do, just when I very badly needed something to do to keep my mind off my feeling of guilt and insecurity.

Galleys or "proofs," for those of you who don't know, are long sheets on which the contents of a book are printed, usually two and a half pages or so to each galley sheet. The writer is supposed to read over them carefully, trying to catch all the typos made by the printer and all the infelicities made by himself. Such "proofreading" and corrections are meant to ensure that the final book will be free of errors.

I suspect that most writers find galleys a pain, but I like them. They give me a chance to read my own writing. The problem is that I'm not a good proofreader, because I read too quickly. I read by "gestalt," a phrase at a time. If there is a wrong letter, a displaced letter, a missing letter, an excessive letter, I don't notice it. The small error is lost in the general correctness of the phrase. I have to force myself to look at each word, each letter separately, but if I relax for one moment I start racing ahead again.

The ideal proofreader should be, in my opinion, knowledgeable about every aspect of spelling, punctuation, and grammar, while being slightly dyslexic.

Asimov's Guide to Shakespeare was published in two volumes in 1970, and whenever I use it, or even look at it, I find myself back in those very early days in New York, uncertain of the future and a little frightened.

Twenty-Nine.
NEW EXPERIMENTS IN WRITING

[During a visit to a secondhand bookstore] I came up with a secondhand Modern Library edition of Lord Byron's *Don Juan*. I had read the first couple of cantos in college, but I had never read the whole thing (or at least the sixteen cantos Byron had written—he never finished it). It struck me that since I could rarely sleep through the night at the [hotel], I could use the time to read *Don Juan*. Who knows? It might put me to sleep.

I tried it that very night, and only got through the dedication and into a few verses of the first canto before I realized that nobody could possibly get the full flavor of the poem without understanding all the allusions Byron was constantly making to current affairs, to recent history, and to classic learning.

I remembered Martin Gardner's recommendation [to try annotating something, because it's fun to do], and fell into an absolute lust to annotate *Don Juan*.

[At a lunch with Larry Ashmead, his Doubleday editor] I advanced my notion of annotating *Don Juan*, explaining that it was the greatest comic epic in the English language, and perhaps in any language, and that its wealth of contemporary and classical allusion, which had made it all the funnier to an educated man of the 1820s, was lost on us a century and a half later.

Larry put it up to the editorial board and in due time I heard that they were willing to let me go ahead. In fact, I couldn't help but notice on Larry's desk a comment (handwritten) by Betty Prashker, one of the senior editors. All it said in connection with the *Don Juan* annotation was, "Oh let Isaac have his fun."

[*Ellery Queen's Mystery Magazine* asked Isaac to write a story for them.]

It occurred to me . . . that I might use the Trap Door Spiders [the stag club that met once a month in New York]. I could have a similar organization, which I would call "The Black Widowers," have similar members, and a similar routine . . .

Where I departed from reality was to have the guest come up with a mystery . . . I also invented a waiter, who solved the mystery . . . he was an incarnation of Wodehouse's immortal Jeeves . . .

I had never thought of the story as the first of a series . . . but [after it appeared] I decided to try more of what I instantly began to think of as the "Black Widowers" stories.

It wouldn't be easy. Each story would have to be told during a banquet; each would have to be analyzed in armchair fashion, with the solution . . . sufficiently forceful to be accepted at once.

I managed. In the end the Black Widowers stories grew to be more in number than those of any other series of stories I had ever written—and the most enjoyable for me.

[Among other things, Isaac wrote a story for a science-fiction anthology. The story turned out to be too long.]

Larry . . . phoned me and told me that anthologization was out. He wanted the story expanded into a novel.

I didn't want to expand it into a novel, however. "The Gods Themselves" fit the twenty thousand words perfectly and if I tried to pump it up to three or four times its length, I would ruin it by making it incredibly spongy.

I thought very rapidly and said, "Look, Larry, the story involves an energy source that depends on communication between ourselves and another universe, and it ends downbeat. What I can do is retell the story from the standpoint of the other universe and still leave it downbeat. Then I can take it up a third time in still a third setting and this time make it upbeat."

"Are you sure you can do this?" said Larry.

Well, I wasn't. I had just made that all up on the spur of the moment, but it wouldn't have done to say so.

"Absolutely positive," I said (well, if I couldn't, I wasn't Isaac Asimov), so on March 8, 1971, I dropped in at Doubleday and signed a contract to do the novel.

Larry had shown the first part [of *The Gods Themselves*] to a paperback house and they had expressed interest, but had said, "Will Asimov be putting some sex into the book?"

Larry said, firmly, "No!"

When Larry told me this I instantly felt contrary enough to want to put sex into the book. I rarely had sex in my stories and I rarely had extraterrestrial creatures in them, either, and I knew there were not lacking those who thought that I did not include them because I lacked the imagination for it.

I determined, therefore, to work up the best extraterrestrials that had ever been seen for the second part of my novel . . . not . . . just human beings with antennae or pointed ears, but utterly inhuman objects in every way. And I determined to give them three sexes and to have that entire section of *The Gods Themselves* revolve about sex—*their* sex.

That is exactly what I did, and I began to feel myself moved by the story I was writing.

Thirty.
MORE WORKING WITH WORDS

 [At Breadloaf Writer's Conference] Not only did I have to give talks, I also had to read material submitted to me and to discuss it intelligently and helpfully both with the students in private and with the class in public.

Every member of the faculty took his turn in delivering an evening speech to the entire student body. My turn came on August 28.

I had noted with some discomfort that each faculty member read from his works at some point in his speech.

I had not brought any works to read from, but I had done [an] article on Ruth. I therefore gave my talk on the Book of Ruth as a commentary on intolerance, went on to the parable of the Good Samaritan, and ended with my own discussion of love overcoming the barriers of difference in "The Ugly Little Boy."

Of all the talks I had ever given, that one was the best.

I do not look at an audience, as it happens, I always focus in midair, but I *listen* to them. From the rustling, the coughing, the laughing, the murmuring, I have my way of judging the effect of what I am saying, and I adjust to suit. None of it is conscious; it is an unconscious and unspoken dialog between myself and my audience and, when it is working well, it guides me and I cannot miss.

But if you were to ask what I listen for that tells me that I am exactly right, I would answer, "Silence!"

There are rare times when an audience falls entirely silent, when there is not a laugh, not a cough, not a rustle, when nothing exists but a sea of ears—and then I know I have reached speaker's heaven.

I haven't achieved this more than four or five times in all my life, but the one time I remember most clearly of all was that August 28, 1971, when I talked on the subject of intolerance at Breadloaf. And when I finished by quoting (from memory) the final climax to "The Ugly Little Boy," the silence was finally broken, for I heard sobbing.

I got the first standing ovation (I was told) that Breadloaf had ever seen.

The whole thing was summed up afterward when one of the students came to me and, with absolutely no sign of sarcasm at all, said, "Thank you for a wonderful sermon, Reverend."

[Isaac's advice, in a letter, about "limping transitions" in first drafts] So what if it limps. Its purpose is to get you into the next stage of the story and you take off from there. Time enough when you go through the novel again to correct the transition. For all you know, the material that you will write much later in the novel will make it plain to you exactly how the transition ought to have been. No amount of rewriting and repolishing now will get it right in the absence of knowledge of the course of the entire book. So let it limp and get on with it . . .

Think of yourself as an artist making a sketch to get the composition clear in his mind, the blocks of color, the balance, and the rest. With that done, you can worry about the fine points.

The only education a writer gets is in reading other people's writing. You should read not through your opinion of whether or not you like something, but to see how the writer does it, why it's effective.

Of course, sometimes it's awfully hard to tell golden drops from shit.

I was in Rochester [to talk to the New York State Librarians Association] in a two-room hotel suite with (at the moment) nothing to do.

... I sat there with the strong urge to write a tenth Black Widowers story—and I had not brought a typewriter with me.

I was tempted to try to write the story with pen and ink, but it seemed to me that this would be far too tiring and that the mechanical detail of moving my hand to form the letters would interfere with the creative process.

I was desperate enough to try, though. I used the hotel writing paper provided guests and began to write—and continued to write—and kept on writing until the story (the first draft at least) was finished.

I rushed into the next room and woke Janet. "Janet," I said, you know how noisy writing is. Well, it isn't the writing that's noisy, it's the *typewriter*." When I wrote by pen and ink, I was conscious of writing in a profound and, to me, an utterly unaccustomed silence.

From that point on, I never took my typewriter with me on trips but relied on pen and ink if I wanted to write.

[Isaac's reaction to the last Apollo shot—at night] The giant rocket stood out against the flat Florida coast like a misplaced Washington's monument. The day darkened; night came; clouds banked on the eastern horizon; and there was a continuous display of faraway lightning-without-thunder ducking in and out of the distant thunderheads. Launch was [put on hold] . . . Midnight came and we were into December 7, the thirty-first anniversary of Pearl Harbor, and no one seemed to be aware of this bit of ill omen but myself. In a short time, the launch would have to be postponed to the next night, the ship would have to move away, and we would miss the sight.

At 12:20 A.M., the hold was lifted and the countdown proceeded to zero. A cloud of vapor enveloped the rocket and I held my breath for fear Pearl Harbor Day would do its work.

It didn't. The rocket slowly rose and the vast red flower at its tail bloomed. What was surely the most concentrated man-made night light on an enormous scale that the world had ever seen blazed out over the nightbound shores of Florida—and the night vanished from horizon to horizon.

We, and the ship, and all the world we could see, were suddenly under the dim copper dome of a sky from which the stars had washed out, while below us the black sea had turned an orange-gray.

In the deepest silence, the artificial sun that had so changed our immediate world rose higher and higher, and then—forty seconds after ignition—the violent shaking of the air all about the rocket engines completed its journey across the seven-mile separation and reached us. With the rocket high in the air, we were shaken with a rumbling thunder so that our private and temporary daytime was accompanied by a private and temporary earthquake.

Sound and light ebbed majestically as the rocket continued to rise until it was a ruddy blotch in the high sky. Night fell once more; the stars were coming out, and the sea darkened. In the sky there was a flash as the second stage came loose, and then the rocket was a star among stars; moving, and moving, and moving, and growing dimmer . . .

In all this, it was useless for me to try to say anything, for there was nothing to say. The words and phrases had not been invented that would serve as an accompaniment to that magnificent leap to the Moon, and I did not try to invent any. After all, I had nothing more at my disposal than the language of Shakespeare.

Some young man behind me, however, was not hobbled by my disadvantage. He had a vocabulary that the young of our day had developed to express their own tastes and quality and he used it to the full.

"Oh, *shit*," he said, as his head tilted slowly upward. And then, with his tenor voice rising over all the silent heads on board, he added eloquently, "Oh, shi-i-i-it."

To each his own, I thought.

There had always been one aspect of the robot theme I had never had the courage to tackle, although Campbell and I had sometimes discussed it. The laws of robots refer to human beings. Robots must not harm them and they must obey them, but what, in robot eyes, is a human being. Or, as the Psalmist asks of God, "What is man that thou art mindful of him?" . . .

I began a robot story entitled, "That Thou Art Mindful of Him."

[On the Canberra in 1973 for the solar eclipse off the coast of Africa] The sight of the total eclipse was wonderful. There were two things that were unexpected. The eclipsed Sun, with its corona spectacularly visible, looked smaller than I expected, and at total eclipse, it did not seem to be night but, rather, twilight.

I was excited enough to be shouting wildly, at the moment of eclipse. There were people there with tape recorders and I was allowed, afterward, to listen to the deathless prose that issued from my lips.

One exclamation was, "Yes, that's it. That's it. That's the way it's supposed to look," as though I were congratulating the cosmic director who was running the show.

The other, when the brighter stars began to be visible was, "That proves it. The stars *do* shine in the daytime."

To me, the most exciting split second was the reappearance of the Sun. For five minutes of totality we waited and then at the western edge of the Sun there was a flash of light. The "diamond ring" effect lasted for a bare moment. The blaze broadened, and in two seconds one could not look at the Sun anymore.

[Reaction to his mother's death in 1973] My mother had died four years and two days after my father, and just one month short of her seventy-eighth birthday.

Her death didn't affect me as badly as my father's had. The slow deterioration of her health had made the event inevitable, her sad and lonely life without my father had made it welcome to her, and I had to recognize that prolonging its meaninglessness was not what she wanted . . .

[His brother and sister and spouses arrived] My deep depression stirred the inevitable gallows humor within me and I said, suddenly, "If Mama had known that all six of us were going to be here today, she would have waited." It got a rather hysterical laugh.

Thirty-One.
ISAAC, HIMSELF

[At a *Family Weekly* awards luncheon full of celebrities] I looked up . . . and there . . . not six feet from where we were sitting, was Alan Alda, the star of the *M*A*S*H* show . . .

I bounced up. "Mr. Alda," I said, "I'm Isaac Asimov."

He said, "Why aren't you at home writing a book?" so I knew he knew who I was.

"It's my wife's fault," I said. "She's deeply in love with you and she's sitting right there and wants your autograph." . . .

Alan Alda said, "Poor woman," and signed.

When I was returning from a dinner in New Jersey, I hastened, in order to get home before midnight and the last news broadcast of the day [hoping for Nixon's impeachment]. Walking into the apartment at a quarter of midnight, I turned on the radio at once so that I would not forget.

My attention was caught at once by the statements being made by whoever it was on the program in progress. I listened for a while and called out, "Janet, there's a joker here spouting my ideas."

Janet came in, listened two seconds, and said, "It's *you*, Isaac."

And so it was. About a month earlier I had taped an interview with Casper Citron and had forgotten about it. It was running now and as usual I didn't recognize my own voice when unprepared for it.

At NBC, I had been working on and off, for some months, with a producer, Lucy Jarvis, writing a special on the cult of youth for television. I didn't enjoy it. . . . Naturally, when I did arrive at NBC for story conferences, I eased my unhappiness by engaging the various pretty young ladies in light-hearted banter, and my role was clearly that of the "sensuous dirty old man" concerning whom I had written.

When I took Robyn to NBC . . . the young women in Lucy Jarvis's office were horrified. There I was with my arm around a very young woman of spectacular appearance and with every evidence of extreme affection on my part—and the instant feeling was that I was flaunting every canon of good taste by bringing my latest starlet-conquest with me.

There was an almost palpable explosion of relief when I introduced Robyn as my daughter.

[While on a trip to England] We went out to the Forest of Dean at the Welsh border . . . it had been raining on and off all day, mild sprinkles that never lasted long and were not very annoying. Interspersed were sunshine and summer clouds. After dinner, Janet and I took a walk among the beeches of the forest and the bluebells on the ground, until another sprinkle drove us under one of the trees.

The Sun was out even while it sprinkled, and a rainbow appeared in the eastern sky. Not one rainbow, either, but *two*. For the first time in my life I saw both the primary and secondary bows, separated, as they should be, by a distance of ten degrees of arc. Between them, the sky was distinctly dark, so that, in effect, we saw a broad band of darkness crossing the eastern sky in a perfect semicircle, bounded on either side by a rainbow, with the red side of each bordering the darkness and the violet side fading into the blue.

It lasted several minutes and we watched in perfect silence. I am not a visual person, but that penetrated—and deeply. Two months later, in fact, the incident inspired my 197th *F & SF* essay, "The Bridge of the Gods."

[In a taxi, after a TV interview] The driver had seen me come tearing out of the Channel 13 building, and asked me what I was doing there.

"Being interviewed," I said, with businesslike conciseness.

"You an actor?"

"No, I'm a writer."

"I once wanted to be a writer," said the cabbie, "but I never got around to it."

"Just as well," I said consolingly. "You can't make a living as a writer."

The taxi driver said argumentatively, "Isaac Asimov does."

I had no answer.

[At a motel in West Virginia] After dinner, we wandered out on the grounds and managed to make our way to a rocky ledge (well-fenced) and stared down into a gorge through which a river wound its way.

The cloudless sky was still bright, but the twilight was deepening; the vista was absolutely bursting with green; the river was a silver curve; and around the bend of a mountain there slowly came a long freight train dragged by four locomotives. It crawled its way precariously along the narrow space between mountain and river, with its busy chug-chug far enough away to sound like the panting of a giant anaconda.

After a long while, Janet said, in an awed whisper, "Isn't this amazing?"

"You bet," I said briskly. "One hundred sixty-six cars! Longest freight train I ever saw."

I finally began "The Bicentennial Man." It seemed to me that to avoid the actual 1976 bicentennial, I would need another kind of bicentennial, and I chose to deal with a two-hundredth birthday. That would mean either a man with an elongated life span or a robot, and I chose a robot. Why, then, the "man" in the title? I decided to write about a robot who wanted to be a man and who attained that goal on the two-hundredth anniversary of its construction.

My vague original notion was to make it a somewhat humorous story, but once again, as in the case of *The Gods Themselves*, the thing got away from me. It was a seventy-five-hundred-word story that had been commissioned, but I had no way of stopping it before fifteen thousand words though I dug in my heels as hard as I could. For another, it turned into a moving story that had me almost in tears when I finished.

["The Bicentennial Man" won both the Hugo and the Nebula in 1977.]

Thirty-Two.
MORE ON WRITING

[Isaac became involved with anthologies, especially those devised by his dear friend Martin H. Greenberg.]

[Marty's] encyclopedic knowledge of science fiction, and of other types of genre fiction, too, has enabled him to prepare many anthologies in science fiction, fantasy, horror, mystery, Western, and other fields . . . there is no question that he is far and away the most prolific and, in addition, the best anthologist the world has ever seen.

He has the knack of thinking up useful "theme" anthologies—that is, collections of stories that cluster about some particular subject. What's more, he has the ability to persuade editors and publishers to do these anthologies. What is still more, he has the industry required to obtain permissions, negotiate contracts, take care of all payments, and disperse them to coeditors and to authors.

In all of this, Marty usually works with coeditors, who are always writers in the field of the anthology, who have names that are valuable on the book covers, but who don't have the time, energy, or the inclination, or all three, to do the scut work involved.

I'm a natural for this sort of thing, and Marty and I have coedited over a hundred anthologies . . . there is no one else I would trust to display the industry, the reliability, the competence, and the absolute trustworthiness that Marty does.

. . . All the stories are sent to me and I read them over carefully, since I have veto rights . . . [but] I am chary of making use of that veto. I might not like a story and yet it might be well written, and I must place the writing above my own tastes.

I then write a more or less elaborate introduction to the anthology and, very often, headnotes for each story.

. . . There would appear to be some people who are of the opinion that my sole function in these anthologies is to let my name be used and that I get a free ride. This is *not* so. Any anthology on my list [of books he's done] is one for which I have done significant work.

There are indeed books with my name in the title where I have done no work, where I have selected no stories and exerted no editorial function. Those are *not* listed among my books. If I have written an introduction to a book but have done no editorial work, I do not list it. Any book on the list is a book I have worked on either as a writer or as an editor, or as both.

But why do I do all these anthologies? Of what value are these endless collections of old stories?

Remember that many science-fiction short stories (even very good ones) tend to fade into oblivion. The issues of the magazines in which they appeared are in landfills somewhere. Collections in which they may have appeared in book form are often out of print and unavailable. Anthologies bring back these old stories to an audience that has never read them, or perhaps to some who have indeed read them years or even decades before and would like the chance to read them again. Furthermore, writers, many of whom may be past their best years and may not be writing much, will have the benefit of having their early stories brought before the public, something that will brighten their fame and earn them a little extra money too.

I am willing to lend my name, and to do the work necessary to accomplish these things. I am very fortunate to be one of the handful of authors whose books continue to sell and whose stories, however old, continue to be reprinted. It is my pleasure and, even more, my *duty* to do what I can to help other writers not quite as well situated as I am.

And it's Marty who makes it possible for me to do so, and who does his further part in hundreds of anthologies in which I am not involved.

One advantage of being prolific is that it reduces the importance of any one book. By the time a particular book is published, the prolific writer hasn't much time to worry about how it will be received or how it will sell. By then he has already sold several others and is working on still others and it is these that concern him. This intensifies the peace and calm of his life.

Then, too, once enough books are published, a kind of "ever-normal granary" is established. Even if one book doesn't do well, all the books, as a whole, are bringing in money, and one fall-short isn't noticeable. Even the publisher can take that attitude.

It also makes it easier to experiment. If an experimental short story goes sour—well, what's one story in hundreds?

An experiment I kept wanting to try was that of writing a funny science-fiction story. I don't really know why but I have this strong drive to make people laugh . . .

I've even written a reasonably successful jokebook, containing not only 640 funny stories but endless advice about how to tell them, what to do, and what not to do. The book is *Isaac Asimov's Treasury of Humor* (Houghton Mifflin, 1971) . . .

The humor in all three [of the early humorous stories written in the forties] was quite infantile and, in quality, they stand very close to the bottom of the list of my stories.

The trouble was that I was trying to imitate the slapsticky humor I found in other science-fiction stories and I wasn't good at that. It was not until I realized that my favorite humorist was P. G. Wodehouse and that the proper way for me to be humorous was to imitate him—use my full vocabulary and say silly things with a straight face—that I began to write successful humor.

My first Wodehousian story was "The Up-to-Date Sorcerer"

(*F & SF*, July 1958). Thereafter, things were easier for me. In the 1980s I began to write a whole series of stories about a tiny demon named Azazel, who was constantly being asked to help people and who did as he was told—but always with disastrous results . . . they were just as Wodehousian as I could possibly make them.

I'm not ashamed of being "derivative" in this respect and I never try to hide the fact that I am. Sam Moskowitz, who has written many historical accounts of science fiction, says, with some bitterness, that I am the *only* science-fiction writer who will admit to being influenced. All the others, he says, imply that their writing is the original production of a mind that owes nothing to anyone.

I have to allow for Sam's exaggeration in this respect. I'm sure that any writer, if pressed, will admit to being influenced by some other writer whom he admires (usually it's Kafka, Joyce, or Proust, although with someone as humble as I am it's Cliff Simak, P. G. Wodehouse, and Agatha Christie). And why not? Why not take someone worthy as a model? And no imitation is truly slavish. I'm sure that no matter how Wodehousian a story I write may be, I can't prevent it from being somewhat Asimovian as well. (As an example, my humor is distinctly more cruel than Wodehouse's is.)

It is, of course, difficult to tell why there should be this strong drive to write humor, not only in myself but in many other writers as well. After all, humor is difficult. Other kinds of stories don't have to hit the bull's-eye. The outer rings have their rewards too. A story can be fairly suspenseful, moderately romantic, somewhat terrifying, and so on.

This is *not* the case with humor. A story is either funny or it is not funny. Nothing in between. The humor target contains only a bull's-eye.

Then, too, humor is entirely subjective. Most people will agree on the suspense content of a story, on the romantic nature, on the mystery or horror of it. But over humor there is bound to be violent disagreement. What is howlingly funny to one person is merely stupid to another, so that even my best humorous stories are often skewered by readers who dismiss them as silly. (Of course, they are dull, humorless clods to whom I pay no attention.) . . .

I have said I am a good raconteur, and in this my fiction writing is of great help. I have a fund of a number of complex stories that are actually mini-short stories that have to be told with skill, because I must make sure that humor exists throughout the narrative . . . holding audience interest, before exploding the final punch line. I love these stories because the people who listen to them can never repeat them with success . . .

And where do I get such a story from? Why, from someone who told it to me in bald, abbreviated form, which I then elaborate into a short story. I once watched a person listen with delight to a story I was telling, and when I was done, I said to him, "But you told me that joke." And he replied, still laughing, "Not like that."

Out of a vast number of stories about the Dutch Treat [club], I'll tell you about the time when one of the regulars had missed a luncheon or two on the petty excuse of his wife's being in the hospital. I said, haughtily and with typical male (false) grandiosity, "The only reason *I* would miss a lunch would be if the gorgeous babe in bed with me simply wouldn't let me leave."

Whereupon Joe Coggins said, sepulchrally, "Which accounts for Isaac's perfect attendance record."

I saw that coming as soon as I made the remark, but it was too late to force it back in my mouth. There was nothing left but to join the group in their laughter.

Despite my prolificity, one thing I never experimented with was vulgarity and sex.

In the days when I started writing, writers, whether for the printed or the visual media, found it impossible to use vulgar language or even some proper words. It was for this reason that cowboys were always saying, "You gol-darned, dag-nabbed, ding-busted varmint," when undoubtedly no cowboy ever said anything like that. We know what they really said but it was unprintable and unusable.

Words like "virgin," "breast," and "pregnant" were also unprintable and unsayable. It was even impossible, in some quarters, to say, "He died." One had to say, "He passed away," or "He went to his reward," or "He was gathered unto his fathers."

This type of prissiness was a great bother to writers, who found themselves unable to present the world as it was, and there was enormous relief in the 1960s when it became possible to use vulgarisms in writing, and even, to an extent, on television. The prissy were horrified, but they live in some never-never land and I am in no mood to worry about them.

And yet, despite all that, I have not joined the revolution. This is *not* out of prissiness of my own. I have published five books of naughty limericks that I constructed myself and that are quite satisfactorily obscene. . . . Those, however, are limericks. In my other writing, sex and vulgarity are absent.

Despite Susan Calvin [in his robot stories], my early science-fiction stories were sometimes considered sexist because of the absence of women. A few years ago, a feminist wrote to excoriate me for this. I replied gently, explaining my utter inexperience with women at the time I began to write.

"That's no excuse," she replied angrily, and I dropped the matter. Clearly, there is no percentage in arguing with fanatics.

As my writing progressed, I became more successful with women characters. In *The Naked Sun*, I introduced Gladia Delmarre as a romantic interest, and I think I did her well.

She appeared again in *The Robots of Dawn* . . . where she was even better, in my opinion. In *The Robots of Dawn* I even made it clear that the hero and heroine had sex (adulterous sex at that, for the hero was a married man), but I gave no clinical details and the episode was absolutely essential to the plot. It was *not* included for titillation.

In fact, in my last few novels, I have made it a practice to exclude not only all vulgarisms but all expletives of any kind. I exclude even "dear me" and "gee whiz." It is difficult to do this, for people use such expressions (and much worse) almost routinely. I do it partly out of deliberate rebellion against the literary freedom of today and partly as an experiment. I was curious to see if any readers would notice. Apparently, they do not.

All throughout [*Isaac Asimov's Treasury of Humor*], I stressed the desirability of *not* using vulgarisms unnecessarily. They were likely to embarrass some in the audience and did not add to the humor of the story. In fact, I pointed out, the humor was more effective when the ribaldry was merely hinted at. The listener fills in the lacunae in his mind according to his own tastes, and I give several examples of jokes where the wicked details are left out to the improvement of the joke.

The last two jokes in the book, however, were examples of cases where the use of vulgarisms was necessary. The last joke, in fact, illustrated the manner in which overuse of a particular vulgarism deprives it of all meaning.

Somewhere in Tennessee, the *Treasury of Humor* was violently attacked. An attempt was made to indicate that the last two jokes were typical of the book as a whole, and no mention was made of my strictures against the use of vulgarisms.

This is not surprising. Bluenose censors, in their attempt to cut off anything they don't like, do not hesitate to distort, deceive, and lie. In fact, I think they would rather. They failed, however. The *Treasury of Humor* was removed from the junior high school shelf but remained in the town library. I hope the publicity meant that more students read it, though they must have been disappointed if they expected real obscenity.

(What strikes me in this is that the junior high school kids, if they are like all the junior high school kids I've ever known, know and freely use the wicked word found in those last two jokes. So, I suspect, do the censors themselves, for they are undoubtedly steeped in every possible aspect of hypocrisy.)

The Robots of Dawn also took its lumps. Parents in some town in the state of Washington found themselves appalled by the book and demanded it be withdrawn from the school library. Some who made this demand admitted they didn't read the book, because they wouldn't read "trash." It was enough to *call* it trash and burn it.

One school board member actually had the guts to read the book. He said he didn't like it (having to stay on the side of the angels if he wanted to keep his job) but actually had the surprising courage to say that he found nothing in it that was obscene. So it stayed.

At a time when obscene books are published without remark and are openly read by young women on buses, the fact that anyone, anywhere, can waste their time over my harmless volumes amazes me. Sometimes, though, I wish that the people who did this weren't the pitiful and petulant pipsqueaks they are and that they made a real stink over some book of mine. How that would improve sales!

[As a fiction writer] I have never joined the gloom and doom procession. This is not because I don't believe that humanity can destroy itself. I believe this heartily and have written numerous essays on different aspects of the problem (particularly on the subject of overpopulation). It is just that I think there are enough science-fiction writers shrieking, "The day of judgment is at hand!" and I won't be missed if I am not of their number.

To be sure, in *Pebble in the Sky*, I described an Earth all but destroyed by radioactivity, but humanity is pictured in that book as existing in a great Galactic Empire, so that the fate of one small world means little to humanity as a whole.

My books tend to celebrate the triumph of technology rather than its disaster. This is true of other science-fiction writers as well, notably Robert Heinlein and Arthur Clarke. It seems odd, or perhaps significant, that the Big Three are all technological optimists.

Thirty-Three.
HEART ATTACK

[In 1977, to Isaac's dismay, he was told he had to go to the hospital because he'd had a mild heart attack.] "I can't," I said. "I have to give a commencement address at Johns Hopkins day after tomorrow."

"No, you won't" [said his doctor].

"Why not? I've lived a week. I can live two days more."

"What if you die on the platform as you give your talk?"

"It will be a professional death," I said firmly.

[He was sent to the hospital.] It was the first time I had ever cancelled speaking engagements and the Johns Hopkins cancellation was intensely embarrassing to me. I eventually wrote them a letter of apology in which I said that I owed them one talk without charge. In 1989, the university called in the debt and, though twelve years had passed, I came through. I went to Baltimore and delivered a talk without charge.

In 1977 Ben Bova pitched in and gave some of my talks for me, doing a great job. But then the villain had the nerve to ask those in charge of the speaking engagements to send the checks to *me*. Fortunately, they called me in the hospital to see if they were really supposed to do that, and I was furious. Ben had to keep the checks himself, and serve him right.

After three hours of ["rest and recuperation"] I was dreadfully bored and said so. —Voluminously.

[With his doctor's permission, the first draft of his autobiography was photocopied so he could edit it in the hospital.] Day after day, I worked on it, and it was so wonderful to feel that I wasn't wasting time.

Ben Bova visited me and, noticing the manuscript spread out over the bed, asked what I was doing. I explained. "In this autobiography," I said, "I'm including every stupid thing I can remember having said or done."

"Oh?" he said, eyeing the pages. "No wonder it's so long."

Paul [his doctor] did insist on my cutting down in one respect. "Isaac," he said, "two things. First, you must cut down on your speaking engagements. They take a lot out of you. Just give fewer talks and raise your fees so you don't lose income, and don't let personal friends talk you into giving talks for nothing. Do you understand?"

"Yes," I said, "and what's the second thing?"

"My group, the New York University Medical School Alumni Association, would like you to give them a talk. Would you?"

I burst out laughing. It was for nothing, of course, but I accepted the talk instantly, for two reasons. First, because Janet was also an alumna, and second, because Paul [the doctor] seemed completely unaware of the mutual exclusivity of his two points.

I eventually gave the talk on May 12, 1979, and I told the story of the two points, imitating Paul's distinctive voice, and that evoked gales of laughter. It seems also that all the alumni wore badges that gave the month and year of their graduation. Paul had graduated during World War II in an accelerated course and he got out in the month of March, which was unusual. I asked him why he alone seemed to have an M on his badge, and he explained.

But that's not the way I told it. What I said was this: "I said to Paul, 'Why do you have an M on your badge, Paul?' and he answered, 'It stands for mediocre.'" More gales of laughter (especially since he was, in actual fact, an honor student), and I felt I had punished him adequately for having pushed me into the hospital, making me miss the Johns Hopkins commencement.

(Paul forever threatens to sue me for something he calls "patient malpractice.")

Once I got out of the hospital, I lived life normally, except that I took better care of myself. Even so, I would occasionally feel a twinge of angina when I walked too rapidly, and I would stop to let it pass.

When I wrote up the tale of my heart attack in the second volume of my autobiography, one of the reviewers said that I had described it "with characteristic lack of self-pity."

I was glad he had noticed . . . I detest self-pity, and when I find myself falling into it, I make every possible effort to fight it off.

And, after all, what reason have I to feel self-pity? What if I had not survived? I had had a reasonably good life, a secure childhood, loving parents, a happy marriage, a delightful daughter, and a successful career. I had had some disappointments and sadness in my life, but, I honestly think, far less than is true for the average human being, and I have had far more success and gladness than most . . .

It seems to me that people who believe in immortality through transmigration of souls have a tendency to think that they were all Julius Caesar or Cleopatra in the past and that they will be equally prominent in the future. Surely, that can't be so. Since some 90 percent of the human race lives (and has always, in time past, lived) in various degrees of poverty and misery, the chances are weighed against any transmigrating personality ending up in happiness. If my personality, on my death, were to transfer into the body of a newborn baby, chosen at random, the chances that I would lead a new life that was far more miserable than the one I had left would be enormous. It's a roulette game that I do not wish to play.

Many people believe that good people are assured of a better life at death and wicked people a worse one. If that were true I would strongly suspect I must have been a very good person in a past life to have deserved the happy life I have led this time, and if I continue to be noble and virtuous, I will have a still happier life the next time. And where will it end? Why, in that happiest state of all—Nirvana; that is, nothingness.

But it is my opinion that we all achieve Nirvana at once, at the moment of the death that ends a single life. Since I have had a good life, I'll accept death as cheerfully as I can when it comes, although I would be glad to have that death painless. I would also be glad to have my survivors—relatives, friends, and readers—refrain from wasting their time and poisoning their lives in useless mourning and unhappiness. They should be happy instead, on my behalf, that my life has been so good.

Thirty-Four.
EXTENDING TWO SERIES

The two volumes of my autobiography had appeared and done quite well, and went on to be published as trade paperbacks under the Avon label, but Doubleday wasn't satisfied. They still wanted novels.

Mind you, I hadn't been neglecting Doubleday, with whom I published *The Road to Infinity*, a new collection of science essays, and *Casebook of the Black Widowers*, a third collection of Black Widower tales. In press was still another collection of science essays, *The Sun Shines Bright*, and a collection of essays on science fiction, *Asimov on Science Fiction*, and an anthology, *The Thirteen Crimes of Science Fiction*. I was also working madly on another edition of *Asimov's Biographical Encyclopedia of Science and Technology*, so Doubleday couldn't say I was neglecting the firm.

Nor was I neglecting other publishers, by the way, for in 1980 and 1981, I had published twenty-four books. These included *Extraterrestrial Civilizations* for Crown; *A Choice of Catastrophes* for Simon and Schuster; *Isaac Asimov's Book of Facts* for Grosset and Dunlap; *The Annotated Gulliver's Travels* for Clarkson Potter; and four *How Did We Find Out About . . . ?* books for Walker and Company.

So I was certainly working full-time, as I always do.

[At Doubleday] Betty Prashker wanted to see me. Betty was high up in the editorial scale and a very respected editor in the field. This mild middle-aged woman smiled at me and said, "Isaac, we want you to write a novel for us."

I said, "But, Betty, I don't know if I can write novels anymore."

Betty said, in the usual refrain, "Don't be silly, Isaac. Just go home and start thinking up a novel."

I was shoved out of the office. That evening, Pat LoBrutto, who was in charge of science fiction at Doubleday, phoned me. "Listen, Isaac," he said, "let me make it clear. When Betty said 'a novel,' she meant 'a science-fiction novel'; and when we say 'a science-fiction novel,' we mean 'a Foundation novel.' That's what we want."

I heard him, but I couldn't make myself take it seriously. I had written only one science-fiction novel in twenty-two years, and I had not written a word of any Foundation story in thirty-two years. I didn't even remember the content of the Foundation stories in any detail.

What's more, I had written the Foundation stories, from beginning to end, between the brash ages of twenty-one and thirty, and had done so under John Campbell's whip. Now I was sixty-one years old, and there was no John Campbell any longer, or any present-day equivalent either.

I had a terrible fear that I would, if I were forced, write a Foundation novel, but that it would be entirely worthless. Doubleday would hesitate to reject it, and would publish it; but it would be lambasted by the critics and the readers; and I would go down in science-fiction history as a writer who was great when he was young, but who then tried to ride the coattails of his youth when he was old and incompetent, and proceeded to make an utter jackass of himself.

What's more, my income was high as a result of my vast number of nonfiction books, twenty times as high, in fact, as in the days when I was writing novels. I felt that I might badly damage the state of my private economy if I returned to writing novels.

The only thing I could do was to lie low and hope that Doubleday would forget about it. They didn't, however . . .

I was given a check for half the advance (the other half to be handed to me on delivery of the manuscript), and after that there was no longer any chance to fool around. As soon as I could complete projects I was then engaged on, I would have to get started.

And before I got started, I would have to reread *The Foundation Trilogy*. This I approached with a certain horror. After all, I was convinced it would seem rough and crude to me after all these years. It would surely embarrass me to read the kind of tripe I wrote when I was in my twenties.

So, wincing, I opened the book on June 1, 1981, and within a few pages I knew I was wrong. To be sure, I recognized the pulpy bits in the early stories, and I knew that I could have done better after I had taken a few more years to learn my craft, but I was seized by the book. It was a page-turner.

My memory of it was just sufficiently insufficient for me not to be certain how my characters were going to solve their problems and I read it with steady excitement.

I couldn't help noticing, of course, that there was not very much action in it. The problems and resolutions thereof were expressed primarily in dialogue, in competing rational discussions from different points of view, with no clear indication to the reader which view was right and which was wrong. At the start, there were villains, but as I went along, both heroes and villains faded into shades of gray and the real problem was always: What is best for humanity?

For that, the answer was never certain. I always supplied an answer, but the whole tone of the series was that, as in history, no answer was final.

When I finished reading the trilogy on June 9, I experienced exactly what readers had been telling me for decades—a sense of fury that it was over and there was no more. Now I *wanted* to write a fourth Foundation novel, but that didn't mean I had a plot for it . . .

[He went over the fourteen pages of a fourth Foundation novel started years before.] That gave me the beginning of a novel without an ending. (Always, it's the other way around.) So I sat down to make up an ending, and the next day I forced my quivering fingers to retype those fourteen pages—and then to keep on going.

It was not an easy job. I tried to stick to the style and the atmosphere of the earlier Foundation stories. I had to resurrect all the paraphernalia of psychohistory, and I had to make references to five hundred years of past history. I had to keep the action low and the dialogue high (the critics often complained about that in my novels, but to perdition with them), and I had to present competing rational outlooks and describe different worlds and societies.

What's more, I was uneasily conscious that the early Foundation stories had been written by someone who knew only the technology of the 1940s. There were no computers, for instance, though I did presume the existence of very advanced mathematics. I didn't try to explain that. I just put very advanced computers in the new Foundation novel and hoped that nobody would notice the inconsistency. Oddly enough, no one did.

There were also no robots in the early Foundation novels, and I didn't introduce them in the new one either.

During the 1940s, you see, I had had two separate series going: the Foundation series and the robot series. I deliberately kept them different, the former set in the far future without robots and the latter in the near future with robots. I wanted the two series to remain as separated as possible so that if I got tired of one of them (or if the readers did), I could continue with the other with a minimum of troubling overlap. And indeed, I did get tired of the Foundation and I wrote no more after 1950, while I continued to write robot stories (and even two robot novels).

In writing the new Foundation novel in 1981, I felt the absence of robots to be an anomaly, but there was no way I could bring them in suddenly and without warning. Computers I could; they were side issues making only brief appearances. Robots, however, would be bound to be principal characters and I had to continue to leave them out. Nevertheless, the problem remained in my head and I knew that I would have to deal with it someday.

I called the new novel *Lightning Rod*, for what seemed to me to be good and sufficient reasons, but Doubleday vetoed that instantly. A Foundation novel had to have "Foundation" in the title so that the readers would know at once that that was what they were waiting for. In this case, Doubleday was right, and I finally settled on *Foundation's Edge* as the title.

It took me nine months to write the novel and it was a hard time not only for me but for Janet, for my uncertainty concerning the quality of the novel reflected itself in my mood. When I felt that the novel wasn't going well, I brooded in wretched silence, and Janet admitted that she longed for the days when I wrote only nonfiction, when I had no literary problems, and when my mood was generally sunny.

[After it was published] Doubleday reported large preliminary orders, but I took that calmly and without excitement. Such large orders might well be followed by large returns and actual sales could be small.

I was wrong.

For over thirty years, generation after generation of science-fiction readers had been reading the Foundation novels and had been clamoring for more. All of them, thirty years' worth of them, were now ready to jump at the book the instant it appeared.

The result was that in the week of its publication, *Foundation's Edge* appeared in twelfth place on the *New York Times* Best-Seller List, and I honestly couldn't believe my eyes. I had been a published writer for forty-three years and *Foundation's Edge* was my 262nd book. Having escaped any hint of best-sellerdom for all that time, I scarcely knew what to do with one.

Incidentally, when [the editor, Hugh O'Neill] showed me the proof of the cover, I burst into laughter, because it announced *Foundation's Edge* as the fourth book of the *Foundation Trilogy*. When Hugh asked me why I laughed, I pointed out that "trilogy" meant "three books," so that introducing a fourth book was a contradiction in terms.

Hugh was horribly embarrassed and said it would be changed. I said, "No, no Hugh. Leave it. It will create talk and will be good publicity."

But Doubleday didn't want that kind of publicity. It was changed to a fourth book of the "Foundation Saga."

There was, of course, one little flaw in all the excitement of a best-seller. My name on the *Times* Best-Seller List set off a small tocsin of alarm in my brain and I knew I was doomed. Doubleday would never let me stop writing novels again—and they never did.

Even before *Foundation's Edge* was published, Doubleday was satisfied on the basis of advance sales and on the sale of foreign rights that it was going to be a big moneymaker. I wasn't, simply because I couldn't believe that one of my books could be a best-seller. Having 261 non-best-sellers in a row rather established the pattern, to my way of thinking.

[But it was a best-seller, and he was given a contract for a new novel.] Nothing in the contract, or in any verbal communication from Doubleday, however, had said it must be another Foundation novel and I certainly didn't want to do one. Instead, I thought of another series I had never finished.

I had published the book version of *The Caves of Steel* in 1954, and its sequel, *The Naked Sun*, in 1957. In 1958, I had a contract for a third novel about Elijah Baley and R. Daneel Olivaw (the detective and his robot assistant), for my intention was to make another trilogy out of it. I began the third volume in 1958 and bogged down after I had done eight chapters. Nothing more would come and what I had written I felt was unsatisfactory. This was the book for which I tried to return the $2,000 advance Doubleday had paid me. They eventually transferred the advance to my first Doubleday nonfiction book, *Life and Energy*.

Now, in 1982, twenty-four years after I had failed with the third book of the robot trilogy, my thoughts turned to it once more. If I could successfully add a fourth book to the Foundation saga, then surely I could successfully add a third book to the robot saga.

What had stopped me in 1958 had been my intention to have a

woman fall in love with a humaniform robot like R. Daneel Olivaw. I had seen no way in 1958 of being able to handle it, and as I wrote the eight chapters I grew more and more frightened of the necessity of describing the situation.

The climate in 1982 has changed, however. Writers were more freely able to discuss sexual situations, and I had become a better writer. I didn't go back to those lost eight chapters (as I had gone back to the fourteen pages of Foundation material). I just didn't want them at all. I decided to start afresh.

I had been been asked to make *Foundation's Edge* longer than my early novels, which had been 70,000 words apiece, except for *The Gods Themselves*, which was 90,000 words. For that reason I had made *Foundation's Edge* 140,000 words long. I assumed that my instructions held for later novels and it was my intention to make the third novel 140,000 words long too—that is, as long as the first two robot novels put together. This would give me more room in which to describe the minutiae of the new societies I would deal with, and more leisure to work out the complexities of plot.

I called the new novel *The World of the Dawn*, because the chief setting was on a planet named Aurora, who was the Roman goddess of the dawn. However, Doubleday again had the final word. A robot novel would have to have the word "robot" in the title, they said. The novel was therefore named *The Robots of Dawn*, which turned out to be even more suitable.

I enjoyed writing the new novel considerably more than I had enjoyed writing *Foundation's Edge*. Partly this was because, with an actual best-seller under my belt, I had more confidence this time around. Then, too, *The Robots of Dawn*, like the first two robot novels, was essentially a murder mystery and I am particularly comfortable with mysteries.

I finished the novel on March 28, 1983, and by that time *Foundation's Edge* had done so well, and *The Robots of Dawn* was so well liked by the Doubleday editors, that I resigned myself totally to the writing of novels.

My pleasure with *The Robots of Dawn* led me to write a fourth robot novel. In the fourth book, Elijah Baley would be dead, but I had already decided that the robot, Daneel Olivaw, was the real hero of the series, and he would continue to function.

Still, the fact that my robots were becoming increasingly advanced with each robot book, made it seem stranger and stranger that there were no robots in my Foundation series.

Carefully, I worked out a reason for it and, in doing so, I could see that it was going to be necessary to tie my robot novels and my Foundation novels together into a single series. I intended to begin that process with the upcoming fourth robot novel, and to give a hint of my intention I was going to call it *Robots and Empire*.

[Various friends and editors disapproved of combining the two series, but his new Doubleday editor told him to write what he wanted.]

I went ahead and wrote *Robots and Empire* and clearly began the process of fusing the two series . . .

I returned to the Foundation series and wrote *Foundation and Earth*, which was a sequel to *Foundation's Edge*, and the fifth book of the series.

Thirty-Five.
TRIPLE BYPASS

 Six years had passed since my heart attack, and I had been living a normal life, just as before. My schedule was full of out-of-town lectures, business lunches and dinners, interviews and social engagements. In those six years, I had published about ninety books, including two novels that made the best-seller lists.

Why didn't I take it easier? Surely, a heart attack is a legitimate excuse to slow down.

First, I didn't want to. I dreaded slowing down.

Second, I'm a denier. I had known some hypochondriacs who enjoyed ill health, who insisted upon it, who abandoned any doctor who told them nothing was wrong with them, who used the ill health to garner pity and to force others into the position of servants. I was determined not to be like that. I treated any kind of illness as an insult to my masculinity, and so I was a denier—I denied it ever happened. I insist that I am well when I am obviously not well, and if I am forced into illness despite everything I can say or do, I retreat into sullen silence, until I recover—when I promptly deny I was ever sick. As you see, then, my heart attack was a source of serious embarrassment to me and I pretended, as far as I could, that it had never happened and that I could live an uncaring normal life.

Third, I was in a hurry, for despite everything I couldn't rid myself of the feeling that I was mortal; in fact, a lot more mortal than I had felt earlier. When I was young, I looked forward to living till the science-fictional year of 2000; in other words, till I was eighty years old. I took it for granted I would make it.

But when both of my parents died in their seventies and I had my first operation on a cancerous thyroid [in 1972], I had to admit that eighty was perhaps unrealistic and that perhaps it was safer to hope I lived to be seventy. Then, with a heart attack at fifty-seven, I couldn't help but wonder if I would have to be satisfied with sixty. There was therefore an urge to speed up rather than slow down, in order that I might get as much work done as possible before I was forced—most unwillingly—to abandon my typewriter.

So put all that together and you can see that my years after the heart attack had to be crammed as tightly with work as I could manage.

But despite all denials, I had one heritage of the heart attack that I could not ignore. That was my angina. It wasn't very bothersome, but if I walked too far, or too quickly, or up an incline, the pain clamped down upon my chest and I was forced to wait in order to let that pain subside. I raged against that evidence of old age and mortality, but there was nothing I could do about it.

For years, however, it remained a minor irritation, since I could avoid it by simply walking at a moderate pace and counting on a natural pause at red lights (so that I could pretend I wasn't forced to stop for internal reasons).

The trouble was that the situation grew slowly worse and finally in 1983 it reached a point where it couldn't be ignored. I could no longer deny very effectively. My coronary arteries were becoming narrower with accumulating plaque and my heart was being more and more starved for oxygen.—And yet I couldn't bring myself to mention the matter in my diary; I couldn't make myself put the truth down in writing.

Over the Labor Day weekend, I went to the World Science-Fiction Convention in Baltimore. On September 4, 1983, *Foundation's Edge* won the Hugo by a narrow margin, despite competition from both Heinlein and Clarke. It was my fifth Hugo.

What made the convention memorable for me, however, was that it was spread over two adjacent hotels, so that we had to travel from one to another constantly over walkways, and I had the greatest difficulty managing it.

On September 12, I spent some time with George Abell, the astronomer, whom I had met on earlier occasions through Carl Sagan. He was a very intelligent man and very friendly. He was younger than I and seemed absolutely fit, for he kept up a regime of exercise and he lacked any sign of a potbelly.

I thought of my own sedentary and flabby life, and of my increasing martyrdom to angina, and I suppose I would have felt envy if it weren't that I was well aware that my condition was my own fault in that it was the result of a lifetime of dietary and sedentary abuse. I had no right to indulge in envy. Nor need I have done so, for on October 7, poor George died of a heart attack and I lived on. He was only fifty-seven, the age of *my* heart attack.

On September 18, I attended "New York is Book Country," the annual book-promoting extravaganza along a temporarily closed Fifth Avenue. Robyn showed up with two of her friends and we all went afterward to have dinner. However, I had to beg them all to slow down and creep along, for I could not walk any faster. That was more embarrassment for me, I'm afraid, to say nothing of my concern over the fact that I was clearly frightening Robyn.

On September 24, I actually mentioned my angina in my diary.

Life went on, however, and I even continued to pretend that I was well. I kept up my drumfire of lectures, traveling to Connecticut, and to Boston (to give one last talk for the medical school on October 3, 1983), and even as far as Newport News, Virginia.

On September 23, I met Indira Gandhi at a meeting she requested with a number of authors, and we gave her some books. She was a gracious, intelligent woman.

On October 17, on my monthly visit to [his doctor] I finally broke down and admitted . . . that I was having anginal problems.

[He was sent to a cardiologist, flunked a stress test, got little benefit from nitroglycerine patches, and his angina increased in intensity.]

In my diary . . . I recorded that 1983 was on its way to being far and away my best year as far as income was concerned, but, alas, "I don't expect to long survive it."

Yet life goes on, and even at this crisis I made a trip to Philadelphia to give a talk. On the other hand, I was cautious enough to prepare a new will on November 4.

On November 14, I went to University Hospital for an angiogram. The coronary blockage was pronounced, but still not so bad as to deprive me of what [the cardiologist] called "options." I could have a triple bypass operation or I could choose to live on nitroglycerine tablets and perhaps live out a normal lifetime without an operation, but I'd be more or less a "cardiac cripple."

I said, "What are the chances of dying on the operating table . . . ?"

[The cardiologist] said, "About one in a hundred . . ."

"And what do you suppose my chances are of dying within a year if I don't have an operation?"

"My guess . . . is one in six."

"All right," I said. "I'll have the operation." So [the cardiologist] made an appointment for me with a surgeon.

[Janet's note. Fearful of the dangers of surgery, I objected to this decision.]

I ought to have started a new novel by now, but I refused to do so until I knew for sure that I would live long enough to finish it. I was *not* going to leave an unfinished novel behind me, as Charles Dickens did, if I could help it. That was why there was a one-year gap before *Robots and Empire* was published. However, I didn't loaf. I was working madly those months on the revision of the *Guide to Science*, hoping to complete a fourth edition before I died.

[The heart surgeon] asked if I wanted to wait till after Christmas–New Year's for the operation. Actually, I had reason to wait, for I wanted to attend the annual banquet of the Baker Street Irregulars [BSI, an organization of the fans of the Sherlock Holmes stories] on January 6. I was preparing a song to be sung to the tune of "Danny Boy" and I wanted desperately to deliver it.

However, I dared not take a chance. I said, "No . . . I want the operation at the earliest possible date."

I completed the song, sang it into a cassette, and told Janet that she must deliver it to the BSI if I couldn't make it.

A few days before I was due for the operation, I forgot my condition, and because I was having trouble getting a taxi, I ran for one that finally stopped at a red light. My intention was to get it before someone else did and before it drove away.

The flow of adrenaline kept me going, but after I got into the cab, announced my destination, and settled back, the adrenaline stopped and my heart, unable to get the oxygen it needed, yelled at the top of its voice. I had the worst anginal attack ever, and as I clutched at my chest and gasped for breath, I decided that this was it. I was going to have a second attack and this time it would kill me.

It seemed to me that the driver would reach Doubleday, where I was heading, and find he would have a dead man in his cab. Unwilling to go through the red tape of reporting me (so it seemed in my imagination), he would continue his drive, taking me to the East River, tumble me into it, and drive away—leaving Janet to go into a frenzy when I never came home.

I reached for my pad to write my name and address on it in large letters, with directions for calling Janet's number, but as I was about to do so, I felt the pain ebbing and when we got to Doubleday I was normal.—I was badly shaken, of course.

On the afternoon of [surgery], I was wheeled to the elevators and my last words to Janet were: "Remember, if anything happens to me, I have a $75,000 advance for a new novel that you will have to return to Doubleday."

(When it was all over, I told Doubleday this, to impress them with the fact that I had no intention of taking money from them for a book I couldn't do. And they replied, as I might have guessed, with the old refrain: "Don't be silly, Isaac. We wouldn't have accepted the money.")

I had been filled with sedatives and I remember nothing at all after I got into the elevator. I was told afterward, however, that I wouldn't let the operation begin until I had sung a song.

"A song?" I said in surprise. "What song?"

"I don't know," said my informant. "Something about Sherlock Holmes."

Obviously my parody for the BSI was much in my mind. In fact, the evening before my operation, I indulged in an involuntary daydream. I had died on the operating table in my reverie, and Janet, all in black, came to the BSI to deliver the cassette.

"My late husband," she would say, brokenly and in tears, "with the BSI in his last thoughts, asked me to deliver this."

And they would play my parody to the tune of "Danny Boy." The first few lines were:

Oh, Sherlock Holmes, the Baker Street Irregulars
     Are gathered here to honor you today,
For in their hearts you glitter like a thousand stars,
     And like the stars, you'll never fade away.

The song would be played and I knew that the audience would be in tears and that when it was done they would stand and applaud and applaud and applaud for twenty minutes. And, in my reverie, I listened to all twenty minutes of applause, and my eyes filled with tears of happiness.

Then I had the operation and the next thing I knew I was opening my eyes and I realized that I was in the recovery room. I had survived. And my first thought was that now I wouldn't get the kind of applause I would have gotten if I had been dead.

"Oh—expletive deleted," I said in disappointment.

I have always thought of that moment as the ultimate testimony to the ultimate ham that I was.

[He went to the BSI banquet.] Everyone flocked about me to tell me how wonderful I looked (a sure sign that I looked terrible, indeed) and I sang my song rather hoarsely, for I'd had a tube down my throat for six hours while I was on the operating table. I got the applause, but it was only for two minutes, not twenty. There are disadvantages to being alive.

Thirty-Six.
HUMANISTS

[While suffering what could be called intimations of mortality, Isaac did not give up his humanist beliefs.]

I've never been particularly careful about what label I placed on my beliefs. I believe in the scientific method and the rule of reason as a way of understanding the natural universe. I don't believe in the existence of entities that cannot be reached by such a method and such a rule and that are therefore "supernatural." I certainly don't believe in the mythologies of our society, in Heaven and Hell, in God and angels, in Satan and demons. I've thought of myself as an "atheist," but that simply describes what I *didn't* believe in, not what I did.

Gradually, though, I became aware that there was a movement called "humanism," which used that name because, to put it most simply, Humanists believe that human beings produced the progressive advance of human society and also the ills that plague it. They believe that if the ills are to be alleviated, it is humanity that will have to do the job. They disbelieve in the influence of the supernatural on either the good or the bad of society, on either its ills or the alleviation of those ills.

I received a copy of the "Humanist Manifesto" decades ago when I was still quite young. I read its statement of the principles of humanism, found that I agreed with them, and signed it. When, in the 1970s, an updated statement, "Humanist Manifesto II," was sent to me, I agreed with it and signed it as well. That made me an avowed Humanist, something in which Janet, entirely of her own accord (and as a result of principles she had developed before she ever met me), joins me . . .

My humanism doesn't extend merely to the signing of statements, of course. I have written essays by the dozen that support scientific reasoning and in which I denounce all kinds of pseudoscientific trash. In particular, I have argued vehemently against those religious Fundamentalists who back the Babylonian worldview of the first chapters of the Book of Genesis. These essays have appeared in a number of places, even in the June, 14, 1981, issue of the *New York Times Magazine.*

I also wrote an Op-Ed piece in the *Times* in which I disputed strenuously (and with justice, I think) the views of a prominent astronomer who published a book in which he maintained that the Big Bang theory was somehow anticipated by the biblical writers of Genesis and that astronomers were hesitant to accept the Big Bang because they didn't want to support the conventional religious view.

I expanded that Op-Ed piece into a book, *In the Beginning,* in which I went over every verse in the first eleven chapters of Genesis, in as evenhanded and unemotional a method as possible, and compared the literal interpretation of its language with the modern beliefs of science. It was published by Crown in 1981.

Then, of course, there was my earlier two-volume *Asimov's Guide to the Bible*—written from a strictly humanist point of view.

All this resulted in the American Humanist Association selecting me as the "Humanist of the Year" in 1984, and I went to Washington to receive the honor and to speak to the group on April 20, 1984. It was a small group, of course, for we Humanists are few in number. At least, those of us who are willing to identify ourselves as Humanists are few. I suspect that huge numbers of people of Western tradition are Humanists in so far as the way they shape their lives is concerned, but that childhood conditioning and social pressures force them to pay lip service to religion and do not allow them even to dream of admitting that it *is* only lip service.

Previous "Humanists of the Year" included Margaret Sanger, Leo Szilard, Linus Pauling, Julian Huxley, Hermann J. Muller, Hudson Hoagland, Erich Fromm, Benjamin Spock, R. Buckminster Fuller, B. F. Skinner, Jonas E. Salk, Andrei Sakharov, Carl Sagan, and a number of others of equal note, so I was in select company.

I gave a humorous talk on the occasion, dealing with the kinds of letters I received from religionists, letters that went to the extreme of praying for my soul, on the one hand, to that of consigning me to Hell, on the other. The talk was a huge success; too huge, for it meant that I was eventually asked to become president of the American Humanist Association.

I hesitated, explaining that I didn't travel and that I would be totally unable to attend conventions held anywhere but in New York City, and that, moreover, my schedule was so heavy that I couldn't engage in extended correspondence or involve myself in the political disputes that are inevitable in all organizations.

I was assured that I would not be expected to travel or to do anything I didn't want to do. What they wanted was my name, my writings (which I did anyway), and my signature attached to fund-raising letters.

Even with that settled, I still had to wonder what would happen if I heightened my profile in the Humanist movement to such an extent. My magazine, *IASFM* [*Isaac Asimov's Science Fiction Magazine*], was still quite young and one or two people had already cancelled their subscriptions "because Isaac Asimov is a Humanist." Would I be killing the magazine altogether if I became president of the AHA?

Then I thought that my editorials in the magazine were completely outspoken—so what worse could my presidency do? Besides, I didn't want to make a decision that was influenced by cowardice. I therefore agreed and I have been president of the American Humanist Association ever since.

[Isaac remained president until his death. Now he is prominent in the huge book, *Who's Who in Hell: A Handbook and International Directory for Humanists, Freethinkers, Naturalists, Rationalists, and Non-Theists*, compiled by Warren Allen Smith and published in 2000.]

Thirty-Seven.
SENIOR CITIZEN AND HONORS

 I passed my sixtieth birthday safely, a milestone I had feared I might not reach after my 1977 heart attack. Then I approached my sixty-fifth birthday, another milestone I had feared I might not reach in the nervous month before my triple bypass.

Now here it was. On January 2, 1985, I turned sixty-five, an age that is often considered the official dividing line beyond which a person is a "senior citizen," a phrase I detest with all my heart.

What I was, at sixty-five, was *an old man*.

Sixty-five is, of course, the traditional age for retirement, but that is only true if someone is in a position to fire you and call it retirement. As a freelance writer, I can be rejected, but not fired. Publishers may refuse to put out my books, but they cannot prevent me from writing them.

So I threw a "nonretirement party" for over a hundred people. Janet and I specified "no presents" and "no smoking." A smoke-free party was the best present I could get and it went off magnificently, with all my publishers and friends smiling at me, and my brother, Stan, making a funny speech, and so on.

And my writing career passed right through my sixty-fifth birthday as though there was nothing there.

On February 7, 1985, however, the government caught up to me and I was called in to see some officials who wanted to look at my birth certificate and my tax returns. (I might have mailed them in, but my birth certificate, a fragile piece of old paper from Russia, was not something I cared to trust to the mails—or to the government officials, for that matter.)

I was told that I qualified for Medicare and I accepted that with a certain guilt since I buy ample medical insurance . . . [but] I had just gone through a nasty and expensive medical procedure and might have to go through more . . . so when the officials told me I *had* to accept Medicare, I acquiesced.

Social security was another thing. I flatly refused to accept that. I said, "I have not retired. I make a good deal of money and will continue to do so. The social security payments are not needed by me and they are needed by others, so keep my payments in the social security fund and pay it out to those others."

The person behind the desk said, "If that's what you want, all right, but only till you're seventy. After you turn seventy, you will have to take your social security payments."

I shrugged that off and forgot about it until January 1990 when a government check arrived that I couldn't account for until I remembered the social security bit. I consulted my accountant, and he said, "You paid for it, Isaac. It's your money."

So it was. And then I thought of the [money] I pay each year in taxes and how much of it finds its way into the pockets of greedy politicians and businessmen—and I hardened my heart and accepted the payment, which, believe me, is not a large one.

One can't live a normal lifetime and accomplish anything at all above the level of being a drunken bum without getting awards for something. I have been at numerous conventions in the course of my oratorical adventures and there are few of them where awards aren't handed out to various people—sometimes in gratitude (I think) for their consenting to retire.

Even in science fiction, awards keep proliferating. There is the Hugo Award (given in ever increasing categories) and the Nebula

Award. In addition, there are awards in the names of dead superstars of science fiction; awards named for John Campbell, Philip Dick, Ted Sturgeon, and so on. Perhaps in time to come there will be an Isaac Asimov Award. [yes]

Naturally, I have collected a number of awards (and would collect more if I were willing to travel more than I do). Some are quite trivial, and the most trivial of them, and one I rather like just the same, is a fancy plaque that says on it: "Isaac Asimov, Lovable Lecher." That's something to get an award for, isn't it?

I've also collected diplomas; not only my own legitimate Ph.D., which is framed and up on the wall, but fourteen honorary doctorates as well, stored in a trunk.

I never had an academic robe of my own (I refused to attend my own graduations) and so each school for which I gave a commencement address had to supply me with one, and with a mortarboard and tassel. When I got my honorary degree from Columbia, however, they let me keep the academic robe instead of taking it back at the end of the proceedings. What a pleasure! Now I could wear my own.

However, the very first time I wore it at another commencement, it started raining during the address, for the first time it had ever rained on such an occasion. I had to put up an umbrella while speaking so as to protect my precious robe.

I have never worn it again, because I am getting too old to sit in the sun for two hours and watch hundreds of youngsters get diplomas, just so that I could make a twenty-minute speech.

There were also honors I got for reasons that had nothing to do with my accomplishments, but simply came to me because of where I was born, or the circumstances of my childhood.

Thus, when projects arose for renovating Ellis Island as a kind of museum to honor the achievements of immigrants who had come to the United States during the years when it was the Golden Door to the Promised Land, *Life* magazine decided to find some people who had actually come through Ellis Island. It meant finding old people, for Ellis Island had been shut down decades before.

I was one of the old people they found. On July 28, 1982, I was taken down to the lower tip of Manhattan (in a driving rainstorm, as it happened) and was ferried over to Ellis Island. It was the first time I had set foot on it since that time in 1923 when I arrived and got the measles to celebrate the fact. The buildings were in a state of shabbiest decay and I was photographed sitting rather glumly in the middle of one of them.

The photograph appeared in *Life*, and everyone who saw it asked, "Why are you wearing rubbers?"

And I said, "Because it was raining heavily. Why else?"

A couple of years later, I was awarded some sort of medal or other for having (a) been an immigrant and (b) done something to make the United States not too sorry that I had arrived.

Perhaps the most surprising honor I got was to have my name inscribed on a slab of rock on a pathway in the Brooklyn Botanic Gardens. I was not the only one, of course. As one went along that path, there was rock after rock with the names of Brooklyn-born people who had become famous. (Mae West's name was there, for instance.)

When I was told my name was being added, I said I hadn't been born in Brooklyn. They told me that since I had been brought up in Brooklyn from the age of three and had been educated in Brooklyn public schools, that was enough . . .

On June 8, 1986 . . . I was asked to say a few words, but the real star present was Danny Kaye, whom I had always admired, and whom I now met for the first and only time. He called me *payess* (Yiddish for "sideburns") and then gave a charming talk.

However, he looked ill and, as a matter of fact, he died on March 3, 1987, only nine months later, at the age of seventy-four.

By the time I was sixty-seven years old, it might have seemed I had everything I could possibly want as far as the science-fiction world was concerned. I had Hugos, Nebulas, and best-sellers. I was one of the Big Three. I was treated as a monument at science-fiction conventions, and young newcomers to the game of science-fiction writing viewed me with awe. Thanks to my prominent white sideburns I was routinely recognized on the street and I was sure that, if I traveled, I would find myself recognized all over the world. I was as popular in places like Japan, Spain, and the Soviet Union as I was in the United States, and my books have been translated into over forty languages.

What remained?

One thing! In 1975, the Science Fiction Writers of America instituted a very special Nebula to be called the Grand Master Award. This was to go to some science-fiction superstar at a Nebula Awards banquet for his life's work, rather than for any single production.

The first one went, inevitably, to Robert Heinlein. There was no argument about that. He was the general favorite among science-fiction readers and he had pioneered the advance of our kind of science fiction into the slicks and the motion pictures. He was respected outside science fiction as well as inside . . .

Other Grand Master Awards were handed out in later years . . . all were well deserved . . . what's more, all were well stricken in years but had fortunately survived to receive the honor. In fact, I can only think of two people in magazine science fiction who would surely have deserved the honor but who had died before 1975. They were E. E. Smith and John W. Campbell himself . . .

The awards were not given every year. In the eleven years from 1975 to 1986 inclusive, only seven awards had been handed out. All seven Grand Masters were older than I was, and all had begun publishing in the 1930s or 1940s, so I had no quarrel with their getting the awards. Of the writers that remained, two worthy candidates I could think of that were older than I were Lester del Rey and Frederik Pohl, and that might delay my turn anywhere from two to four years.

I was nervous about that. I was having a rash of medical problems that did not fill me with much confidence as to my chance of surviving three or four years, and I certainly didn't want people to go about saying, "We should have given him a Grand Master Award before he died." A fat lot of good that would have done me.

It may sound rather greedy of me to hunger for the award, but I'm human too. I wanted it. I honestly thought I deserved it. However, I kept my hunger entirely within myself. In no way did I campaign for it, and by no word or deed did I ever indicate openly that I was interested.

But the time came at last, and I was still alive. On May 2, 1987, at the Nebula Awards banquet, I received my Grand Master Award. I was the eighth Grand Master and all of us were still alive, a point I made gleefully in my acceptance speech. (It was the last opportunity to say that, alas, for in the next year two of the Grand Masters, Robert Heinlein and Clifford Simak, died . . .)

In my acceptance speech, incidentally, I said we all looked for special distinction. Thus, though Robert Heinlein was the first Grand Master, Arthur Clarke was the first British Grand Master, and Andre Norton was the first woman Grand Master. I, although the eighth all told, was the first Jewish Grand Master.

After the banquet, Robert Silverberg . . . said, "Now that you're the first Jewish Grand Master, where does that leave me?" . . .

I said to him, "Bob, you will be the first *handsome* Jewish Grand Master," and he broke into a smile and was pleased.

Thirty-Eight.
WORKING ON
IN GATHERING SHADOWS

Harper & Row asked me to write a history of science, year by year . . . [including] in each year something of what was going on in the world outside science. That filled me with excitement. It would be a kind of *history* book, a general one, and not just one about science.

With my novels going at a hot pace, I couldn't start it, but I kept thinking about it, and dreaming about it.

I was going up in my apartment elevator one day when a young man said to me that he had read the Foundation series and he always wanted to know what had happened to Hari Seldon when he was young and how he had come to invent psychohistory (the fictional science that underlies the series).

I seized on that, and when the time came to sign contracts for new novels, I suggested that I go back in time and write *Prelude to Foundation*, which would deal with events that took place fifty years before the first book in the series and with Hari Seldon and the establishment of psychohistory. . . . It was published in 1988.

[In the meantime] I cast aside caution and began the book I called *Science Timeline*. Eventually Harper & Row gave it the ungainly, but descriptive name of *Asimov's Chronology of Science and Technology*. I have rarely had so much fun in my life.

I tried to write it along with *Nemesis* when it came time to do that novel, alternating the two. I used *Nemesis* as a bribe and the *Chronology* as a reward. If I managed to do ten pages of *Nemesis*, I felt free to do twenty of the *Chronology*, and so on. The advantage was all on the side of the *Chronology*. I knew that *Nemesis* would make ten times as much money as the *Chronology*, but my heart was with non-fiction . . .

[*Nemesis*] was placed closer to our time than was true of either the robot novels or the Foundation novels. It dealt with the colonization of a satellite that circled a Jovian-type planet that, in turn, circled a red-dwarf star. My protagonist was a teenaged girl and I also had two strong adult women characters. I placed considerably more emotion in the novel than was customary for me.

[Since the publication of *Asimov's Biographical Encyclopedia of Science and Technology* in 1972] I developed the habit of keeping my eye on the *New York Times* obituary page . . . I had to know when one of the still-living scientists dealt with in the final pages of the book died. I would then enter the exact day and place of death in a special copy of the book I used for that purpose. This kept me ready for future editions, and I have followed the system ever since.

I began reading the obituaries with a sense of detachment, for death, of course, was something for old people. I was only fifty-two years old when I began my obituary reading and death still seemed far away. However, as I grew older, the obituary page slowly became at once more important to me and more threatening. It has become morbidly obsessive with me now.

I suspect this happens to a great many people. Ogden Nash wrote a line that I have always remembered: "The old men know when an old man dies."

With the years, that line has become ever more poignant to me. After all, an old person to one who has known him for a long time is not an "old person" but is much more likely to be thought of as the younger person who inhabits our memory, vigorous and vibrant. When an old person dies who has been a part of your life, it is part of your youth that dies. And though you survive yourself, you must watch death take away the world of your youth, little by little.

There may be some morbid satisfaction in being a last survivor, but is it so much better than death to be the last leaf on the tree, to find yourself alone in a strange and hostile world where no one remembers you as a boy, and where no one can share with you the memory of that long-gone world that glowed all about you when you were young?

Thoughts like that would beset me, now and then, after I passed my sixty-ninth birthday on January 2, 1989, and knew myself to be within a year of the biblical threescore years and ten.

Mind you, I hadn't turned completely morbid. For the most part, I maintained my cheery and ebullient outlook on the world. I kept up my busy schedule of social get-togethers, speaking engagements, editorial conferences, and endless writing, writing, writing. But in the dead of night sometimes, when sleep wouldn't come, I might think of how few there remained who remembered, with me, how it all was in the beginning . . .

I don't expect to live forever, nor do I repine over that, but I am weak enough to want to be remembered forever.—Yet how few of those who have lived, even of those who have accomplished far more than I have, linger on in world memory for even a single century after their death.

This, as you see, verges dangerously on what is to me the most hated of sins—self-pity—and I fight it.

[Janet's note: Isaac always fought self-pity and fears of death. When much younger, he wrote in a letter] Of the five heaps of snow in my driveway, one is almost gone and two more are pretty sickly. That always makes me feel sad. I'm delighted to see the snow go, you understand, but I can't help empathizing with the heaps. I tend to personify them ever since I was a little kid. The snow (in my mind) was always fighting and eventually losing the fight with the sun.

Occasionally it would receive reinforcements from the heaven, but as March wore on, the retreats would be farther than the one before. The army would break into separate contingents and I would imagine them exhorting each other and keeping each other's courage up. I would even imagine the largest heap to be rather scornful of the others as faint-hearts giving in to the enemy and coming down in its pride to humiliating defeat . . .

Even now, mature and rational as I am, each morning I make a little round of inspection to view the army and feel the pang of sympathy for the defeated . . .

[I answered: "All things change—every thing trying to remain immutable is fighting a losing fight. All of which sounds very wise and doesn't explain why I get annoyed when things wear out, and walls need repainting, etc."]

[Isaac's reply to my letter] Fighting to stay alive is fighting the inevitable. The good fight has its own values. That it must end in irrevocable defeat is irrelevant.

[By 1989, Isaac was beginning to feel that irrevocable defeat was coming closer.]

[It was] difficult to bear up under the increasingly rapid drumfire of deaths that come with the passing years. [He lists many] And so it went. I held more and more passionately to the dwindling group of old friends who survived . . .

Unquestionably, twilight was drawing on and the shadows were gathering—and deepening.

These gloomy ruminations of mine; these sad thoughts of death and dissolution and of an approaching end; were not entirely the result of philosophic thought and of the bitter experience that came to me with the years. There was something more concrete than that. My physical health was deteriorating.

I would not be a good "denier" if I had admitted that deterioration and you can be sure I didn't admit it. Through the summer and fall of

1989, I stubbornly continued my accustomed course, pretending that I did not feel my years . . .

Of course, I kept up my writing . . . I also started *Forward the Foundation*, and helped with the novelization of "Nightfall." In addition I worked endlessly on my huge history book.

Yet all through that summer and autumn, I felt an unaccountable and increasing tendency to weariness. I walked slowly and with an effort. People commented on my loss of ebullience now and then, and, in embarrassment, I tried to be more lively, but only with an ever-increasing effort.

Indeed, I caught myself thinking, now and then, that it would be so pleasant simply to lie down and drift quietly off to sleep and not waken again. Such a thought was so alien to me that, whenever it occurred to me, I shoved it away in horror. I did so with a kind of double horror, in fact, for I could not help but think how Janet and Robyn would react, for one thing, and for another I realized, with complete consternation, that I would be leaving behind unfinished work.

But the thought kept returning.

Yet not a word of the gathering weariness managed to find its way into my diary. I refused to admit openly that it existed. Just the same, there was something wrong that I could not deny because [there were physical manifestations].

[He experienced more and more sickness and "wipeouts."]

All through that unhappy December [1989] I kept thinking "I'm so close, so close, but I won't make it to seventy." . . . What is so magic about seventy? The trouble is that Psalm 90:10 reads: "The years of our life are threescore and ten."

This has been taken, on biblical authority, to be the normal span of human life. Actually, it's not so. The average life span of human beings did not reach seventy over a large section of the population till well into the twentieth century. It took modern medicine and science to see to it that seventy is really the years of our life. But the Bible says seventy, and that figure became magic.

Comparatively early in life, I managed to have it ground into my brain that there was no disgrace in dying after seventy, but that dying before seventy was "premature" and was a reflection on a person's intelligence and character.

It was unreasonable, of course; quite irrational.

Still, I had reached sixty when, after my heart attack, I thought I might not. Then I reached sixty-five when, before my triple bypass, I thought I might not. And now seventy was within reach and I thought, "I won't make it." (It reminded me of the days in 1945 when I was racing to reach twenty-six before I could be drafted—and failed.)

January 2, 1990, finally dawned and I was seventy years old after all—officially. Janet, Robyn, and I had a celebration dinner at our Chinese restaurant and we had Peking duck. . . . I ate a small quantity only, for it had salt in it, so it was not exactly a happy birthday even though I was greatly relieved at having reached it.

I had come to a momentous decision. On January 11, 1990, I went to see Paul [his doctor, and], almost in tears, I made a rather long and eloquent speech, the tenor of which was that I didn't want to take tests, didn't want hospitalization, I didn't want anything. I just wanted to be allowed to die in peace, and not be made a football to be bounced from doctor to doctor while all of them experimented with me and began to employ more and more heroic measures to keep me alive.

I had reached seventy, I said, and it was no longer a disgrace to die.

[He was sent to the hospital anyway.]

My big problem came on January 16, which was the sixth day of my hospital stay. For months, Doubleday had been planning a party on that day to celebrate both my seventieth birthday and the fortieth anniversary of my first book, *Pebble in the Sky*. It was to be held at Tavern on the Green and it was, to my horror, to be black tie.

[He and I and his doctor conspired to get him out of the hospital for that evening. At Tavern on the Green] all my buddies from various publishing houses, all my pals from the Dutch Treat Club and the Trap Door Spiders, all my friends and neighbors, near and far, were waiting . . .

I launched into my talk. I discussed my earlier near-scrapes with death, going into full detail about my fantasy involving the Baker Street Irregulars at the time of my bypass and what a flash of disappointment I experienced on realizing that I had survived and would not get the applause a dead man would have gotten.

There was wild laughter and applause from everyone, of course, and the only negative comment I got was from Robyn [who said] "You may think it's funny to talk about dying, because you're crazy, but *I* don't think it is."

Well, everyone else laughed!

By 9 P.M., I was back in my room, feeling I had handled everything perfectly and no one in the hospital would know.

However, the *New York Times* knew about the party. It appeared in the paper the next day and everyone in the hospital apparently read it, so that I was lectured by the nurses. Lester del Rey (whose own condition wouldn't allow him to attend) called up and raved at me for doing it and endangering my life. All I could say was, "Lester! I didn't know you cared!" and that didn't seem to soothe him.

What bothered me most, though, was a matter involving my syndicated column. It was time to do it and the only way I could manage it was to choose a topic that required no reference material, write it out longhand, and then call the *Los Angeles Times* and read it into their recording machine.

I did exactly that, but when I called, I got a young woman at the paper who said to me, as soon as I announced my name, "Oh, you bad boy! Why did you sneak out of the hospital?"

It just about broke my heart. I couldn't even carry out an innocent little deception without the whole world knowing.

[He started the third volume of his autobiography while in the hospital.] By the time I was ready to leave the hospital I had written over 250 long pages in reasonably small printing. Not only did this keep me from going mad but it actually put me into a jovial and good-natured mood.

[Nevertheless] It was one miserable winter. They had to continue the intravenous drip for four weeks. Twice each day, material was dribbled through a heplock into my veins for an hour or two at a time.

Then, on February 15, the doctors came to me with further news. In view of the fact that no infection could be found [in the mitral valve], they did not think it wise to subject me to the operation and take a chance on further kidney damage with the heart-lung machine. Therefore, I would not have the operation to replace the leaking mitral valve. They said I could live with mitral regurgitation, that there was no chance that it would suddenly give way and kill me. At the most it would weaken further, my symptoms would get worse, and they would bring me in again for surgery.

On March 3, then, I was back at home and ready to renew my life—with a leaking valve and faulty kidneys. The doctors warned me against involvement in anything beyond my strength, but they agreed that writing (even to the extent that I wrote) was not physically strenuous and that I could continue.

[Isaac ended his autobiography with a chapter called "New Life." He had been told he might live another three or four years.]

It's not really a new life I have returned to, for I am doing my best to make it as much like my old life as possible. But it's new in that it is considerably modified, and for the worse, I suppose. I am a septuagenarian now, with a leaky heart valve and imperfect kidneys.

[He recounted some of the pleasant things he'd done after leaving the hospital, and mentioned the premature and sudden death of an old friend.]

My turn will come too, eventually, but I have had a good life and I have accomplished all I wanted to, and more than I had a right to expect I would.

So I am ready.

But not *too* ready . . . I shall hope.

EPILOGUE
by Janet Asimov
(Revised as of 2001)

One of the deepest desires of a human being is to be known and understood. Hamlet instructs Horatio to tell his story. A child asks to be told a story and is most thrilled when the one he hears has a character like himself in it.

In May 1990, Isaac ended the last volume of his autobiography with the word "hope." He knew, however, that he did not have long to live. He hoped for several more years, but his heart and kidney failure worsened and he died on April 6, 1992.

Within a day of Isaac's death, Arthur Ashe revealed that he had contracted HIV infection from a blood transfusion during surgery. The resulting public shock and publicity made it difficult to reveal that Isaac had also died of the consequences of HIV infection.

When Isaac had his bypass surgery on December 14, 1983, very little was known about HIV. The blood used for transfusion was not taken from him, earlier, or from known donors. Furthermore, screening tests for HIV contamination of blood were not done.

The surgery itself went well. He woke up from anesthesia with his brain functioning perfectly, and was happy because he'd been worried about the known possibility of brain damage from bypass surgery. He even tested his mental prowess by making up a ribald limerick for his internist.

The next day he had a high fever. He felt so terrible that he kept telling me he was going to die. The doctors were puzzled. They worried about some unknown postsurgical inflammation. Within a few days, he seemed well. Only years later, in hindsight, did we realize that the posttransfusion HIV infection had taken hold.

The now well-known quiescent period of HIV set in. Isaac went back to work and was his usual happy self. In the spring of 1984, however, he did have ankle edema, corrected by diuretics and attributed to the removal of the large leg vein used for the bypass. He also had blood test results (like an abnormally high sedimentation rate) that the doctors could not understand.

The water retention increased and generalized. By 1987, results on blood tests indicated that his kidneys were not functioning normally. By 1989, as he stated in the autobiography which I have recorded, he knew he was not well. In fact, he admitted that he was seriously sick.

He had developed a heart murmur. After several tests, he was told that he had a serious problem with the mitral valve of his heart. He was given intravenous antibiotics and was scheduled for heart valve surgery.

For several years I had been reading about HIV and worrying that some of Isaac's symptoms could be due to it, thanks to those blood transfusions during surgery in 1983. I wanted Isaac to be tested for HIV, but it was not done until February 1990, shortly before he was to have valve surgery.

After the test was done, the doctor told us that Isaac had tested positive for HIV, with only half the normal number of T cells. The surgery was canceled.

From February 1990 until he died in April 1992, he and I and Robyn (and a few others) lived with the knowledge that Isaac had AIDS. The doctors advised against going public on this, and Isaac went along with them.

In those days there seemed to be much fear of and prejudice against AIDS patients. I heard even well-educated people say they would be afraid to touch an AIDS patient (although you can't get AIDS that way). Some people said that they would not even want to be in the same room with an AIDS patient, or touch anything he touched (including phones).

The doctors told me that, although I tested negative several times, there would be prejudice against me. In spite of my misgivings about hiding truth, I agreed to keep the matter secret.

They were, frankly, horrible years—from 1989, when he was very seriously ill, to his hopelessly sick last years (from 1990 to 1992) when we also lived with the knowledge that he had AIDS. He received the best of care possible at the time, but only now are AIDS patients living longer and better thanks to combinations of new drugs.

Well, those years were not entirely horrible. He managed to complete first or final drafts of many important works. The third volume of his autobiography was finished *after* he knew his true diagnosis.

As I said in the first version of this epilogue, Isaac wanted the autobiography published right away, so that he could see the book before he died, but this was not done.

Isaac's 1990 diary records May 30 as the day he finished typing the final copy of the autobiography. He writes, "It is now all ready to hand in, 125 days after I started it. Not many can write 235,000 words in that time, while doing other things as well." I would add—and while coping with terminal illness.

He managed to do several enjoyable things, like going to Washington, D.C., for a luncheon at the Soviet Embassy. The trip made Isaac feel, for a while, that he was back from illness and part of life again. He was particularly happy about meeting Gorbachev because the ending of the Cold War gave hope to the world. Isaac strongly believed all peoples should work together for the common good of humanity.

There were other special occasions—like going to the Rensselaerville Institute "Asimov Seminar," where he sang and explained all the verses of "The Star Spangled Banner."

And in spite of increasing weakness, he wrote every day until almost the end. Writing *Asimov Laughs Again* lifted his spirits, but (in April 1991) he concluded the manuscript with the words, "I'm afraid that my life has just about run its course and I don't really expect to live much longer. . . . In my life, I have had Janet and I have had my daughter, Robyn, and my son, David; I have had a large number of good friends; I have had my writing and the fame and fortune it has brought me; and no matter what happens to me now, it's been a good life, and I am satisfied with it.

"So please don't worry about me, or feel bad. Instead I only hope that this book has brought you a few laughs."

After he finished and turned in *Asimov Laughs Again*, he became more withdrawn. The handwriting in his diary became more and more deteriorated, and there were fewer, shorter entries—until the summer of 1991, when he stopped.

When typing was difficult, he dictated to me, especially his last piece for the *Magazine of Fantasy and Science Fiction*. It was a poignant "Farewell—Farewell" to all his "Gentle Readers." In it he said, "It has always been my ambition to die in harness with my head face down on a keyboard and my nose caught between two of the keys, but that's not the way it worked out."

The last months were filled with hospitalizations and physical deterioration. It is almost true—as I said in the first epilogue—that he did not suffer pain.

He probably died, not of infection due to the destruction of his immune system, but of terminal heart and kidney failure, causing a kind of merciful apathy.

He slept a great deal, but there were many unpleasant symptoms and disabilities, and in the last hospital days, he did often suffer when he was awake.

His sense of humor surfaced at times. The day before he died, Robyn, his brother Stan, and Stan's wife Ruth were in Isaac's hospital room when I said to him, "Isaac, you're the best there is."

Isaac smiled and shrugged. Then, with a mischievous lift of his eyebrows, he nodded yes, and we all laughed.

The next day he seemed to be in pain, especially when trying to breathe. Medication eased the pain and may have made it possible for him to die peacefully late that night.

Robyn and I were there when he died, holding his hands and telling him we loved him. His last complete sentence was: "I love you too."

Many years ago, Isaac wrote in a letter that he had seen the movie *Lili* and cried during the dream ballet:

"I know why it makes me cry. It's like life—people go one by one and you say goodbye and goodbye, until the time comes when it's your turn to go and they say goodbye. I guess the important thing is Carpe Diem—seize the day—and then let it go."

He also said, "the soft bonds of love are indifferent to life and death. They hold through time so that yesterday's love is part of today's and the confidence in tomorrow's love is also part of today's. And when one dies, the memory lives in the other, and is warm and breathing. And when both die—I almost believe, rationalist though I am—that somewhere it remains, indestructible and eternal, enriching all of the universe by the mere fact that once it existed."

And he also wrote: "At various times of life, we find ourselves with a handful of blocks of different sizes and shapes, out of which we can build some aspect of life, and it behooves us to build it as beautifully as we can . . ."

Writing what he wanted to write was an act of joy for him, during which he relaxed and forgot his troubles. *Forward the Foundation* was hard on him, because in killing Hari Seldon he was also killing himself, yet he transcended the anguish.

He told me what the end of *Forward the Foundation* was going to be—that as Hari Seldon dies, the equations of the future swirl around him, and he knows he is looking into the future that he himself has discovered and helped to bring about.

Knowing his own death was imminent, Isaac said, "I don't feel self-pity because I won't be around to see any of the possible futures. Like Hari Seldon, I can look at my work all around me and I'm comforted. I know that I've studied about, imagined, and written down many possible futures—it's as if I've been there."

Once when Isaac and I talked about old age, illness, and death, he said it wasn't so terrible to get sick and old and to die if you've been part of life completing itself as a pattern. Even if you don't make it to old age, it's still worthwhile; there's still pleasure in that vision of being part of the pattern of life—especially a pattern expressed in creativity and shared in love.

He also said, "I suppose there are people who are so 'lucky' that they are not touched by phantoms and are not troubled by fleeting memory and know not nostalgia and care not for the ache of the past and are spared the feather-hit of the sweet, sweet pain of the lost, and I am sorry for them—for to weep over what is gone is to have had something prove worth the weeping."

When I weep—and I still do—I try to remember that Isaac was right when he said, "It's been a good life."

THE END

Appendix A.
ESSAY 400—
A WAY OF THINKING
by Janet and Isaac Asimov

Science is much more than a body of knowledge. It is a way of thinking.

—Carl Sagan

INTRODUCTORY NOTE

Isaac had written 399 science essays for *Fantasy and Science Fiction* but was too ill to write the 400th. This troubled him deeply, so—because I was already writing one of his regular science columns—I suggested that we write the 400th essay together, recording his thoughts about science and science writing. Unfortunately, the essay was never written.

Because I still want that 400th essay, I've finally put one together from our discussions and letters.

My comments are marked by brackets, and this "essay" is not polished because the letters were not. Long ago, he wrote me about this: "My letters to you are first drafts; straight as it comes and completely unpolished; and I leave it to you to get past the maunderings and potterings and see my meaning. In fact, it is very wonderful to be able to leave it to you to do that—in full confidence and trust."

I leave it to Isaac's readers, in full confidence and trust.

[From a commencement speech] Science with all its faults has brought education and the arts to more people—a larger percentage—than has ever existed before science. In that respect it is science that is the great humanizer. And, if we are going to solve the problems that science has brought us, it will be done by science and in no other way.

[Telling me what he said in a letter to Carl Sagan] The brotherhood of science is one of the few ideals that transcends national boundaries and points the way to possible safety amid the dangers that threaten us.

[This is the quote from a published work—*I. Asimov: A Memoir* (which Isaac had called "Scenes of Life") published by Doubleday in 1994] . . . science *can't ever* explain everything and I can give you the reasons for that decision . . . I believe that scientific knowledge has fractal properties; that no matter how much we learn, whatever is left, however small it may seem, is just as infinitely complex as the whole was to start with. That, I think, is the secret of the universe.

[Helping people understand science had its difficulties. This is from a letter about an article he'd written for *Playboy* and which they wanted revised.] . . . I wrote a letter to *Playboy* suggesting that in my opinion they ought to do the article I sent them as it stands because I wasn't going to rewrite it into a silly sensational piece of the kind they were asking for. I explained that I had dedicated my life to educating the public and that science must not be viewed as a mysterious black box out of which came toys and goodies, for that way laymen would view scientists as a kind of lab-coated priesthood—and, eventually, fear and hate them. I couldn't connive at that view. I had to *explain* science and *Playboy* owed a duty to its public to have science explained, and if most of their readership would rather not trouble their rusty heads, they could look at the Playmate of the Month. That's what she was there for.—Anyway, it was a very stubborn and self-righteous letter and I haven't received any answer.

[In an article] I made fun of a reviewer who wanted less of a bang of statistics . . . and more of a moan of delight. I got a letter from a fan today who sympathized with me and who sent the following quotation from Alfred Noyes (you know, the *Highwayman* guy—which, by the way, turns out to be the favorite poem of Gene Roddenberry, and one he loves to recite thumpingly). I never came across the quotation and I think it is beautiful and I want to pass it on to you:

> Fools have said
> That knowledge drives out wonder from the world;
> They'll say it still, though all the dust's ablaze
> With miracles at their feet.

[About a critical letter] . . . from someone who says indignantly that if s.f. [science fiction] were scientifically accurate it wouldn't be s.f. and if she wants an education she would go to school. I scowled formidably and sent back a postcard saying, "There is a difference between fiction and ignorance. If you want to be ignorant, that's your business." I work so hard to educate and here are people who would rather be stupid.

[I don't know if the following is Isaac's or something he read, but he said it with fervor] Uncertainty that comes from knowledge (knowing what you don't know) is different from uncertainty coming from ignorance.

[About a talk he gave at a college] I traced the history of science and man (science and *ordinary* man, not science and scholars) through three stages. First there was the stage where science meant *nothing* to the man in the streets and he turned to his various religious leaders for help in protecting him against the universe. The turning point came (according to my thesis) with Franklin's invention of the lightning rod—the first victory of science over a menace to man which had till then seemed unavertable and which had, indeed, been considered the direct artillery of Zeus, Thor, and Yahveh.

And, I added impressively, when the average man saw lightning rods rising over the steeples of the great cathedrals of Europe, he could see with his own eyes that the priests themselves trusted in science rather than in their own holiness, and the battle was over right there. In the last two centuries, religion has retreated steadily before science. Also it led to nineteenth-century Utopianism with regard to science. Science was Good and could solve everything.

The fact that science was also Bad, I traced to 1915 and the development of gas warfare, the first time that the average man could see, with the shock of sudden recognition, that a pure development of science could be outrageously bad and without mitigating good.

Since then we have lived in an ambivalent society where science is both Good and Bad, where it poses us insuperable problems and dangers but where only it offers us the slightest hope of solution. I then looked into the future and pictured a possible ideal society in which work and risk were abolished and in which men slowly lost interest and declined in numbers while robots, who grew to be more and more manlike in appearance and ability, took over the work of the world.

Finally the last man was gone and only the robots, self-repairing and self-perpetuating, were left. And they puzzled over their dim memories of a Golden Age, as the centuries passed. Surely there had once been a race of demigods, who never had to work, who never suffered from disease, who did not die but who just fell asleep. How had all that been lost, and left their own race forever condemned to brutal labor?

One of the robots finally got an idea. "You see," he began, "there was this snake. . ."

And with that I ended the talk.

Would you like to know what writing problems are like to someone who never suffers from a writing block? Well, I am working on a book on physical biochemistry (of sorts) which involves chapter upon chapter upon chapter dealing with thermodynamics to begin with. Now I am using the historical approach and historically the second law of thermodynamics was discovered before the first law, *but* it makes much more sense to discuss the first law first. How then can I discuss the first law first and the second law second without giving the impression that I am zigzagging in time, which I am? See?

I've just written my article called "Selenize or Die," which briefly states my thesis that it is important [for scientists] to start a Moon colony, for they will show us how to *really* construct a managed economy and it will be on them that the brunt of further space exploration will fall. The peroration is "Why spend billions to place a man on the moon? If we don't, we may lose Earth. If we do, we may gain the universe. You couldn't ask for better odds."

[About giving a talk to a small audience that seemed to possess "unsullied gravity"] . . . since I don't prepare my talks I am guided entirely by audience reaction and not even consciously. I just automatically get more and more funny if the audience laughs . . . or less and less funny if the audience doesn't laugh. This time I got less and less funny and began an increasingly sober discussion of the possible usefulness of the Moon program, ending with the hope that the Moon colony would teach mankind how to live an ecologically sane existence, which brought me into the problems of overpopulation and overpollution and I grew very intense indeed . . . I spoke rapidly and pulled no punches and everyone left shaken up and saying they wouldn't be able to sleep that night.
They should have laughed.

[About an interview with a reporter for a European magazine] She whipped out a recorder and asked if I'd mind and I said "No." (What the heck, I'm not ashamed of anything I say.) Then I talked freely for two hours, giving her my feelings that . . . exploring space was something for all mankind and I hated to see it made a football for national rivalries, but perhaps that was the only way in this insane world of doing it at all; and I said that the Moon could never support enough men to make it a way of absorbing our population excess, and that the population explosion had to be solved by 2000 C.E. or else, and that we could not look for help from outer space but had to solve it by then right here on Earth; and that we had to stop polluting water and air and crowding other species recklessly off the face of the earth; and that extending the life span to 200 years would be of dubious benefit since the population would explode that much faster and extending the life span of a small minority of worthwhile people would create such a problem of "who is to decide" that I dreaded the thought of it; and that in an automated world, boredom would be a painful epidemic disease, and that the worst punishment would be to take a criminal off the "work-lists" for the number of years required to fit the crime.—All like that there.

[The reporter] kept saying enthusiastically, "You're the first American who has said such things to me." It made me nervous . . . people can spout official statements, . . . but I can say what I please; or at least I *will* say what I please.

[About the flap over whether or not flatworms automatically became conditioned if they ate pieces of other, conditioned worms] . . . I viewed this with severe suspicion (my "built-in doubter," you know) but finally decided that the only way it could happen was that RNA molecules (the key to memory) were incorporated whole into the cannibalistic worms since their organization was so low-key that they probably didn't require digestion when their food was so like themselves. To my delight, this turned out to be the most popular explanation by "real scientists." However, [a "very good scientist"] now insists that the work of the worm-runners can't be confirmed; that flatworms can't be conditioned. This gives me some sardonic amusement for, of course, John Campbell jumped on this at the very beginning, convinced that there was some explanation that would upset all of "orthodox science." (He is for anything far-out, not because he values the far-out, but because he wants to see the amateur—like himself—win over the professionals who wouldn't let him finish MIT.)

Also, have you read that the meteorite in which traces of life were discovered turns out to have been hoaxed a century ago? It is another example of the value of routine doubting. My thesis, in case you've forgotten, is not doubt-for-doubt's-sake, but doubt as a necessary barrier which the valid can overcome and the nonvalid cannot. The more a finding seems to destroy the basis of the scientific structure, the higher the barrier of doubt. Of course one must remember that "doubt" is *not* synonymous with "refusal to listen."

I was on a two-hour radio show and discussed the origin of life . . . talked learnedly and rapidly about the development through chance of nucleic acid molecules, of evolution by natural selection, etc. etc. etc. In the second hour the listeners phoned in questions, and some of them were from Fundamentalists who were simply furious with me. They quoted from the Bible and denounced me as someone who would steal the beauty of the universe (as though the conceptions of evolution and the long history of the stars was not infinitely more beautiful than the story of a petulant God making and destroying a pint-sized basketball of a world). One questioner, her voice shaking, would refer to me only as *that man* and addressed her questions (or rather her denunciations) only to the announcer. You would have been proud of me, though. I was calm and polite and smooth and in answering these people I kept saying, "[Scientists] neither back the Bible nor refute it. The Bible doesn't concern us one way or the other." Of course that reduced them to gibbering fury and the announcer would then cut them off.

The trouble is these people have a comfortable little world of miracles and literal-word-of-the-Bible and associate only with others who live in the same world and go to a tiny, Fundamentalist church on Sunday and (like the green peas in the pod who thought the whole universe was green) honestly think that all the world thinks as they do. They don't read books on the scientific view, or go to lectures, or attend courses—and then, they have the radio on and to their disbelief and horror, someone is spouting blasphemy at them and speaking of life originating by chance and mankind developing through the blind forces of natural selection and never mentioning God.

It's a wonder they don't break down at the mere fact that I am not being struck by lightning. Anyway, I think I brought some fresh air into the minds of a number who were not irrevocably wedded to ignorance. It was an interesting experience.

I have just received a very strange fan letter from a "Bible Fundamentalist" who says "After years of admiring you and your goodness in putting your knowledge into layman's terms so many of us could enjoy this great world of science with you, I am finally dropping these lines to tell you how much I appreciate what you have contributed to my faith in the literal word of God."

Dearest doctor—where have I gone wrong?

[In a letter I wrote to Isaac about an argument I'd had with a Fundamentalist relative: . . . Some people will always believe any insane system if it happens to fit their needs enough, especially if their needs are very neurotic . . . but fewer people would be taken in if they got a thorough grounding in scientific principles in childhood. Every single child born in this age should have a rough idea of what scientific method is, so that their thinking runs along—at least vaguely—lines similar to those used by scientists when confronted with hypotheses, new data, new questions, etc. Not that scientists aren't prey to emotionalism and other forms of distorted thinking, but at least they have the *tools* of thinking which they *can* use if they are not too anxious and frightened. My cousin doesn't have these tools and there is no use arguing with him, because he has no adequate means of appraising your reasoning or his own.]

[Isaac's response] . . . You and I are alike children of Thales, for he was the first known rationalist; the first to attempt to explain the universe without calling upon the supernatural; the first to believe, *by faith*, that the workings of the universe could be understood by reason. We share the same heritage, you and I, and our ancestors are men who withstood persecution and derision, who labored under difficulties and often without any sort of appreciation, who were rarely enriched and often impoverished by their work. In writing my biographies [of great scientists], I was in a sense writing the story of our ancestors and was aware, as I was doing so, of a Mystic bond (well, I can think of no other word) that bound me to all those men of the past and to all the men of the time yet to come—those very, very few who are rationalists and who work at it.

A friend of mine commented idly that my book *The Human Brain* had made clear the meaning of EMF [electromotive force] for the first time. As soon as I could get hold of the book myself I quickly looked up EMF in the index and turned to the page and read it, with great delight; feeling that I was sharing a learning experience.

How sad it is that for one reason or another (social, personal, philosophical. I don't know—*you're* the psychiatrist) learning usually becomes associated with pain, work, and boredom so that as soon as school is over and enforced learning put to an end, the average person thankfully puts it all behind and proceeds to forget whatever he or she has learned, above the barest minimum of reading, writing, and third-grade arithmetic. (Really, for most people, there is no way of telling from their conversation or work that they have ever progressed beyond the third grade.) But I am not saying this to criticize; but rather to sympathize; for the loss is theirs, not mine.

It is not even *knowing* that really adds a joy to life, but the ability and eagerness to *learn*. For instance . . . [A friend's astronomy article] works out calculations that are of only minimal interest to me; but what does stay with me is the idea of Earth and Moon as two islands in the empty volume of a single body circling the Sun. It's just a way of looking at matters that never occurred to me but which fascinates me now that it has been put into my mind. It adds to my picture of the universe; it gives me all the pleasure of new knowledge that a poem might give to one of literary bent or a sudden revelation might give to one of mystical bent.

I am now writing an *F&SF* article on . . a subject I do not understand very well, but by the time I have written the article, I *will* understand it. In fact, I sometimes think my articles are a vast scheme of self-education. It works, too. There is nothing like writing an article on a subject for forcing yourself to think that subject through clearly.

All that is, has developed out of the random application of the laws of the universe, in my belief. I find the hypothesis of a directing intelligence to be more implausible than the hypothesis of a nondirecting random process that just happens to be here at this point in time. It might have been somewhere else, but it happens to be here. . .

. . . We must distinguish between scientific knowledge and all knowledge. Scientific knowledge is only one subspecies of the genus. It is knowledge gained in a particular way. There is knowledge gained in other ways. For instance, a young man in love *knows* that his young woman is the most wonderful one in the world. He doesn't measure her in any way; he knows by a reaction in himself that is indescribable, let alone measurable.

[About a fan letter] He responds to my recent article in which I take off on mystical explanations of the universe. The fan points out that the Sun corresponds to the brain; the nine planets to the nine major openings in the body (two eyes, two ears, two nostrils, mouth and, I presume, urethra and anus—the young man, apparently, having never looked closely at the feminine urethra and environs, completely missed a tenth opening, in the female at least), the asteroids (as an exploded planet) to the umbilicus, as an opening that once was but is no longer (Hmm, could the asteroids signify that tenth opening, broken up to indicate it is present in only one sex?). He also maintains that if we could count all the asteroids, comets, and smaller bodies these would correspond exactly to the number of pores in the skin—the minor openings.

I am sending back a postcard saying "Excellently reasoned! And as the umbilicus is in the middle of the body, so is the asteroid belt in the middle of the solar system."

[About a review of one of his science books] I sat down and wrote a perfectly furious letter . . . I pointed out that facts were facts and that I was shocked to know that he favored altering facts to fit theory and that this worried me because in the same issue *he* had an article favoring the widespread use of pesticides and I wasn't sure it was safe to listen to him. . .

After I wrote the letter, and addressed an airmail envelope and sealed the envelope, I found my fury evaporating. I reread the review and found it was stupid but not as evil as I had thought. He had even used the adjective "interesting" at one point so that the review was not solidly bad. So now I have to nerve myself to tear up an envelope with a perfectly good stamp on it.

PS I've just torn it up.

[He loved Benjamin Franklin] . . . Just the other day I learned something new about him. During the American Revolution, Captain Cook was engaged in his phenomenal sweeps across the Pacific Ocean. He was the first of the great modern scientific explorers, searching not for gold, trade, or colonies but for knowledge. In those days, American privateers were scouring the seas looking for British craft to sink out of a little bit of patriotism and a whole lot of love of loot. Captain Cook, however, went untouched and undisturbed, officially protected against harm by the American revolutionaries, at the advice and insistence of Benjamin Franklin.

Franklin quite well realized that the search for knowledge (of the universe by scientists, of man's senses and emotions by writers and artists, of man's ethics and behavior by psychologists, philosophers, and—ugh—theologians) was mankind's highest purpose in life and was what made man man and not merely another animal. Most of all he realized, and made the American government realize, that it stood even higher than purely national interest.

We're living in a time when science has made "purely national interest" completely obsolete, only not enough of us realize it.

The thing that gets me is that people are ready to consider scientists evil for their part in the bomb, but scientists are those who have rebelled against the bomb (not all of them, of course) and fought against it. It was the politicians that actually made the decision to use it, and the military that used it—and where is a single politician or military man who has ever regretted publicly his part in the atomic bomb and its use? It is my theory that the type of mind which is today drawn to science, which in ancient times was drawn to philosophy, in medieval times to theology—is not only the best mind but the goodest mind. (Which, of course, does not mean that there are not rats in the ranks of science.)

[About an old science-fiction movie] Earth *can't* leave its orbit and swirl toward the Sun as a result of anything, anything, anything that happens on Earth. An external force must be applied. Earth can be blown into tiny pieces as a result of actions on Earth and some of the pieces may hurtle toward the Sun, but then an equivalent mass must hurtle in the opposite direction and the center of gravity of all the pieces will continue to move majestically about the Sun just as it is doing. Damn it, not to know this (and nobody in the movie capital does) is to be pre-Galilean. It is equivalent in the artistic world of saying that Mozart wrote *Gotterdammerung*. And it's no use saying, "Oh, well, the stupid jerks who watch the picture won't know the difference and wouldn't care if they did." In this present world, scientific illiteracy is a sin and anyone who encourages the spread of scientific illiteracy is a criminal.

. . . A lot of good it does us to try to teach legitimate physics in the schools, when the movies do things that prove they never heard of the conservation of angular momentum.

[About vandalism and terrorism] The whole world is being burned down or torn up or broken to pieces and people don't care. I have reached the point where I can almost hope that the death rate goes up quickly, *very* quickly, with maximum damage to humanity and minimum damage to the rest of the animal kingdom and the inanimate environment so that the old planet has a chance to recover. I am becoming misanthropic. Individual human beings are becoming monsters incapable of any kind of motive except that of grabbing what they can from the universal wreckage.

You must not use the phrase "nineteenth-century mechanists" as though it were a dirty word. The nineteenth-century mechanists were a heck of a lot closer to the mark than were their competitors, the vitalists, the theologians, and the mystics. By a "mechanist" I mean someone who thinks that the behavior of the universe can be interpreted through a series of general statements which we can call "laws of nature." That the universe and its component parts always behave so as to agree with the laws of nature and cannot disobey. This negates any thought of "free will" or a "directing intelligence" or a "god" if you want me to be blunt. It also implies that man, as part of the universe, lacks free will and cannot disobey the laws of nature. In short, the universe has characteristics in common with those we recognize in a machine.

This view of matters was emotionally offensive to many who felt bound and determined to consider themselves as more than machines, as equipped with free will and souls and all the rest. Consequently there was vast relief among many philosophers when it turned out that the nineteenth-century mechanists didn't know as much as they thought they did. (Nobody does, and the odd part is that nineteenth-century mechanists were a lot less arrogant in this respect than their opponents . . .)

The great addition that had to be made can be summed up in the one word "probability." The gas laws weren't as absolute as they seemed, once they were interpreted as the result of random motion of particles. They fuzzed out into probability. The uncertainty principle fuzzed everything out into probability.

This didn't mean the universe was not a machine. It simply meant that we didn't know as much about machines as we thought we did. The universe is governed by uncertainty in that we can't say yes or no, but so are all machines. We can set up mathematical expressions that precisely express the probabilities. We can't stop the fuzziness from being fuzzy, but we can describe the nature of the fuzziness. And the universe is *still* a machine; we just know more about machines, that's all. So I'm a twentieth-century mechanist—and a very thoroughgoing one—and I will not admit that there is any reason to suppose that everything in the universe cannot be satisfactorily explained on the basis of material things (with energy and matter both considered material).

In other words, in order for arrangement, order, interrelationship, and all such abstractions to have meaning, there must be order and arrangement of *certain material objects*. And you will never truly understand order and arrangement until you know what it is you are ordering and arranging.

For instance, it is quite possible to study symptoms and cures of diseases without knowing anything about the cause of the disease. Great successes can be achieved even. Vaccination and quinine were introduced when only superficial knowledge existed concerning smallpox and malaria. However, it was only after the germ theory of disease was introduced that medicine became more than empirical guesswork. Which was more important, good doctor, vaccination or germ theory? And, if it were possible by skimping on research into vaccination to have discovered the germ theory twenty years sooner, would that not have been beneficial in the long run?

The greatest discovery in biology was the theory of evolution which was essentially an order-and-arrangement discovery, yet it could not have been made unless and until the concept of species was introduced.

To be sure, life is more complex than the DNA molecule, just as matter is more complex than the atom, since matter includes all the interatomic forces. However, until the atom is understood, the inter-atomic forces will not be. The study of life will remain fuzzy and mystical until we know exactly what the fundamental basis of life is. *Then* we can turn to the order and arrangement that makes up all the higher subtlety of life and *finally* understand them. And if we skimp on the order and arrangement now in order to more quickly understand what we are ordering and arranging, we will get there faster in the long run.

Or, to give another example, consider that the great advances in chemistry were made in three stages. First, after the concept of element had been introduced; second, after the concept of the atom had been introduced; and third, after the concept of the electronically charged subatomic particle had been introduced. In no case do we say that sulfuric acid is *really* a mixture of elements (it isn't) or *merely* a conglomeration of atoms (it isn't) or *only* a mass of electrons and protons (it isn't). It is all these things plus organization, yes. But everytime we found out a little more about what was being organized, we found out a great deal more about the organization.

Now the traditional biologists can continue what they are doing, but all the problems they strive so painstakingly to solve will fall into place without difficulty when the DNA boys finally solve their molecular biology. And anything we can do to help along the DNA boys is for the benefit of the traditional biologists as well.

[After a similar argument, I agreed with him and he answered:] Thank you for trying to understand my commitment to the battle of Reason against Chaos, even when I show the battle at its worst by dashing suddenly at windmills. And I shall try, with all my heart, to understand your commitment to the battle of the Heart against all the Blindness and Indifference of the world . . . if at times we veer apart in the comparative stress we lay upon Heart and Mind, I know we will find our way back to the common battle of Good (of Heart and Mind) against the Evil (of Indifference and Ignorance).

[In the letter column of a reputable science journal] An argument rages between the traditionalists of biology and the molecular biologists. The traditionalists insist they are not vitalists and point out that the molecular biologists are biochemists by training and know virtually nothing of biology. The molecular biologists insist that the traditionalists *are* vitalists and stubbornly insist on the molecular biological road to ultimate biological truth.

At first blush, I am heart and soul with the molecular biologist, and yet as I think of it in the light of what I have learned [during our arguments], I find both sides incomplete. It is certainly truth that the average molecular biologist is a chemist rather than a biologist, but surely this gives the traditional biologist a wonderful chance. Let him learn molecular biology and adapt it to his own knowledge of traditional biology. Let the two merge; for all learning is one, and though there may be enemies among scholars there can be no enmity among scholarship.

As an example from history, when Pasteur (a chemist) advanced the germ theory of disease, the traditional doctors may well have pointed out that Pasteur was a microscopist who could see answers only in the microscopic world and that he knew nothing about medicine itself. True! But Robert Koch took Pasteur's bacteriological work and applied it to medicine in systematic fashion and revolutionized the art.

[He had complained about the price of fame, so I reminded him of what Henry Fielding said: "Do thou teach me not only to foresee but to enjoy; nay, even to feed on future praise. Comfort me by a solemn assurance that when the little parlour in which I sit at this instant shall be reduced to a worse furnished box, I shall be read with honour by those who never knew nor saw me, and whom I shall neither know nor see." Isaac replied:] How minds can meet and agree across the centuries! Isn't it much greater to be *Homo sapiens* than to be part of any artificial subclass thereof?

[About a fan's letter praising one of his books on science] I am absurdly gratified whenever someone tells me that the book has "reawakened a forgotten joy in learning" because that is what I try to do; that is my mission; only how do I go about saying so without sounding priggish and mawkish? We live in a society in which it is impermissible to be idealistic; where to wish to do good and to help one's fellowman in any way is so laughed out of court that those who most wish to do so (for the very selfish reason that it makes them feel good and gives meaning to their life) must clothe their actions in selfish terminology as I have just done and must live constantly in fear of being accused of hypocrisy or worse . . . Oh, Dr. J., it would be so much better to give than to receive, if it were two different actions; if it weren't that only by giving can one receive, and only by receiving that one can give. I want to give in so many ways, on so many levels, to so many recipients—love and joy and knowledge—and in so doing I find love and joy and knowledge, for in the most concrete of the three, knowledge, it is absolute truth that I have never written a book that didn't teach me far more than it taught any reader.

Appendix B.
Isaac's Personal Favorite
THE LAST QUESTION

The last question was asked for the first time, half in jest, on May 21, 2061, at a time when humanity first stepped into the light. The question came about as a result of a five-dollar bet over highballs, and it happened this way:

Alexander Adell and Bertram Lupov were two of the faithful attendants of Multivac. As well as any human beings could, they knew what lay behind the cold, clicking, flashing face—miles and miles of face—of that giant computer. They had at least a vague notion of the general plan of relays and circuits that had long since grown past the point where any single human could possibly have a firm grasp of the whole.

Multivac was self-adjusting and self-correcting. It had to be, for nothing human could adjust and correct it quickly enough or even adequately enough.—So Adell and Lupov attended the monstrous giant only lightly and superficially, yet as well as any men could. They fed it data, adjusted questions to its needs and translated the answers that were issued. Certainly they, and all others like them, were fully entitled to share in the glory that was Multivac's.

For decades, Multivac had helped design the ships and plot the trajectories that enabled man to reach the Moon, Mars, and Venus, but past that, Earth's poor resources could not support the ships. Too much energy was needed for the long trips. Earth exploited its coal and uranium with increasing efficiency, but there was only so much of both.

But slowly Multivac learned enough to answer deeper questions more fundamentally, and on May 14, 2061, what had been theory, became fact.

The energy of the sun was stored, converted, and utilized directly on a planet-wide scale. All Earth turned off its burning coal, its fissioning uranium, and flipped the switch that connected all of it to a small station, one mile in diameter, circling the Earth at half the distance of the Moon. All Earth ran by invisible beams of sunpower.

Seven days had not sufficed to dim the glory of it and Adell and Lupov finally managed to escape from the public function, and to meet in quiet where no one would think of looking for them, in the deserted underground chambers, where portions of the mighty buried body of Multivac showed. Unattended, idling, sorting data with contented lazy clickings, Multivac, too, had earned its vacation and the boys appreciated that. They had no intention, originally, of disturbing it.

They had brought a bottle with them, and their only concern at the moment was to relax in the company of each other and the bottle.

"It's amazing when you think of it," said Adell. His broad face had lines of weariness in it, and he stirred his drink slowly with a glass rod, watching the cubes of ice slur clumsily about. "All the energy we can possibly ever use for free. Enough energy, if we wanted to draw on it, to melt all Earth into a big drop of impure liquid iron, and still never miss the energy so used. All the energy we could ever use, forever and forever and forever."

Lupov cocked his head sideways. He had a trick of doing that when he wanted to be contrary, and he wanted to be contrary now, partly because he had had to carry the ice and glassware. "Not forever," he said.

"Oh, hell, just about forever. Till the sun runs down, Bert."

"That's not forever."

"All right, then. Billions and billions of years. Twenty billion, maybe. Are you satisfied?"

Lupov put his fingers through his thinning hair as though to reassure himself that some was still left and sipped gently at his own drink. "Twenty billion years isn't forever."

"Well, it will last our time, won't it?"

"So would the coal and uranium."

"All right, but now we can hook up each individual spaceship to the Solar Station, and it can go to Pluto and back a million times without ever worrying about fuel. You can't do *that* on coal and uranium. Ask Multivac, if you don't believe me."

"I don't have to ask Multivac. I know that."

"Then stop running down what Multivac's done for us," said Adell, blazing up, "It did all right."

"Who says it didn't? What I say is that a sun won't last forever. That's all I'm saying. We're safe for twenty billion years, but then what?" Lupov pointed a slightly shaky finger at the other. "And don't say we'll switch to another sun."

There was silence for a while. Adell], put his glass to his lips only occasionally, and Lupov's eyes slowly closed. They rested.

Then Lupov's eyes snapped open. "You're thinking we'll switch to another sun when ours is done, aren't you?"

"I'm not thinking."

"Sure you are. You're weak on logic, that's the trouble with you. You're like the guy in the story who was caught in a sudden shower and who ran to a grove of trees and got under one. He wasn't worried, you see, because he figured when one tree got wet through, he would just get under another one."

"I get it," said Adell. "Don't shout. When the sun is done, the other stars will be gone, too."

"Darn right they will," muttered Lupov. "It all had a beginning in the original cosmic explosion, whatever that was, and it'll all have an end when all the stars run down. Some run down faster than others. Hell, the giants won't last a hundred million years. The sun will last twenty billion years and maybe the dwarfs will last a hundred billion for all the good they are. But just give us a trillion years and everything will be dark. Entropy has to increase to maximum, that's all."

"I know all about entropy," said Adell, standing on his dignity.

"The hell you do."

"I know as much as you do."

"Then you know everything's got to run down someday."

"All right. Who says they won't?"

"You did, you poor sap. You said we had all the energy we needed, forever. You said 'forever.' "

It was Adell's turn to be contrary. "Maybe we can build things up again someday," he said.

"Never."

"Why not? Someday."

"Never."

"Ask Multivac."

"*You* ask Multivac. I dare you. Five dollars says it can't be done."

Adell was just drunk enough to try, just sober enough to be able to phrase the necessary symbols and operations into a question which, in words, might have corresponded to this: Will mankind one day without the net expenditure of energy be able to restore the sun to its full youthfulness even after it had died of old age?

Or maybe it could be put more simply like this: How can the net amount of entropy of the universe be massively decreased?

Multivac fell dead and silent. The slow flashing of lights ceased, the distant sounds of clicking relays ended.

Then, just as the frightened technicians felt they could hold their breath no longer, there was a sudden springing to life of the teletype attached to that portion of Multivac. Five words were printed: INSUFFICIENT DATA FOR MEANINGFUL ANSWER.

"No bet," whispered Lupov. They left hurriedly.

By next morning, the two, plagued with throbbing head and cottony mouth, had forgotten the incident.

Jerrodd, Jerrodine, and Jerrodette I and II watched the starry picture in the visiplate change as the passage through hyperspace was completed in its non-time lapse. At once, the even powdering of stars gave way to the predominance of a single bright marbledisk, centered.

"That's X-23," said Jerrodd confidently. His thin hands clamped tightly behind his back and the knuckles whitened.

The little Jerrodettes, both girls, had experienced the hyperspace passage for the first time in their lives and were self-conscious over the momentary sensation of inside-outness. They buried their giggles and chased one another wildly about their mother, screaming, "We've reached X-23—we've reached X-23—we've—"

"Quiet, children," said Jerrodine sharply. "Are you sure, Jerrodd?"

"What is there to be but sure?" asked Jerrodd, glancing up at the bulge of featureless metal just under the ceiling. It ran the length of the room, disappearing through the wall at either end. It was as long as the ship.

Jerrodd scarcely knew a thing about the thick rod of metal except that it was called a Microvac, that one asked it questions if one wished; that if one did not it still had its task of guiding the ship to a preordered destination; of feeding on energies from the various Subgalactic Power Stations; of computing the equations for the hyperspacial jumps.

Jerrodd and his family had only to wait and live in the comfortable residence quarters of the ship.

Someone had once told Jerrodd that the "ac" at the end of "Microvac" stood for "analog computer" in ancient English, but he was on the edge of forgetting even that.

Jerrodine's eyes were moist as she watched the visiplate. "I can't help it. I feel funny about leaving Earth."

"Why, for Pete's sake?" demanded Jerrodd. "We had nothing there. We'll have everything on X-23. You won't be alone. You won't be a pioneer. There are over a million people on the planet already. Good Lord, our greatgrandchildren will be looking for new worlds because X-23 will be overcrowded." Then, after a reflective pause, "I tell you, it's a lucky thing the computers worked out interstellar travel the way the race is growing."

"I know, I know," said Jerrodine miserably.

Jerrodette I said promptly, "Our Microvac is the best Microvac in the world."

"I think so, too," said Jerrodd, tousling her hair.

It *was* a nice feeling to have a Microvac of your own and Jerrodd was glad he was part of his generation and no other. In his father's youth, the only computers had been tremendous machines taking up a hundred square miles of land. There was only one to a planet. Planetary ACs they were called. They had been growing in size steadily for a thousand years and then, all at once, came refinement. In place of transistors, had come molecular valves so that even the largest Planetary AC could be put into a space only half the volume of a spaceship.

Jerrodd felt uplifted, as he always did when he thought that his own personal Microvac was many times more complicated than the ancient and primitive Multivac that had first tamed the Sun, and almost as complicated as Earth's Planetary AC (the largest) that had first solved the problem of hyperspatial travel and had made trips to the stars possible.

"So many stars, so many planets," sighed Jerrodine, busy with her own thoughts. "I suppose families will be going out to new planets forever, the way we are now."

"Not forever," said Jerrodd, with a smile. "It will all stop someday, but not for billions of years. Many billions. Even the stars run down, you know. Entropy must increase."

"What's entropy, daddy?" shrilled Jerrodette II.

"Entropy, little sweet, is just a word which means the amount of running-down of the universe. Everything runs down, you know, like your little walkie-talkie robot, remember?"

"Can't you just put in a new power-unit, like with my robot?"

"The stars *are* the power-units, dear. Once they're gone, there are no more power-units."

Jerrodette I at once set up a howl. "Don't let them, daddy. Don't let the stars run down."

"Now look what you've done," whispered Jerrodine, exasperated.

"How was I to know it would frighten them?" Jerrodd whispered back.

"Ask the Microvac," wailed Jerrodette I. "Ask him how to turn the stars on again."

"Go ahead," said Jerrodine. "It will quiet them down." (Jerrodette II was beginning to cry, also.)

Jerrodd shrugged. "Now, now, honeys. I'll ask Microvac. Don't worry, he'll tell us."

He asked the Microvac, adding quickly, "Print the answer."

Jerrodd cupped the strip of thin cellufilm and said cheerfully, "See now, the Microvac says it will take care of everything when the time comes so don't worry."

Jerrodine said, "And now, children, it's time for bed. We'll be in our new home soon."

Jerrodd read the words on the cellufilm again before destroying it: INSUFFICIENT DATA FOR MEANINGFUL ANSWER.

He shrugged and looked at the visiplate. X-23 was just ahead.

VJ-23X of Lameth stared into the black depths of the three-dimensional, small-scale map of the Galaxy and said, "Are we ridiculous, I wonder, in being so concerned about the matter?"

MQ-17J of Nicron shook his head. "I think not. You know the Galaxy will be filled in five years at the present rate of expansion."

Both seemed in their early twenties, both were tall and perfectly formed.

"Still," said VJ-23X, "I hesitate to submit a pessimistic report to the Galactic Council."

"I wouldn't consider any other kind of report. Stir them up a bit. We've got to stir them up."

VJ-23X sighed. "Space is infinite. A hundred billion Galaxies are there for the taking. More."

"A hundred billion is *not* infinite and it's getting less infinite all the time. Consider! Twenty thousand years ago, mankind first solved the problem of utilizing stellar energy, and a few centuries later, interstellar travel became possible. It took mankind a million years to fill one small world and then only fifteen thousand years to fill the rest of the Galaxy. Now the population doubles every ten years—"

VJ-23X interrupted. "We can thank immortality for that."

"Very well. Immortality exists and we have to take it into account. I admit it has its seamy side, this immortality. The Galactic AC has solved many problems for us, but in solving the problem of preventing old age and death, it has undone all its other solutions."

"Yet you wouldn't want to abandon life, I suppose."

"Not at all," snapped MQ-17J, softening it at once to, "Not yet. I'm by no means old enough. How old are you?"

"Two hundred twenty-three. And you?"

"I'm still under two hundred.—But to get back to my point. Population doubles every ten years. Once this Galaxy is filled, we'll have filled another in ten years. Another ten years and we'll have filled two more. Another decade, four more. In a hundred years, we'll have filled a thousand Galaxies. In a thousand years, a million Galaxies. In ten thousand years, the entire known Universe. Then what?"

VJ-23X said, "As a side issue, there's a problem of transportation. I wonder how many sunpower units it will take to move Galaxies of individuals from one Galaxy to the next."

"A very good point. Already, mankind consumes two sunpower units per year."

"Most of it's wasted. After all, our own Galaxy alone pours out a thousand sunpower units a year and we only use two of those."

"Granted, but even with a hundred per cent efficiency, we only stave off the end. Our energy requirements are going up in a geometric progression even faster than our population. We'll run out of energy even sooner than we run out of Galaxies. A good point. A very good point."

"We'll just have to build new stars out of interstellar gas."

"Or out of dissipated heat?" asked MQ-17J, sarcastically.

"There may be some way to reverse entropy. We ought to ask the Galactic AC."

VJ-23X was not really serious, but MQ-17J pulled out his AC-contact from his pocket and placed it on the table before him.

"I've half a mind to," he said. "It's something the human race will have to face someday."

He stared somberly at his small AC-contact. It was only two inches cubed and nothing in itself, but it was connected through hyperspace with the great Galactic AC that served all mankind. Hyperspace considered, it was an integral part of the Galactic AC.

MO-17J paused to wonder if someday in his immortal life he would get to see the Galactic AC. It was on a little world of its own, a spider webbing of force-beams holding the matter within which surges of sub-mesons took the place of the old clumsy molecular valves. Yet despite its sub-etheric workings, the Galactic AC was known to be a full thousand feet across.

MQ-17J asked suddenly of his AC-contact, "Can entropy ever be reversed?"

VJ-23X looked startled and said at once, "Oh, say, I didn't really mean to have you ask that."

"Why not?"

"We both know entropy can't be reversed. You can't turn smoke and ash back into a tree."

"Do you have trees on your world?" asked MQ-17J.

The sound of the Galactic AC startled them into silence. Its voice came thin and beautiful out of the small AC-contact on the desk. It said: THERE IS INSUFFICIENT DATA FOR A MEANINGFUL ANSWER.

VJ-23X said, "See!"

The two men thereupon returned to the question of the report they were to make to the Galactic Council.

Zee Prime's mind spanned the new Galaxy with a faint interest in the countless twists of stars that powdered it. He had never seen this one before. Would he ever see them all? So many of them, each with its load of humanity.—But a load that was almost a dead weight. More and more, the real essence of men was to be found out here, in space.

Minds, not bodies! The immortal bodies remained back on the planets, in suspension over the eons. Sometimes they roused for material activity but that was growing rarer. Few new individuals were coming into existence to join the incredibly mighty throng, but what matter? There was little room in the Universe for new individuals.

Zee Prime was roused out of his reverie upon coming across the wispy tendrils of another mind.

"I am Zee Prime," said Zee Prime. "And you?"

"I am Dee Sub Wun. Your Galaxy?"

"We call it only the Galaxy. And you?"

"We call ours the same. All men call their Galaxy their Galaxy and nothing more. Why not?"

"True. Since all Galaxies are the same."

"Not all Galaxies. On one particular Galaxy the race of man must have originated. That makes it different."

Zee Prime said, "On which one?"

"I cannot say. The Universal AC would know."

"Shall we ask him? I am suddenly curious."

Zee Prime's perceptions broadened until the Galaxies themselves shrank and became a new, more diffuse powdering on a much larger background. So many hundreds of billions of them, all with their immortal beings, all carrying their load of intelligences with minds that drifted freely through space. And yet one of them was unique among them all in being the original Galaxy. One of them had, in its vague and distant past, a period when it was the only Galaxy populated by man.

Zee Prime was consumed with curiosity to see this Galaxy and he called out: "Universal AC! On which Galaxy did mankind originate?"

The Universal AC heard, for on every world and throughout space, it had its receptors ready, and each receptor led through hyperspace to some unknown point where the Universal AC kept itself aloof.

Zee Prime knew of only one man whose thoughts had penetrated within sensing distance of Universal AC, and he reported only a shining globe, two feet across, difficult to see.

"But how can that be all of Universal AC?" Zee Prime had asked.

"Most of it," had been the answer, "is in hyperspace. In what form it is there I cannot imagine."

Nor could anyone, for the day had long since passed, Zee Prime knew, when any man had any part of the making of a Universal AC. Each Universal AC designed and constructed its successor. Each, during its existence of a million years or more accumulated the necessary data to build a better and more intricate, more capable successor in which its own store of data and individuality would be submerged.

The Universal AC interrupted Zee Prime's wandering thoughts, not with words, but with guidance. Zee Prime's mentality was guided into the dim sea of Galaxies and one in particular enlarged into stars.

A thought came, infinitely distant, but infinitely clear. "THIS IS THE ORIGINAL GALAXY OF MAN."

But it was the same after all, the same as any other, and Zee Prime stifled his disappointment.

Dee Sub Wun, whose mind had accompanied the other, said suddenly, "And is one of these stars the original star of Man?"

The Universal AC said, "MAN'S ORIGINAL STAR HAS GONE NOVA. IT IS A WHITE DWARF."

"Did the men upon it die?" asked Zee Prime, startled and without thinking.

The Universal AC said, "A NEW WORLD, AS IN SUCH CASES WAS CONSTRUCTED FOR THEIR PHYSICAL BODIES IN TIME."

"Yes, of course," said Zee Prime, but a sense of loss overwhelmed him even so. His mind released its hold on the original Galaxy of Man, let it spring back and lose itself among the blurred pin points. He never wanted to see it again.

Dee Sub Wun said, "What is wrong?"

"The stars are dying. The original star is dead."

"They must all die. Why not?"

"But when all energy is gone, our bodies will finally die, and you and I with them."

"It will take billions of years."

"I do not wish it to happen even after billions of years. Universal AC! How may stars be kept from dying?"

Dee Sub Wun said in amusement, "You're asking how entropy might be reversed in direction."

And the Universal AC answered: "THERE IS AS YET INSUFFI-CIENT DATA FOR A MEANINGFUL ANSWER."

Zee Prime's thoughts fled back to his own Galaxy. He gave no further thought to Dee Sub Wun, whose body might be waiting on a Galaxy a trillion light-years away, or on the star next to Zee Prime's own. It didn't matter.

Unhappily, Zee Prime began collecting interstellar hydrogen out of which to build a small star of his own. If the stars must someday die, at least some could yet be built.

Man considered with himself, for in a way, Man, mentally, was one. He consisted of a trillion, trillion, trillion ageless bodies, each in its place, each resting quiet and incorruptible, each cared for by perfect automatons, equally incorruptible, while the minds of all the bodies freely melted one into the other, indistinguishable.

Man said, "The Universe is dying."

Man looked about at the dimming Galaxies. The giant stars, spendthrifts, were gone long ago, back in the dimmest of the dim far past. Almost all stars were white dwarfs, fading to the end.

New stars had been built of the dust between the stars, some by natural processes, some by Man himself, and those were going, too. White dwarfs might yet be crashed together and of the mighty forces so released, new stars built, but only one star for every thousand white dwarfs destroyed, and those would come to an end, too.

Man said, "Carefully husbanded, as directed by the Cosmic AC, the energy that is even yet left in all the Universe will last for billions of years."

"But even so," said Man, "eventually it will all come to an end. However it may be husbanded, however stretched out, the energy once expended is gone and cannot be restored. Entropy must increase forever to the maximum."

Man said, "Can entropy not be reversed? Let us ask the Cosmic AC."

The Cosmic AC surrounded them but not in space. Not a fragment of it was in space. It was in hyperspace and made of something that was neither matter nor energy. The question of its size and nature no longer had meaning in any terms that Man could comprehend.

"Cosmic AC," said Man, "how may entropy be reversed?"

The Cosmic AC said, "THERE IS AS YET INSUFFICIENT DATA FOR A MEANINGFUL ANSWER."

Man said, "Collect additional data."

The Cosmic AC said, "I WILL DO SO. I HAVE BEEN DOING SO FOR A HUNDRED BILLION YEARS. MY PREDECESSORS AND I HAVE BEEN ASKED THIS QUESTION MANY TIMES. ALL THE DATA I HAVE REMAINS INSUFFICIENT."

"Will there come a time," said Man, "when data will be sufficient or is the problem insoluble in all conceivable circumstances?"

The Cosmic AC said, "NO PROBLEM IS INSOLUBLE IN ALL CONCEIVABLE CIRCUMSTANCES."

Man said, "When will you have enough data to answer the question?"

The Cosmic AC said, "THERE IS AS YET INSUFFICIENT DATA FOR A MEANINGFUL ANSWER."

"Will you keep working on it?" asked Man.

The Cosmic AC said, "I WILL."

Man said, "We shall wait."

The stars and Galaxies died and snuffed out, and space grew black after ten trillion years of running down.

One by one Man fused with AC, each physical body losing its mental identity in a manner that was somehow not a loss but a gain.

Man's last mind paused before fusion, looking over a space that included nothing but the dregs of one last dark star and nothing besides but incredibly thin matter, agitated randomly by the tag ends of heat wearing out, asymptotically, to the absolute zero.

Man said, "AC, is this the end? Can this chaos not be reversed into the Universe once more? Can that not be done?"

AC said, "THERE IS AS YET INSUFFICIENT DATA FOR A MEANINGFUL ANSWER."

Man's last mind fused and only AC existed—and that in hyperspace.

Matter and energy had ended and with it space and time. Even AC existed only for the sake of the one last question that it had never answered from the time a half-drunken computer programmer ten trillion years before had asked the question of a computer that was to AC far less than was a man to Man.

All other questions had been answered, and until this last question was answered also, AC might not release his consciousness.

All collected data had come to a final end. Nothing was left to be collected.

But all collected data had yet to be completely correlated and put together in all possible relationships.

A timeless interval was spent in doing that.

And it came to pass that AC learned how to reverse the direction of entropy.

But there was now no man to whom AC might give the answer of the last question. No matter. The answer—by demonstration—would take care of that, too.

For another timeless interval, AC thought how best to do this. Carefully, AC organized the program.

The consciousness of AC encompassed all of what had once been a Universe and brooded over what was now Chaos. Step by step, it must be done.

And AC said, "LET THERE BE LIGHT!"

And there was light—

Appendix C.
A BIBLIOGRAPHY OF WORKS BY ISAAC ASIMOV

FICTION

Science Fiction Novels

1950	*Pebble in the Sky* Doubleday
1951	*The Stars, Like Dust—* Doubleday
	Foundation Gnome
1952	*David Starr: Space Ranger* Doubleday
	Foundation and Empire Gnome
	The Currents of Space Doubleday
1953	*Second Foundation* Gnome
	Lucky Starr and the Pirates of the Asteroids Doubleday
1954	*The Caves of Steel* Doubleday
	Lucky Starr and the Oceans of Venus Doubleday
1955	*The End of Eternity* Doubleday
1956	*Lucky Starr and the Big Sun of Mercury* Doubleday
1957	*The Naked Sun* Doubleday
	Lucky Starr and the Moons of Jupiter Doubleday
1958	*Lucky Starr and the Rings of Saturn* Doubleday
1966	*Fantastic Voyage* Houghton Mifflin
1972	*The Gods Themselves* Doubleday
1982	*Foundation's Edge* Doubleday
1983	*Norby, the Mixed-up Robot* (with Janet Asimov) Walker
	The Robots of Dawn Doubleday

1984   *Norby's Other Secret* (with Janet Asimov) Walker
1985   *Norby and the Lost Princess* (with Janet Asimov) Walker
        Robots and Empire Doubleday
        Norby and the Invaders (with Janet Asimov) Walker
1986   *Foundation and Earth* Doubleday
        Norby and the Queen's Necklace (with Janet Asimov) Walker
1987   *Norby Finds a Villain* (with Janet Asimov) Walker
        Fantastic Voyage II: Destination Brain Doubleday
1988   *Prelude to Foundation* Doubleday
        Norby Down to Earth (with Janet Asimov) Walker
1989   *Nemesis* Doubleday
        Norby and Yobo's Great Adventure (with Janet Asimov) Walker
1990   *Norby and the Oldest Dragon* (with Janet Asimov) Walker
        Nightfall Doubleday
1992   *The Ugly Little Boy* Doubleday
1993   *Norby and the Court Jester* (with Janet Asimov) Walker
        Forward the Foundation Doubleday
        The Positronic Man Doubleday

Mystery Novels

1958   *The Death Dealers* Avon
1976   *Murder at the ABA* Doubleday

Science Fiction Short Stories and Short Story Collections

1950   *I, Robert* Gnome
1955   *The Martian Way and Other Stories* Doubleday
1957   *Earth Is Room Enough* Doubleday
1959   *Nine Tomorrows* Doubleday
1964   *The Rest of the Robots* Doubleday
1967   *Through a Glass, Clearly* New English Library
1968   *Asimov's Mysteries* Doubleday
1969   *Nightfall and Other Stories* Doubleday
1971   *The Best New Thing* World Publishing

1972   *The Early Asimov* Doubleday
1973   *The Best of Isaac Asimov* Sphere
1974   *Have You Seen These?* NESRAA
1975   *Buy Jupiter and Other Stories* Doubleday
        The Heavenly Host Walker
1976   *"The Dream," "Benjamin's Dream," and "Benjamin's*
            Bicentennial Blast" Private Print
        Good Taste Apocalypse
        The Bicentennial Man and Other Stories Doubleday
1981   *Three by Asimov* Tart
1982   *The Complete Robot* Doubleday
1983   *The Winds of Change and Other Stories* Doubleday
1985   *The Edge of Tomorrow* Tor
        It's Such a Beautiful Day Creative Education
1986   *The Alternate Asimovs* Doubleday
        Science Fiction by Asimov Davis
        The Best Science Fiction of Isaac Asimov Doubleday
        Robot Dreams Byron Press
1987   *Other Worlds of Isaac Asimov* Avenel
1989   *All the Troubles of the World* Creative Education
        Franchise Creative Education
        Robbie Creative Education
        Sally Creative Education
        The Asimov Chronicles Dark Harvest
1990   *Robot Visions* Byron Press

Fantasy Short Story Collection

1988   *Azazel* Doubleday

Mystery Short Story Collections

1974   *Tales of the Black Widowers* Doubleday
1976   *More Tales of the Black Widowers* Doubleday
1977   *The Key Word and Other Mysteries* Walker
1980   *Casebook of the Black Widowers* Doubleday

1983 *The Union Club Mysteries* Doubleday
1984 *Banquets of the Black Widowers* Doubleday
1985 *The Disappearing Man and Other Stories* Walker
1986 *The Best Mysteries of Isaac Asimov* Doubleday
1990 *Puzzles of the Black Widowers* Doubleday

Anthologies (Edited by Isaac Asimov)

1962 *The Hugo Winners* Doubleday
1963 *Fifty Short Science-fiction Tales* (with Groff Conklin) Collier
1966 *Tomorrow's Children* Doubleday
1971 *Where Do We Go from Here?* Doubleday
       The Hugo Winners, Vol. 2 Doubleday
1973 *Nebula Award Stories Eight* Harper
1974 *Before the Golden Age* Doubleday
1977 *The Hugo Winners*, Vol. 3 Doubleday
1978 *One Hundred Great Science-fiction Short-short Stories* (with
       Martin H. Greenberg and Joseph D. Olander) Doubleday
1979 *Isaac Asimov Presents the Great SF Stories, 1: 1939* (with Martin
       H. Greenberg) DAW Books
       Isaac Asimov Presents the Great SF Stories, 2: 1940 (with Martin
       H. Greenberg) DAW Books
       The Science Fictional Solar System (with Martin H. Greenberg and
       Charles G. Waugh) Harper & Row
       The Thirteen Crimes of Science Fiction (with Martin H. Greenberg
       and Charles G. Waugh) Doubleday
1980 *The Future in Question* (with Martin H. Greenberg and Joseph D.
       Olander) Fawcett
       Microcosmic Tales (with Martin H. Greenberg and Joseph D.
       Olander) Taplinger
       Isaac Asimov Presents the Great SF Stories, 3: 1941 (with Martin
       H. Greenberg) DAW Books
       Who Dun It? (with Alice Laurence) Houghton Mifflin
       Space Mail (with Martin H. Greenberg and Joseph D. Olander)
       Fawcett
       Microcosmic Tales (with Martin H. Greenberg and Joseph D.
       Olander) Taplinger

Isaac Asimov Presents the Great SF Stories, 4: 1942 (with Martin H. Greenberg) DAW Books

The Seven Deadly Sins of Science Fiction (with George G. Waugh and Martin H. Greenberg) Fawcett

The Future I (with Martin H. Greenberg and Joseph D. Olander) Fawcett

1981   *Isaac Asimov Presents the Great SF Stories, 5: 1943* (with Martin H. Greenberg) DAW Books

Catastrophes (with Martin H. Greenberg and Charles G. Waugh) Fawcett

Isaac Asimov Presents the Best SF of the 19th Century (with Charles G. Waugh and Martin H. Greenberg) Beaufort

The Seven Cardinal Virtues of Science Fiction (with Charles G. Waugh and Martin H. Greenberg) Fawcett

Fantastic Creatures (with Martin H. Greenberg and Charles G. Waugh) Franklin Watts

Raintree Reading Series I (with Martin H. Greenberg and Charles G. Waugh) Raintree

Miniature Mysteries (with Martin H. Greenberg and Joseph D. Olander) Taplinger

The Twelve Crimes of Christmas (with Carol-Lynn Rössel Waugh and Martin H. Greenberg) Avon

Isaac Asimov Presents the Great SF Stories, 6: 1944 (with Martin H. Greenberg) DAW Books

Space Mail II (with Martin H. Greenberg and Charles G. Waugh) Fawcett

1982   *Tantalizing Locked Room Mysteries* (with Charles G. Waugh and Martin H. Greenberg) Walker

TV: 2000 (with Charles G. Waugh and Martin H. Greenberg) Fawcett

Laughing Space (with J. O. Jeppson) Houghton Mifflin

Speculations (with Alice Laurance) Houghton Mifflin

Flying Saucers (with Martin H. Greenberg and Charles G. Waugh) Fawcett

Raintree Reading Series II (with Martin H. Greenberg and Charles G. Waugh) Raintree

Dragon Tales (with Martin H. Greenberg and Charles G. Waugh)
Fawcett

Big Apple Mysteries (with Carol-Lynn Rössel Waugh and Martin
H. Greenberg) Avon

Isaac Asimov Presents the Great SF Stories, 7: 1945 (with Martin
H. Greenberg) DAW Books

The Last Man on Earth (with Martin H. Greenberg and Charles G.
Waugh) Fawcett

Science Fiction A to Z (with Martin H. Greenberg and Charles G.
Waugh) Houghton Mifflin

Isaac Asimov Presents the Best Fantasy of the 19th Century (with
Charles G. Waugh and Martin H. Greenberg) Beaufort

Isaac Asimov Presents the Great SF Stories, 8: 1946 (with Martin
H. Greenberg) DAW Books

1983   *Isaac Asimov Presents the Great SF Stories, 9: 1947* (with Martin
H. Greenberg) DAW Books

Show Business Is Murder (with Carol-Lynn Rössel Waugh and
Martin H. Greenberg) Avon

Hallucination Orbit (with Martin H. Greenberg and Charles G.
Waugh) Farrar, Straus & Giroux

Caught in the Organ Draft (with Martin H. Greenberg and Charles
G. Waugh) Farrar, Straus & Giroux

The Science Fiction Weight-Loss Book (with George R. R. Martin
and Martin H. Greenberg) Crown

*Isaac Asimov Presents the Best Horror and Supernatural Stories of
the 19th Century* (with Charles G. Waugh and Martin H.
Greenberg) Beaufort

Starships (with Martin H. Greenberg and Charles G. Waugh)
Fawcett

Isaac Asimov Presents the Great SF Stories, 10: 1948 (with Martin
H. Greenberg) DAW Books

The Thirteen Horrors of Halloween (with Carol-Lynn Rössel
Waugh and Martin H. Greenberg) Avon

Creations (with George Zebrowski and Martin H. Greenberg) Crown

Wizards (with Martin H. Greenberg and Charles G. Waugh) NAL

Those Amazing Electronic Machines (with Martin H. Greenberg
and Charles G. Waugh) Franklin Watts

Computer Crimes and Capers (with Martin H. Greenberg and
Charles G. Waugh) Academy

Intergalactic Empires (with Martin H. Greenberg and Charles G.
Waugh) NAL

Machines That Think (with Patricia S. Warrick and Martin H.
Greenberg) Holt, Rinehart and Winston

1984   *100 Great Fantasy Short Stories* (with Terry Carr and Martin H.
Greenberg) Doubleday

Raintree Reading Series III (with Martin H. Greenberg) Raintree

Isaac Asimov Presents the Great SF Stories, 11: 1949 (with Martin
H. Greenberg) DAW Books

Witches (with Martin H. Greenberg and Charles G. Waugh) NAL

Murder on the Menu (with Carol-Lynn Rössel Waugh and Martin
H. Greenberg) Avon

Young Mutants (with Martin H. Greenberg and Charles G. Waugh)
Harper & Row

Isaac Asimov Presents the Best Science Fiction Firsts (with
Charles G. Waugh and Martin H. Greenberg) Beaufort

The Science Fictional Olympics (with Martin H. Greenberg and
Charles G. Waugh) NAL

Fantastic Reading (with Martin H. Greenberg and David C.
Yeager) Scott, Foresman

Election Day: 2084 (with Martin H. Greenberg) Prometheus

Isaac Asimov Presents the Great SF Stories, 12: 1950 (with Martin
H. Greenberg) DAW Books

Young Extraterrestrials (with Martin H. Greenberg and Charles
G. Waugh) Harper & Row

Sherlock Holmes Through Time and Space (with Martin H.
Greenberg and Charles G. Waugh) Blue Jay

Supermen (with Martin H. Greenberg and Charles G. Waugh) NAL

Thirteen Short Fantasy Novels (with Martin H. Greenberg and
Charles G. Waugh) Crown

Cosmic Knights (with Martin H. Greenberg and Charles G. Waugh)
NAL

1985   *The Hugo Winners*, Vol. 4 Doubleday

Young Monsters (with Martin H. Greenberg and Charles G.
Waugh) Harper & Row

Spells (with Martin H. Greenberg and Charles G. Waugh) NAL

Great Science Fiction Stories by the World's Great Scientists (with Martin H. Greenberg and Charles G. Waugh) Donald Fine

Isaac Asimov Presents the Great SF Stories, 13: 1951 (with Martin H. Greenberg) DAW Books

Amazing Stories Anthology (with Martin H. Greenberg) TSR, Inc.

Young Ghosts (with Martin H. Greenberg and Charles G. Waugh) Harper & Row

Thirteen Short Science Fiction Novels (with Martin H. Greenberg and Charles G. Waugh) Crown

Giants (with Martin H. Greenberg and Charles G. Waugh) NAL

1986   *Isaac Asimov Presents the Great SF Stories, 14: 1952* (with Martin H. Greenberg) DAW Books

Comets (with Martin H. Greenberg and Charles G. Waugh) NAL

Young Star Travellers (with Martin H. Greenberg and Charles G. Waugh) Harper & Row

The Hugo Winners, Vol. 5 Doubleday

Mythical Beasties (with Martin H. Greenberg and Charles G. Waugh) NAL

Tin Stars (with Martin H. Greenberg and Charles G. Waugh) NAL

Magical Wishes (with Martin H. Greenberg and Charles G. Waugh) NAL

Isaac Asimov Presents the Great SF Stories, 15: 1953 (with Martin H. Greenberg) DAW Books

The Twelve Frights of Christmas (with Charles G. Waugh and Martin H. Greenberg) Avon

1987   *Isaac Asimov Presents the Great SF Stories, 16: 1954* (with Martin H. Greenberg) DAW Books

Young Witches and Warlocks (with Martin H. Greenberg and Charles G. Waugh) Harper & Row

Devils (with Martin H. Greenberg and Charles G. Waugh) NAL

Hound Dunnit (with Martin H. Greenberg and Carol-Lynn Rössel Waugh) Carroll & Graf

Space Shuttles (with Martin H. Greenberg and Charles G. Waugh) NAL

1988   *Atlantis* (with Martin H. Greenberg and Charles G. Waugh) NAL

Isaac Asimov Presents the Great SF Stories, 17: 1955 (with Martin H. Greenberg) DAW Books

Encounters (with Martin H. Greenberg and Charles G. Waugh) Headline

Isaac Asimov Presents the Best Crime Stories of the 19th Century Dembner

The Mammoth Book of Classic Science Fiction (with Charles G. Waugh and Martin H. Greenberg) Carroll & Graf

Monsters (with Martin H. Greenberg and Charles G. Waugh) NAL

Isaac Asimov Presents the Great SF Stories, 18: 1956 (with Martin H. Greenberg) DAW Books

Ghosts (with Martin H. Greenberg and Charles G. Waugh) NAL

The Sport of Crime (with Carol-Lynn Rössel Waugh and Martin H. Greenberg) Lynx

1989   *Isaac Asimov Presents the Great SF Stories, 19: 1957* (with Martin H. Greenberg) DAW Books

Tales of the Occult (with Martin H. Greenberg and Charles G. Waugh) Prometheus

Purr-fect Crime (with Carol-Lynn Rössel Waugh and Martin H. Greenberg) Lynx

Robots (with Martin H. Greenberg and Charles G. Waugh) NAL

Visions of Fantasy (with Martin H. Greenberg) Doubleday

Curses (with Martin H. Greenberg and Charles G. Waugh) NAL

The New Hugo Winners (with Martin H. Greenberg) Wynwood

Senior Sleuths (with Martin H. Greenberg and Carol-Lynn Rössel Waugh) G. K. Hall

1990   *Cosmic Critiques* (with Martin H. Greenberg) Writers Digest

Isaac Asimov Presents the Great SF Stories, 20: 1958 (with Martin H. Greenberg) DAW Books

NONFICTION

General Science

1959   *Words of Science* Houghton Mifflin

1960   *Breakthroughs in Science* Houghton Mifflin

The Intelligent Man's Guide to Science Basic Books

1964   *Asimov's Biographical Encyclopedia of Science and Technology*
       Doubleday
1965   *The New Intelligent Man's Guide to Science* Basic Books
1969   *Twentieth Century Discovery* Doubleday
       Great Ideas of Science Houghton Mifflin
1972   *Asimov's Biographical Encyclopedia of Science and Technology*
       Rev. ed. Doubleday
       Asimov's Guide to Science Basic Books
       More Words of Science Houghton Mifflin
       Ginn Science Program—Intermediate Level A Ginn
       Ginn Science Program—Intermediate Level B Ginn
       Ginn Science Program—Intermediate Level C Ginn
1973   *Ginn Science Program—Advanced Level A* Ginn
       Ginn Science Program—Advanced Level B Ginn
       Please Explain Houghton Mifflin
1979   *A Choice of Catastrophes* Simon & Schuster
1982   *Exploring the Earth and the Cosmos* Crown
       Asimov's Biographical Encyclopedia of Science and Technology
       2d Rev. ed. Doubleday
1983   *The Measure of the Universe* Harper & Row
1984   *Asimov's New Guide to Science* Basic Books
1987   *Beginnings* Walker
1989   *Asimov's Chronology of Science and Discovery* Harper & Row
1991   *Our Angry Earth* (with Frederick Pohl) Tor

Mathematics

1959   *Realm of Numbers* Houghton Mifflin
1960   *Realm of Measure* Houghton Mifflin
1961   *Realm of Algebra* Houghton Mifflin
1964   *Quick and Easy Math* Houghton Mifflin
1965   *An Easy Introduction to the Slide Rule* Houghton Mifflin
1973   *How Did We Find Out About Numbers?* Walker
1989   *The History of Mathematics* (a chart) Carolina Biological Supplies

Astronomy

1959	*The Clock We Live On* Abelard-Schuman
1960	*The Kingdom of the Sun* Abelard-Schuman
	Satellites in Outer Space Random House
	The Double Planet Abelard-Schuman
1964	*Planets for Man* Random House
1966	*The Universe* Walker
1967	*The Moon* Follett
	Environments Out There Scholastic/Abelard-Schuman
	To the Ends of the Universe Walker
	Mars Follett
1968	*Stars* Follett
	Galaxies Follett
1969	*ABC's of Space* Walker
1971	*What Makes the Sun Shine?* Little, Brown
1973	*Comets and Meteors* Follett
	The Sun Follett
	Jupiter, the Largest Planet Lothrop, Lee & Shepard
1974	*Our World in Space* New York Graphic
1975	*The Solar System* Follett
	How Did We Find Out About Comets? Walker
	Eyes on the Universe Houghton Mifflin
1976	*Alpha Centauri, the Nearest Star* Lothrop, Lee & Shepard
1977	*The Collapsing Universe* Walker
	How Did We Find Out About Outer Space? Walker
	Mars, the Red Planet Lothrop, Lee & Shepard
1978	*How Did We Find Out About Black Holes?* Walker
1979	*Saturn and Beyond* Lothrop, Lee & Shepard
	Extraterrestrial Civilizations Crown
1981	*Venus: Near Neighbor of the Sun* Lothrop, Lee & Shepard
	Visions of the Universe Cosmos Store
1982	*How Did We Find Out About the Universe?* Walker
1985	*Asimov's Guide to Halley's Comet* Walker
	The Exploding Suns Dutton
1987	*How Did We Find Out About Sunshine?* Walker

Did Comets Kill the Dinosaurs? Gareth Stevens
1988   *Asteroids* Gareth Stevens
Earth's Moon Gareth Stevens
Mars: Our Mysterious Neighbor Gareth Stevens
Our Milky Way and Other Galaxies Gareth Stevens
Quasars, Pulsars, and Black Holes Gareth Stevens
Rockets, Probes, and Satellites Gareth Stevens
Our Solar System Gareth Stevens
The Sun Gareth Stevens
Uranus: The Sideways Planet Gareth Stevens
Saturn: The Ringed Beauty Gareth Stevens
How Was the Universe Born? Gareth Stevens
Earth: Our Home Base Gareth Stevens
Ancient Astronomy Gareth Stevens
Unidentified Flying Objects Gareth Stevens
The Space Spotter's Guide Gareth Stevens
1989   *Is There Life on Other Planets?* Gareth Stevens
Science Fiction, Science Fact Gareth Stevens
Mercury: The Quick Planet Gareth Stevens
Space Garbage Gareth Stevens
Jupiter: The Spotted Giant Gareth Stevens
The Birth and Death of Stars Gareth Stevens
Think About Space (with Frank White) Walker
Mythology and the Universe Gareth Stevens
Colonizing the Planets and the Stars Gareth Stevens
Astronomy Today Gareth Stevens
Pluto: A Double Planet Gareth Stevens
Piloted Space Flights Gareth Stevens
Comets and Meteors Gareth Stevens
1990   *Neptune: The Farthest Giant* Gareth Stevens
Venus: A Shrouded Mystery Gareth Stevens
The World's Space Programs Gareth Stevens
How Did We Find Out About Neptune? Walker
1991   *How Did We Find Out About Pluto?* Walker

Earth Sciences

1962   *Words on the Map* Houghton Mifflin
1970   *ABC's of the Ocean* Walker
1971   *ABC's of the Earth* Walker
1973   *How Did We Find Out the Earth Is Round?* Walker
1975   *The Ends of the Earth* Weybright & Talley
1978   *How Did We Find Out About Earthquakes?* Walker
1979   *How Did We Find Out About Antarctica?* Walker
1980   *How Did We Find Out About Oil?* Walker
        How Did We Find Out About Coal? Walker
1981   *How Did We Find Out About Volcanoes?* Walker
1985   *How Did We Find Out About the Atmosphere?* Walker

Chemistry and Biochemistry

1952   *Biochemistry and Human Metabolism* Williams & Wilkins
1954   *The Chemicals of Life* Abelard-Schuman
1956   *Chemistry and Human Health* McGraw-Hill
1957   *Building Blocks of the Universe* Abelard-Schuman
1958   *The World of Carbon* Abelard-Schuman
        The World of Nitrogen Abelard-Schuman
1962   *Life and Energy* Doubleday
        The Search for the Elements Basic Books
1963   *The Genetic Code* Orion Press
1965   *A Short History of Chemistry* Doubleday
1966   *The Noble Gases* Basic Books
        The Genetic Effect of Radiation (with Theodosius Dobzhansky)
           AEC
1969   *Photosynthesis* Basic Books
1974   *How Did We Find Out About Vitamins?* Walker
1985   *How Did We Find Out About DNA?* Walker
1988   *How Did We Find Out About Photosynthesis?* Walker

Physics

1956   *Inside the Atom* Abelard-Schuman
1966   *Inside the Atom* Rev. Ed. Abelard-Schuman
       The Neutrino Doubleday
       Understanding Physics, Vol. 1 Walker
       Understanding Physics, Vol. 2 Walker
       Understanding Physics, Vol. 3 Walker
1970   *Light* Follett
1972   *Electricity and Man* AEC
       Worlds Within Worlds AEC
1973   *How Did We Find Out About Electricity?* Walker
1975   *How Did We Find Out About Energy?* Walker
1976   *How Did We Find Out About Atoms?* Walker
       How Did We Find Out About Nuclear Power? Walker
1981   *How Did We Find Out About Solar Power?* Walker
1984   *How Did We Find Out About Computers?* Walker
       How Did We Find Out About Robots? Walker
1985   *Robots* (with Karen Frenkel) Harmony House
1986   *How Did We Find Out About the Speed of Light?* Walker
1988   *How Did We Find Out About Superconductivity?* Walker
1989   *How Did We Find Out About Microwaves?* Walker
1990   *How Did We Find Out About Lasers?* Walker
1991   *Atom* Dutton

Biology

1955   *Races and People* (with William C. Boyd) Abelard-Schuman
1960   *The Living River* Abelard-Schuman
       The Wellsprings of Life Abelard-Schuman
1963   *The Human Body* Houghton Mifflin
1964   *The Human Brain* Houghton Mifflin
       A Short History of Biology Doubleday
1972   *ABC's of Ecology* Walker
1973   *How Did We Find Out About Dinosaurs?* Walker
1974   *How Did We Find Out About Germs?* Walker

1979   *How Did We Find Out About Our Human Roots?* Walker
1982   *How Did We Find Out About Life in the Deep Sea?* Walker
        How Did We Find Out About the Beginning of Life? Walker
1983   *How Did We Find Out About Genes?* Walker
1987   *How Did We Find Out About Blood?* Walker
        How Did We Find Out About the Brain? Walker
1988   *The History of Biology* (a chart) Carolina Biological Supplies
        Little Library of Dinosaurs Outlet

Science Essay Collections

1957   *Only a Trillion* Abelard-Schuman
1962   *Fact and Fancy* Doubleday
1963   *View from a Height* Doubleday
1964   *Adding a Dimension* Doubleday
1965   *Of Space and Time and Other Things* Doubleday
1966   *From Earth to Heaven* Doubleday
1967   *Is Anyone There?* Doubleday
1968   *Science, Numbers, and I* Doubleday
1970   *The Solar System and Back* Doubleday
1971   *The Stars in Their Courses* Doubleday
1972   *The Left Hand of the Electron* Doubleday
1973   *Today and Tomorrow and—* Doubleday
        The Tragedy of the Moon Doubleday
1974   *Asimov on Astronomy* Doubleday
        Asimov on Chemistry Doubleday
1975   *Of Matters Great and Small* Doubleday
        Science Past—Science Future Doubleday
1976   *Asimov on Physics* Doubleday
        The Planet That Wasn't Doubleday
1977   *Asimov on Numbers* Doubleday
        The Beginning and the End Doubleday
1978   *Quasar, Quasar, Burning Bright* Doubleday
        Life and Time Doubleday
1979   *The Road to Infinity* Doubleday
1981   *The Sun Shines Bright* Doubleday
        Change! Houghton Mifflin

1983   *Counting the Eons* Doubleday
        The Roving Mind Prometheus
1984   *X Stands for Unknown* Doubleday
1985   *The Subatomic Monster* Doubleday
1986   *The Dangers of Intelligence* Houghton Mifflin
1987   *Far as the Human Eye Could See* Doubleday
        Past, Present, and Future Prometheus
1988   *The Relativity of Wrong* Doubleday
1989   *The Tyrannosaurus Prescription* Prometheus
        Asimov on Science Doubleday
1990   *Frontiers* Dutton
        Out of the Everywhere Doubleday
        The Secret of the Universe Doubleday
1993   *Frontiers II* Dutton

Science Fiction Essay Collections

1981   *Asimov on Science Fiction* Doubleday
1989   *Asimov's Galaxy* Doubleday

History

1963   *The Kite That Won the Revolution* Houghton Mifflin
1965   *The Greeks* Houghton Mifflin
1966   *The Roman Republic* Houghton Mifflin
1967   *The Roman Empire* Houghton Mifflin
        The Egyptians Houghton Mifflin
1968   *The Near East* Houghton Mifflin
        The Dark Ages Houghton Mifflin
        Words from History Houghton Mifflin
1969   *The Shaping of England* Houghton Mifflin
1970   *Constantinople* Houghton Mifflin
1971   *The Land of Canaan* Houghton Mifflin
1972   *The Shaping of France* Houghton Mifflin
1973   *The Shaping of North America* Houghton Mifflin
1974   *The Birth of the United States* Houghton Mifflin

Earth: Our Crowded Spaceship John Day
1975   *Our Federal Union* Houghton Mifflin
1977   *The Golden Door* Houghton Mifflin
1991   *The March of the Millennia* (with Frank White) Walker
        Asimov's Chronology of the World HarperCollins

The Bible

1962   *Words in Genesis* Houghton Mifflin
1963   *Words from the Exodus* Houghton Mifflin
1968   *Asimov's Guide to the Bible,* Vol. 1 Doubleday
1969   *Asimov's Guide to the Bible,* Vol. 2 Doubleday
1972   *The Story of Ruth* Doubleday
1978   *Animals in the Bible* Doubleday
1981   *In the Beginning* Crown

Literature

1961   *Words from the Myths* Houghton Mifflin
1970   *Asimov's Guide to Shakespeare,* Vol. 1 Doubleday
        Asimov's Guide to Shakespeare, Vol. 2 Doubleday
1972   *Asimov's Annotated Don Juan* Doubleday
1974   *Asimov's Annotated Paradise Lost* Doubleday
1977   *Familiar Poems, Annotated* Doubleday
        Asimov's Sherlockian Limericks Mysterious Press
1980   *The Annotated Gulliver's Travels* Clarkson Potter
1987   *How to Enjoy Writing* (with Janet Asimov) Walker
1988   *Asimov's Annotated Gilbert & Sullivan* Doubleday

Humor and Satire

1971   *The Sensuous Dirty Old Man* Walker
        Isaac Asimov's Treasury of Humor Houghton Mifflin
1975   *Lecherous Limericks* Walker
1976   *More Lecherous Limericks* Walker
1977   *Still More Lecherous Limericks* Walker

1978   *Limericks Too Gross* (with John Ciardi) Norton
1981   *A Glossary of Limericks* (with John Ciardi) Norton
1984   *Limericks for Children* Caedmon
1992   *Asimov Laughs Again* HarperCollins

Autobiography

1979   *In Memory Yet Green* Doubleday
1980   *In Joy Still Felt* Doubleday
1994   *I, Asimov* Doubleday

Miscellaneous

1969   *Opus 100* Houghton Mifflin
1979   *Opus 200* Houghton Mifflin
       Isaac Asimov's Book of Facts Grosset & Dunlap
1982   *Isaac Asimov Presents Superquiz* (by Ken Fisher) Dembner
1983   *Isaac Asimov Presents Superquiz II* (by Ken Fisher) Dembner
1984   *Opus 300* Houghton Mifflin
1985   *Lining in the Future* (edited) Harmony House
1986   *Future Days* Henry Holt
1987   *Isaac Asimov Presents Superquiz III* (by Ken Fisher) Dembner
1988   *Isaac Asimov Presents: From Harding to Hiroshima* (by
       Barrington Boardman) Dembner
       Isaac Asimov's Book of Science and Nature Quotations (with
       Jason A. Shulman) Blue Cliff
       *Isaac Asimov's Science Fiction and Fantasy Story-a-Month 1989
       Calendar* (with Martin H. Greenberg) Pomegranate
1989   *Isaac Asimov Presents Superquiz IV* (by Ken Fisher) Dembner
       The Complete Science Fair Handbooks (with Anthony D.
       Fredericks) Scott, Foresman

INDEX OF ISAAC ASIMOV'S PUBLISHED WRITING MENTIONED IN THE BOOK